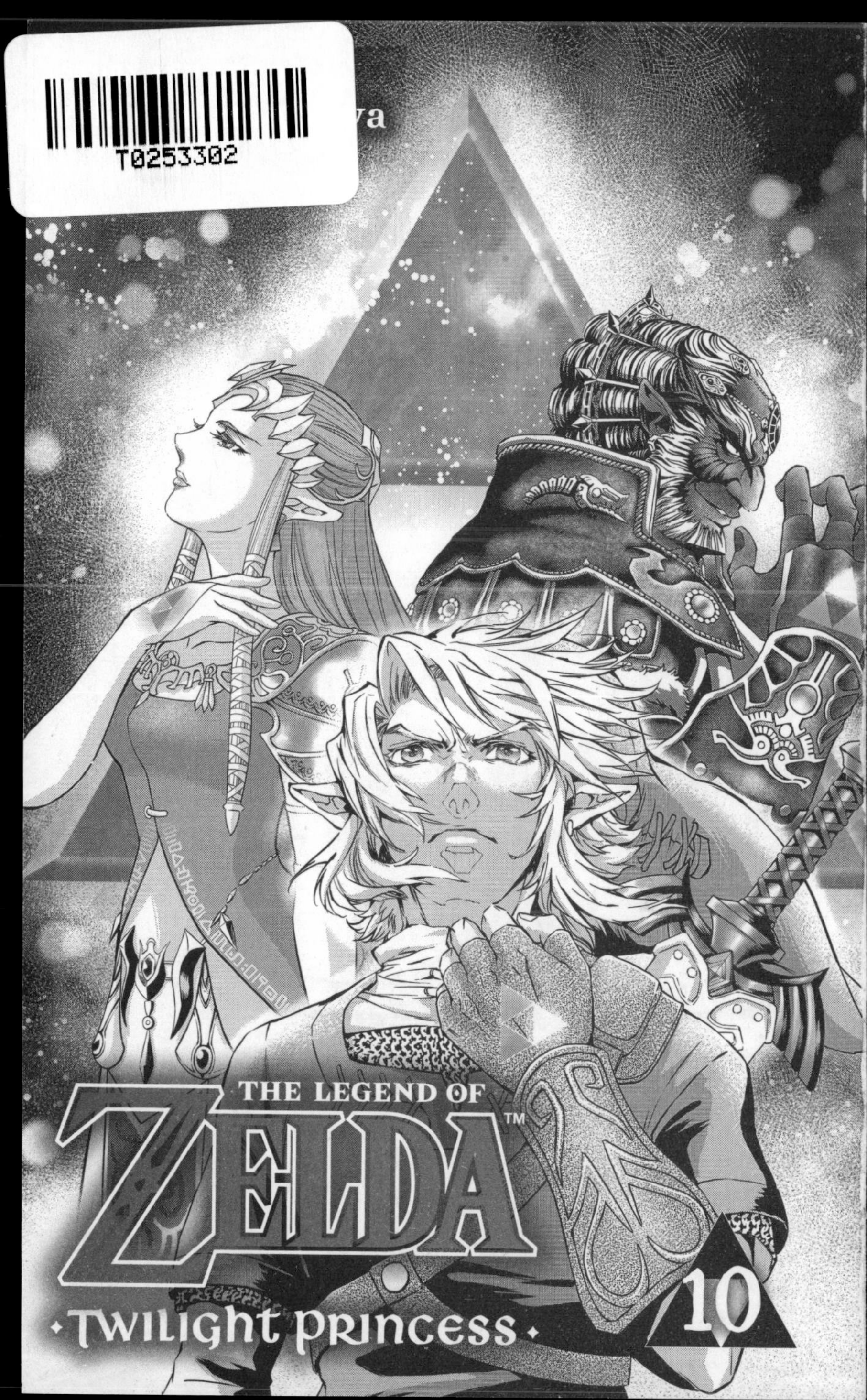
ya
THE LEGEND OF
ZELDA™
·Twilight Princess·
10

THE LEGEND OF
ZELDA™

᛫ TWILIGHT PRINCESS ᛫

10

RRMM

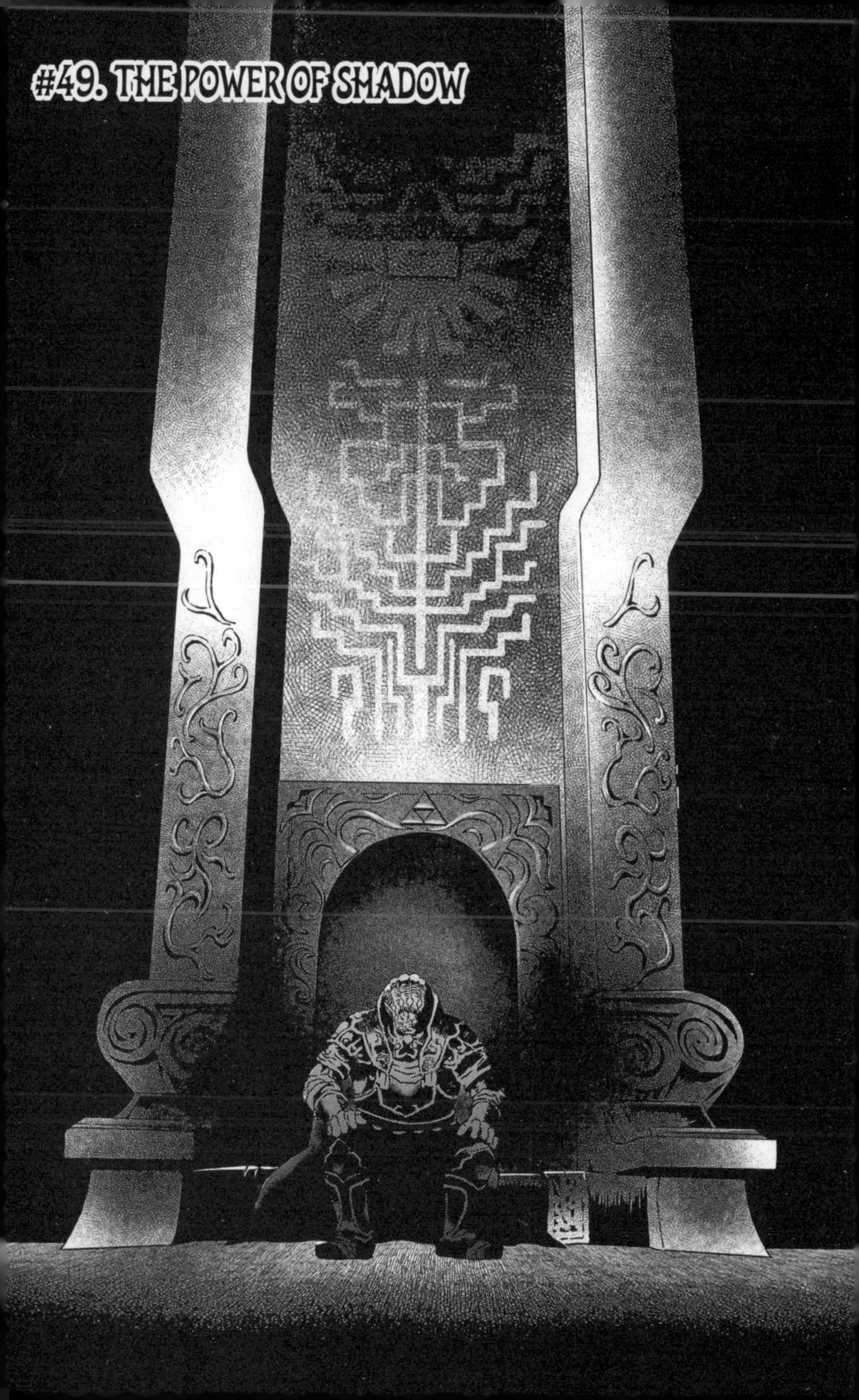
#49. THE POWER OF SHADOW

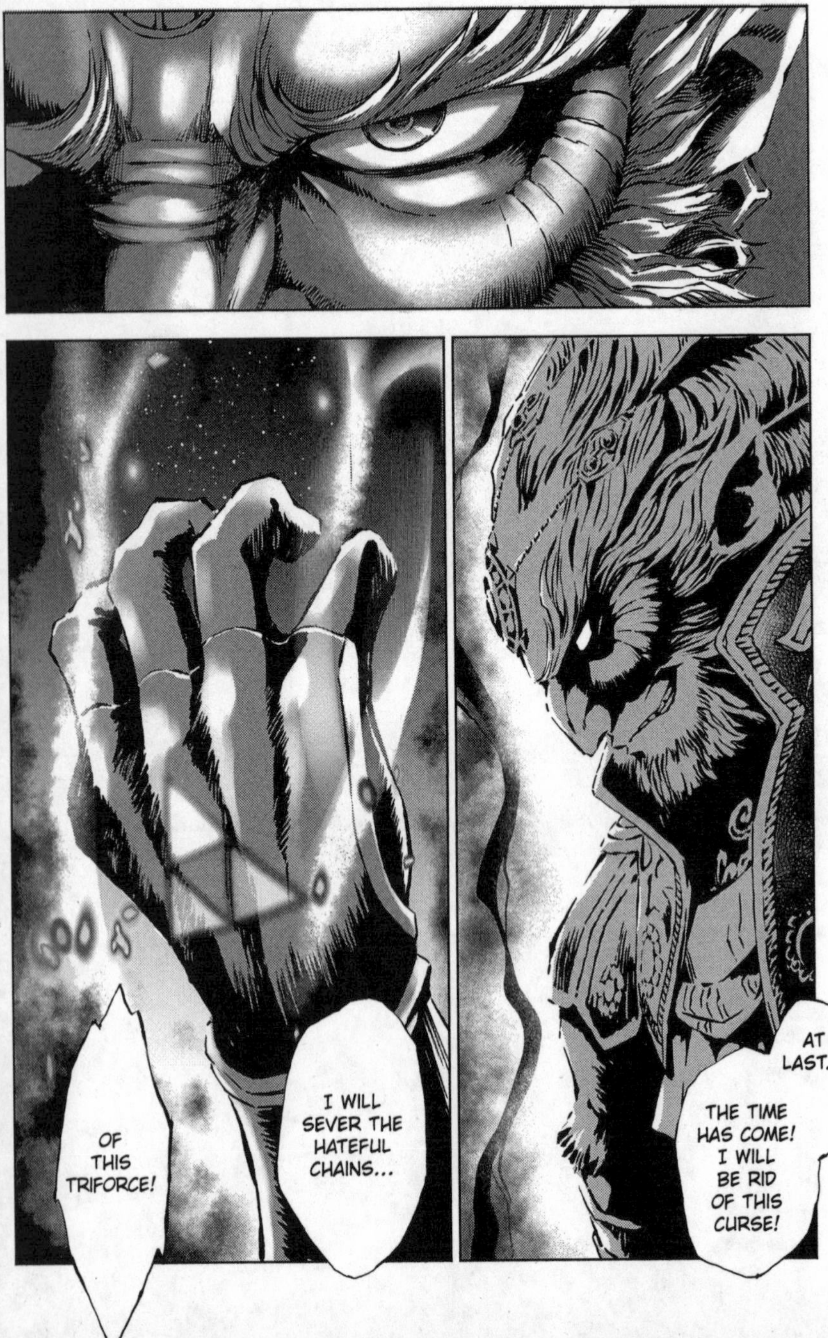
AT LAST...
THE TIME HAS COME! I WILL BE RID OF THIS CURSE!
I WILL SEVER THE HATEFUL CHAINS...
OF THIS TRIFORCE!

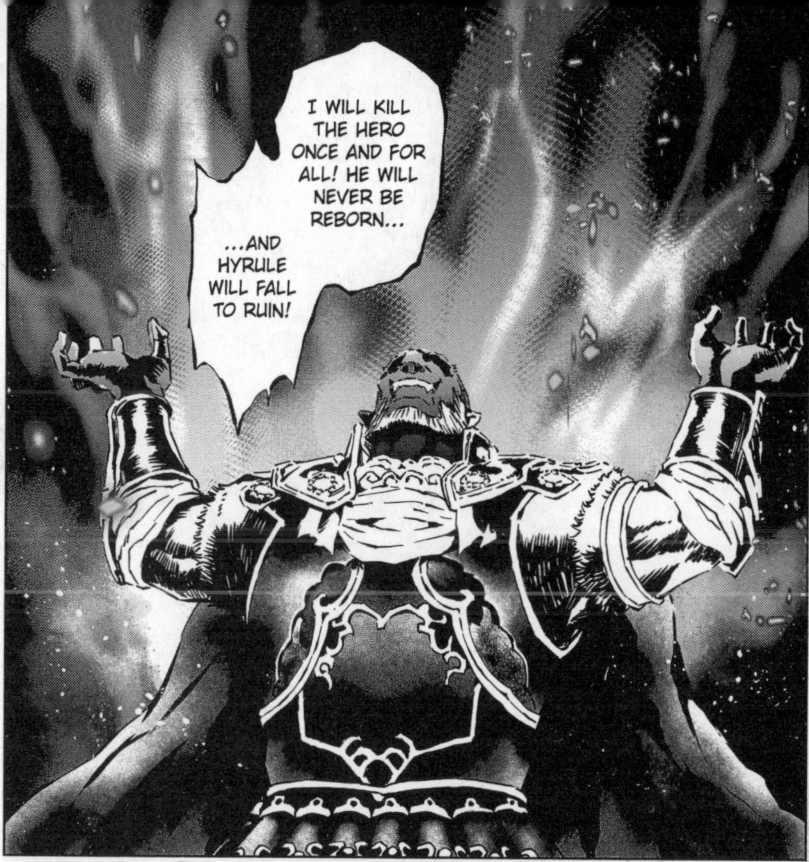
I WILL KILL THE HERO ONCE AND FOR ALL! HE WILL NEVER BE REBORN...
...AND HYRULE WILL FALL TO RUIN!

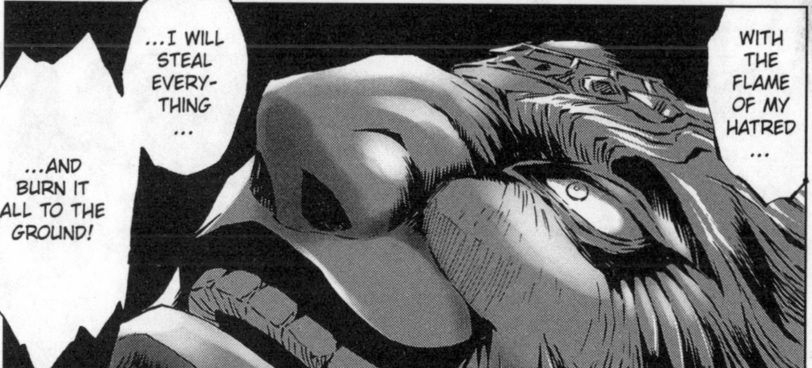
WITH THE FLAME OF MY HATRED...
...I WILL STEAL EVERY-THING...
...AND BURN IT ALL TO THE GROUND!

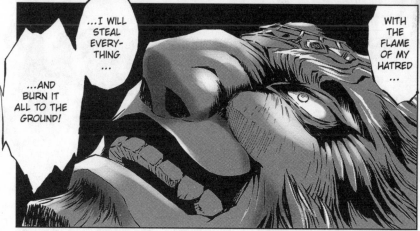

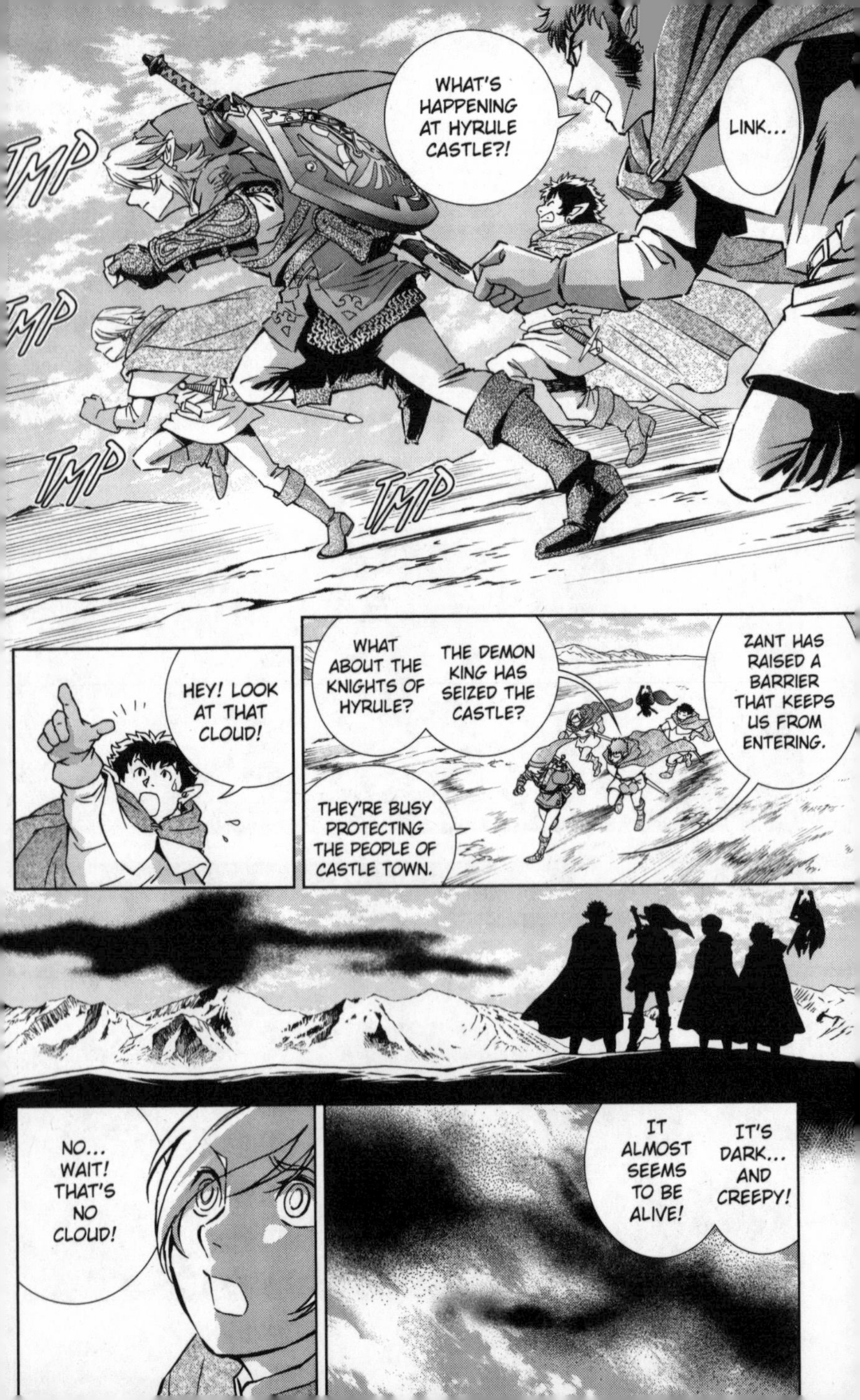
LINK...
WHAT'S HAPPENING AT HYRULE CASTLE?!
TMP
TMP
TMP
TMP
ZANT HAS RAISED A BARRIER THAT KEEPS US FROM ENTERING.
THE DEMON KING HAS SEIZED THE CASTLE?
WHAT ABOUT THE KNIGHTS OF HYRULE?
THEY'RE BUSY PROTECTING THE PEOPLE OF CASTLE TOWN.
HEY! LOOK AT THAT CLOUD!
IT'S DARK... AND CREEPY!
IT ALMOST SEEMS TO BE ALIVE!
NO... WAIT! THAT'S NO CLOUD!

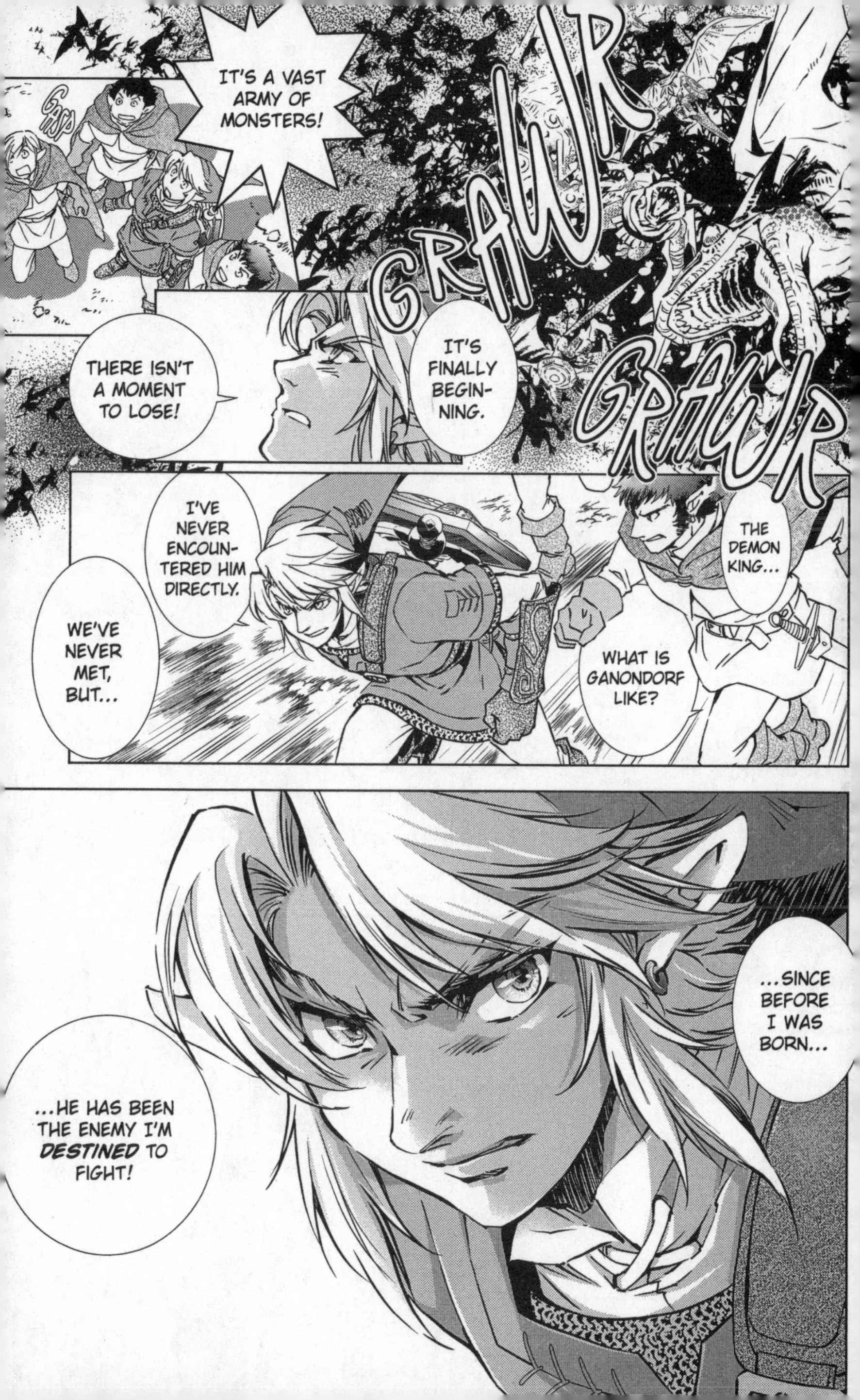
GRAWR
GRAWR
IT'S A VAST ARMY OF MONSTERS!
GASP
IT'S FINALLY BEGINNING.
THERE ISN'T A MOMENT TO LOSE!
THE DEMON KING...
WHAT IS GANONDORF LIKE?
I'VE NEVER ENCOUNTERED HIM DIRECTLY.
WE'VE NEVER MET, BUT...
...SINCE BEFORE I WAS BORN...
...HE HAS BEEN THE ENEMY I'M ***DESTINED*** TO FIGHT!

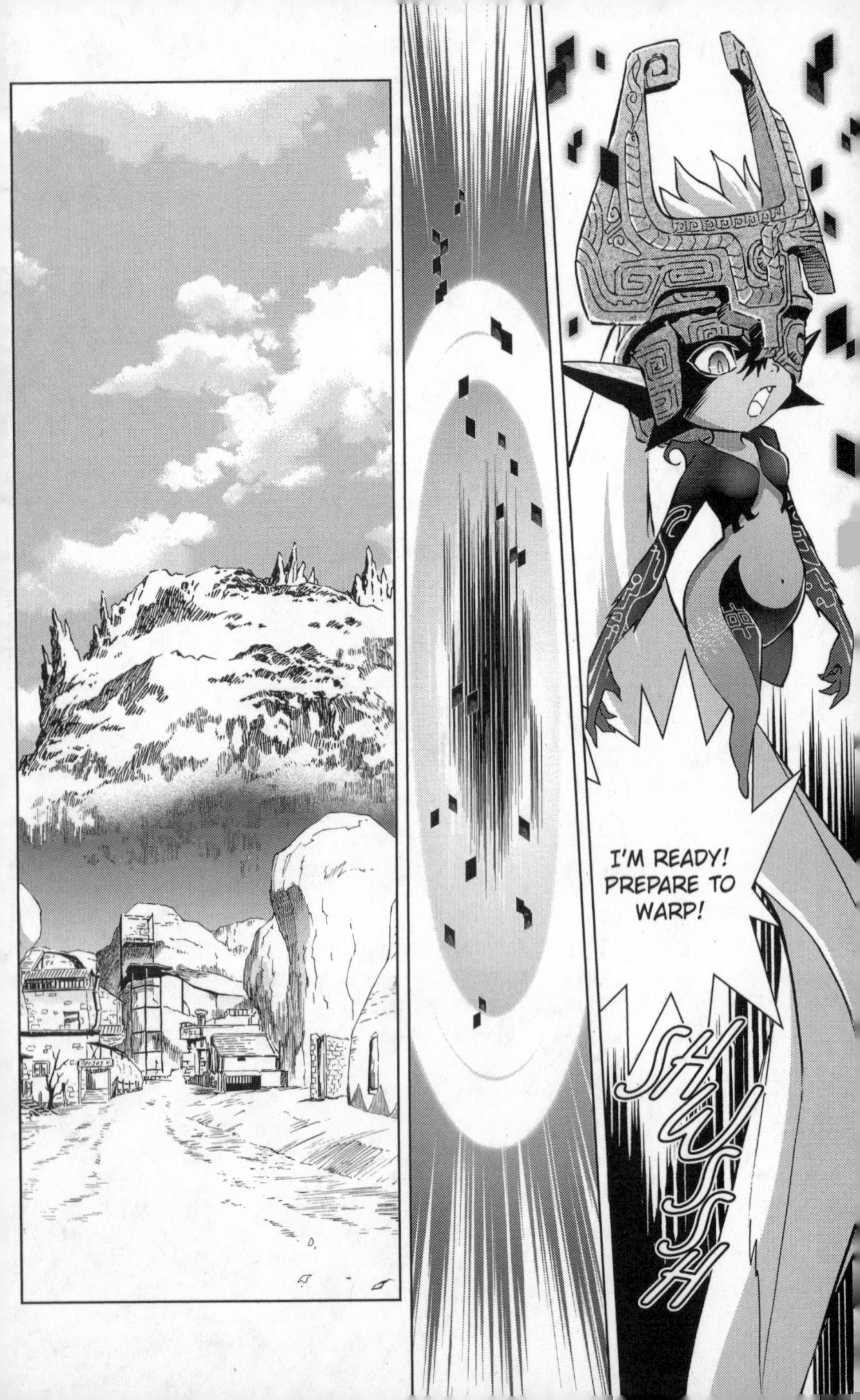
I'M READY! PREPARE TO WARP!
SHWSSH

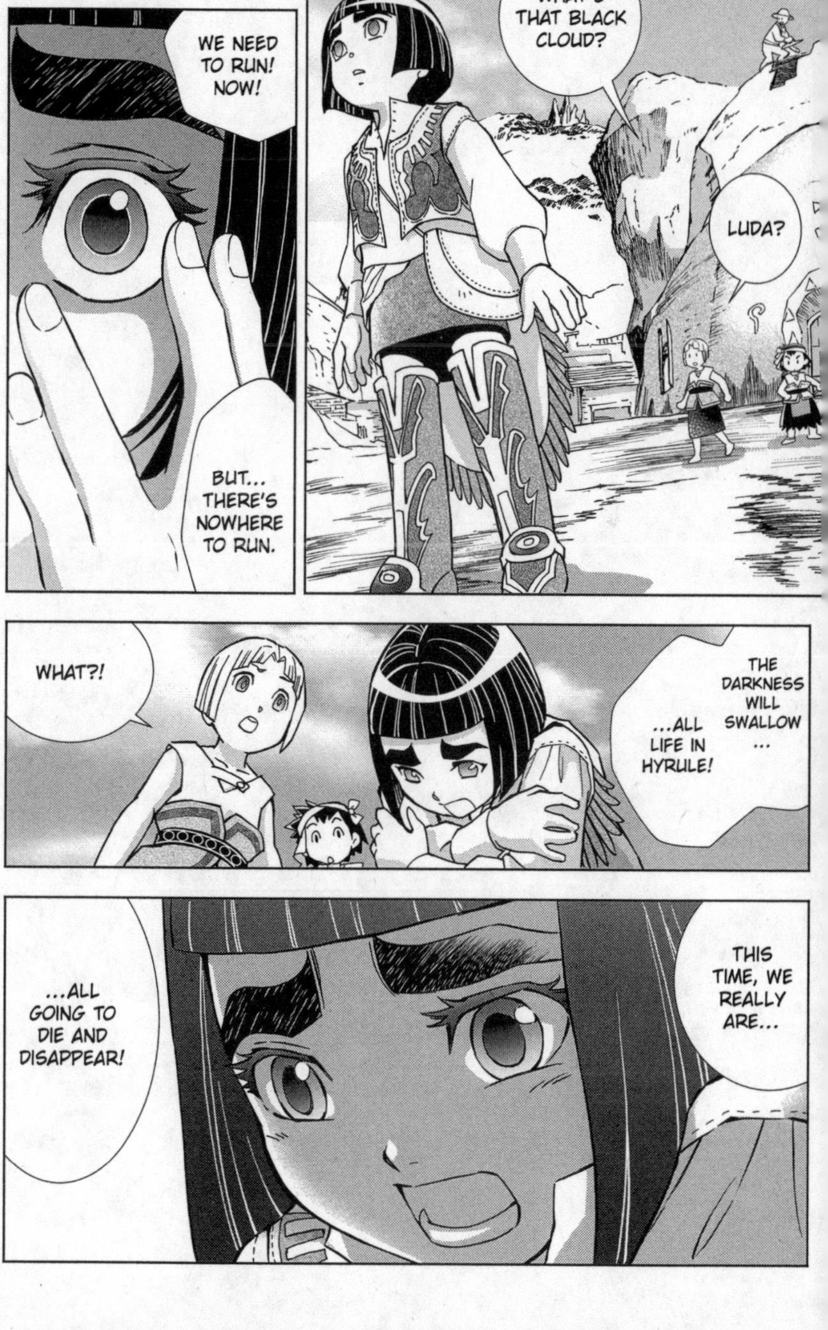
WHAT'S THAT BLACK CLOUD?
LUDA?
WE NEED TO RUN! NOW!
BUT... THERE'S NOWHERE TO RUN.
THE DARKNESS WILL SWALLOW...
...ALL LIFE IN HYRULE!
WHAT?!
THIS TIME, WE REALLY ARE...
...ALL GOING TO DIE AND DISAPPEAR!

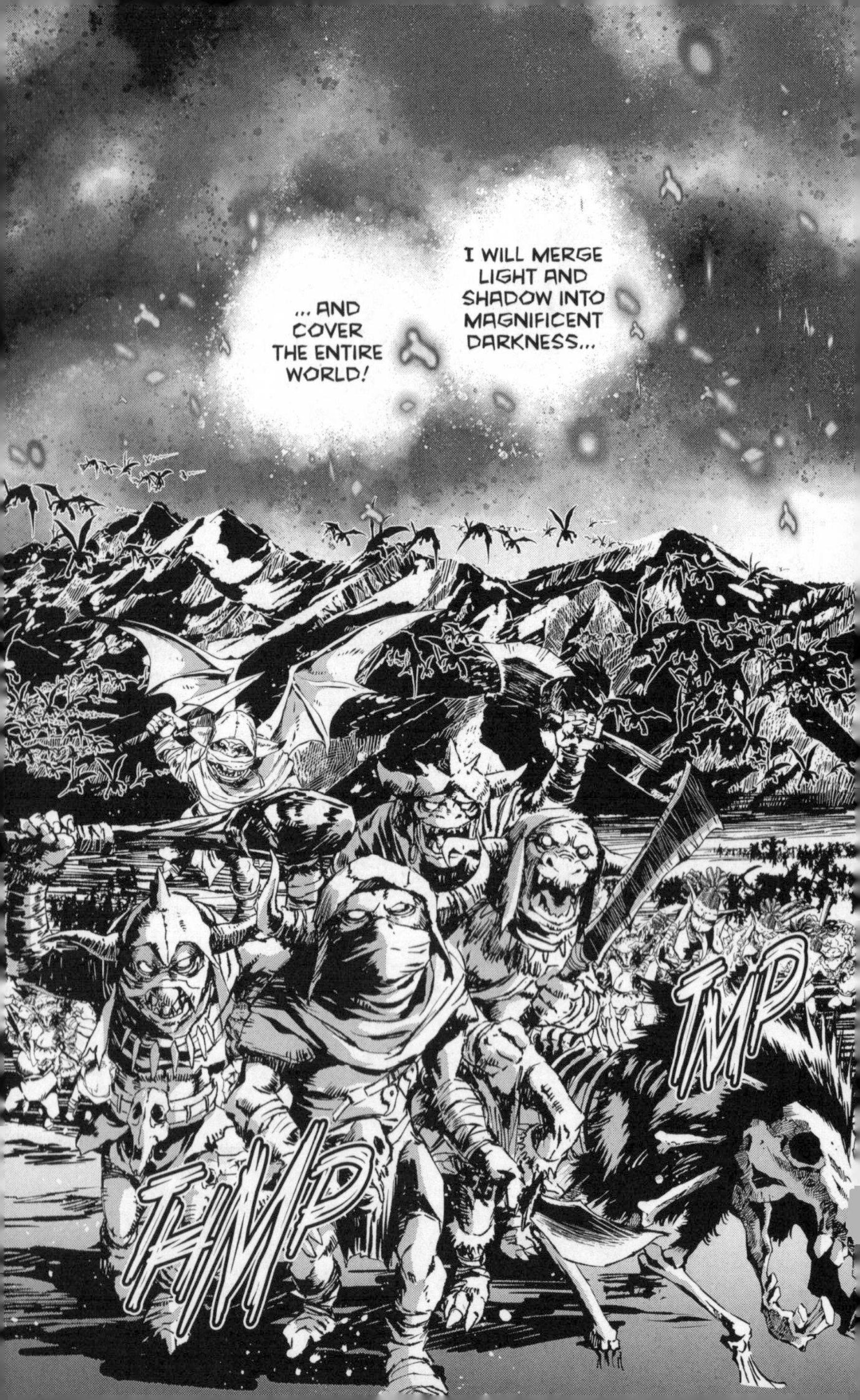
I WILL MERGE LIGHT AND SHADOW INTO MAGNIFICENT DARKNESS...
... AND COVER THE ENTIRE WORLD!
TMP
THMP

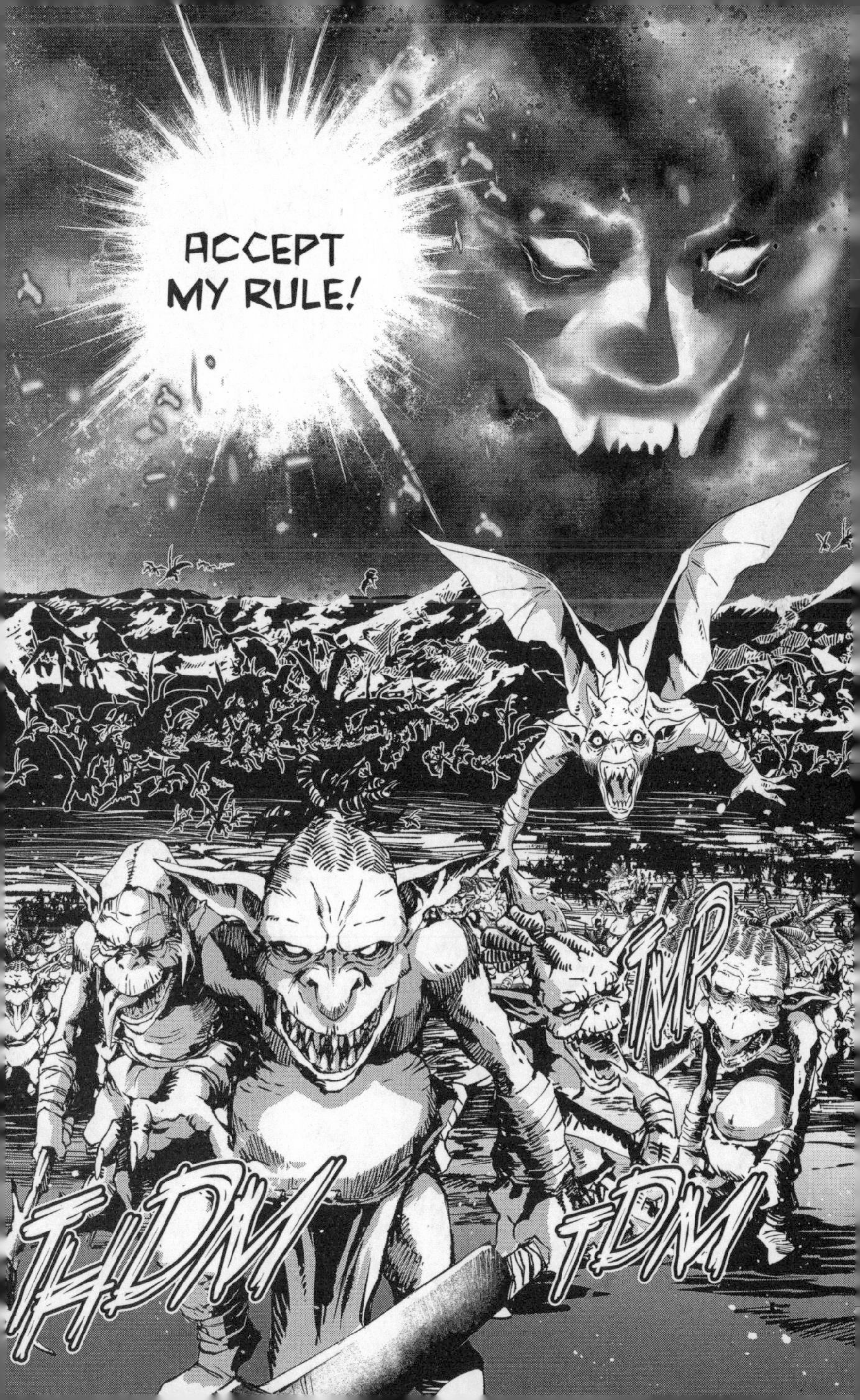
ACCEPT MY RULE!
TMP
TDM
THDM

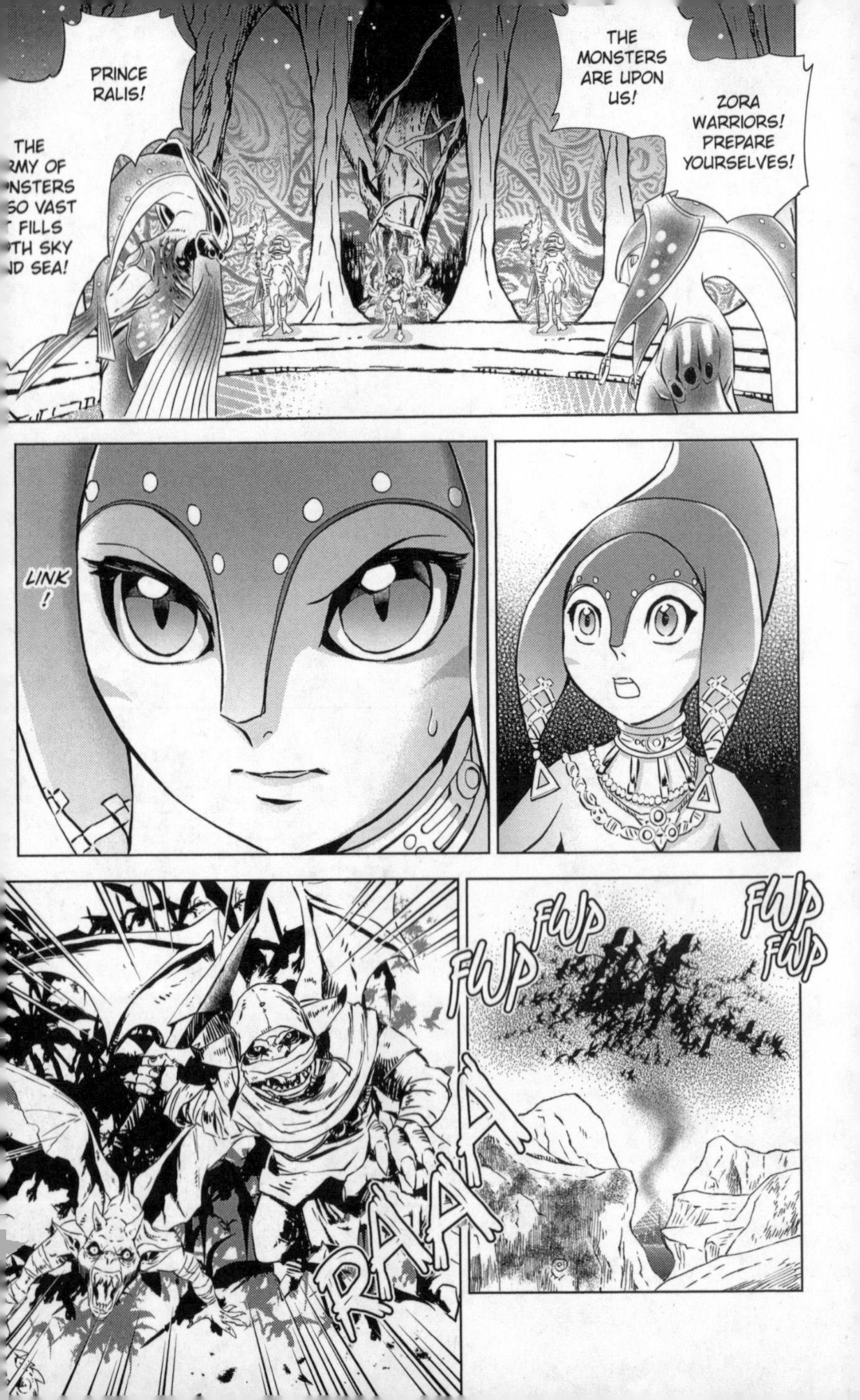

THE MONSTERS ARE UPON US!
ZORA WARRIORS! PREPARE YOURSELVES!
PRINCE RALIS!
THE RMY OF NSTERS SO VAST T FILLS OTH SKY ND SEA!
LINK!
FWP FWP
FWP FWP
RAAAA

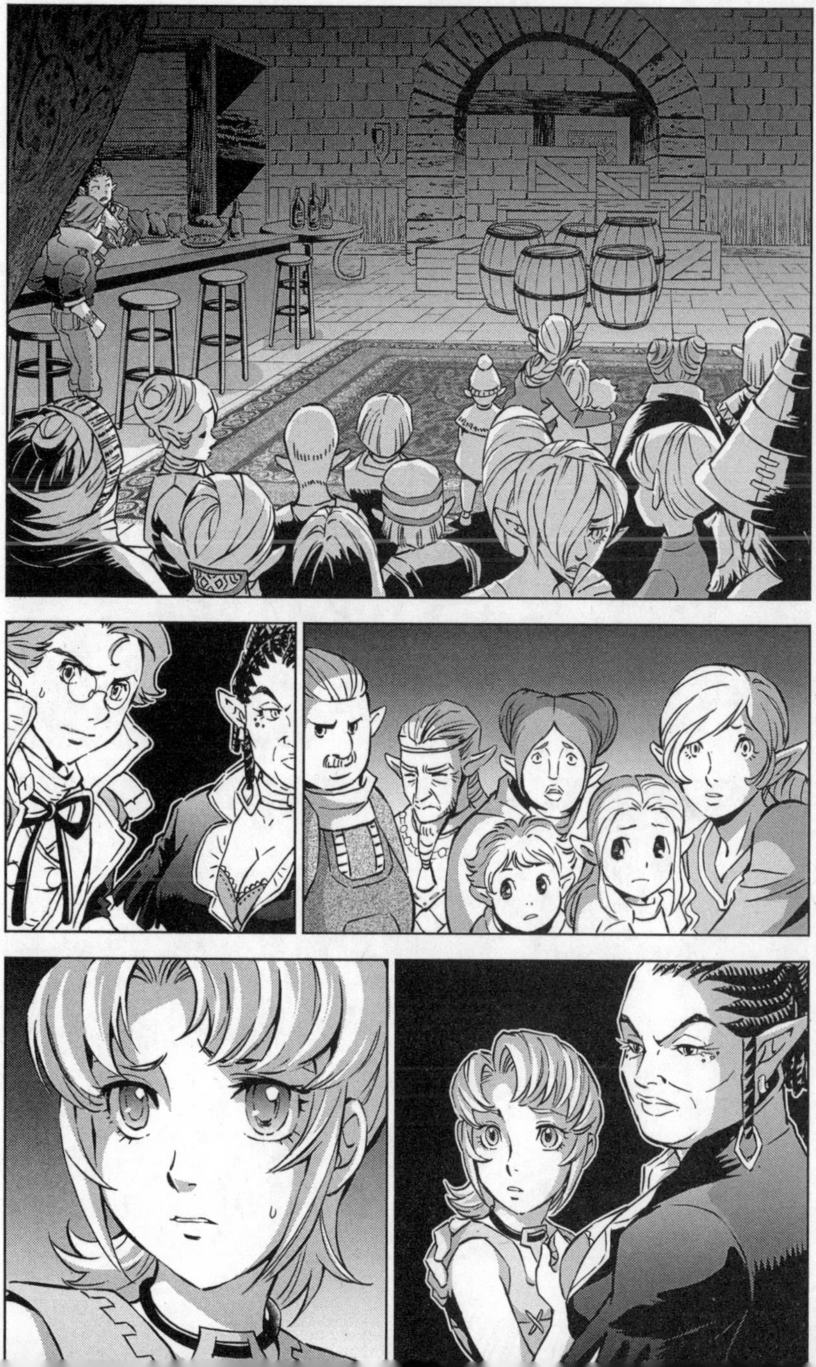

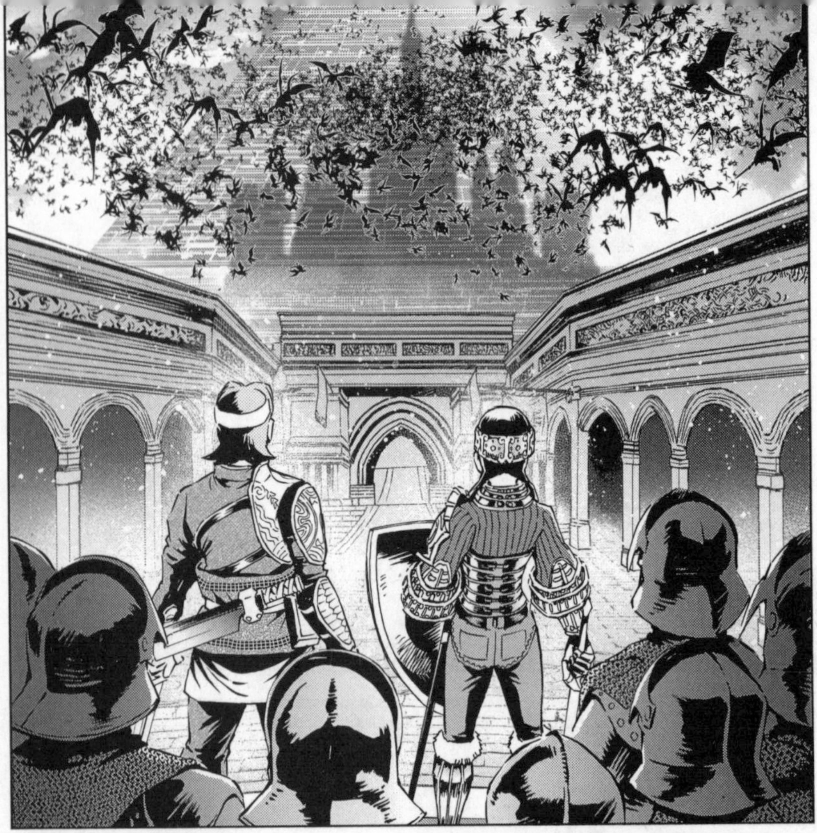

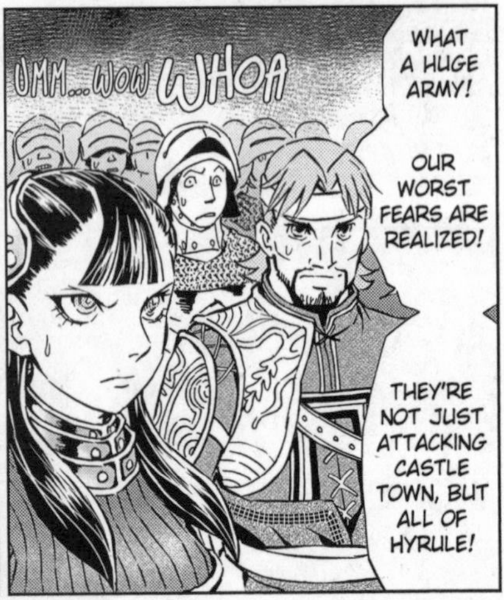
WHAT A HUGE ARMY!
UMM... WOW WHOA
OUR WORST FEARS ARE REALIZED!
THEY'RE NOT JUST ATTACKING CASTLE TOWN, BUT ALL OF HYRULE!

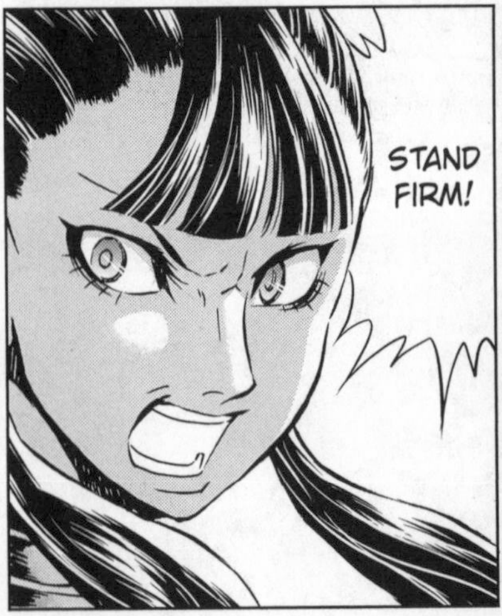
STAND FIRM!

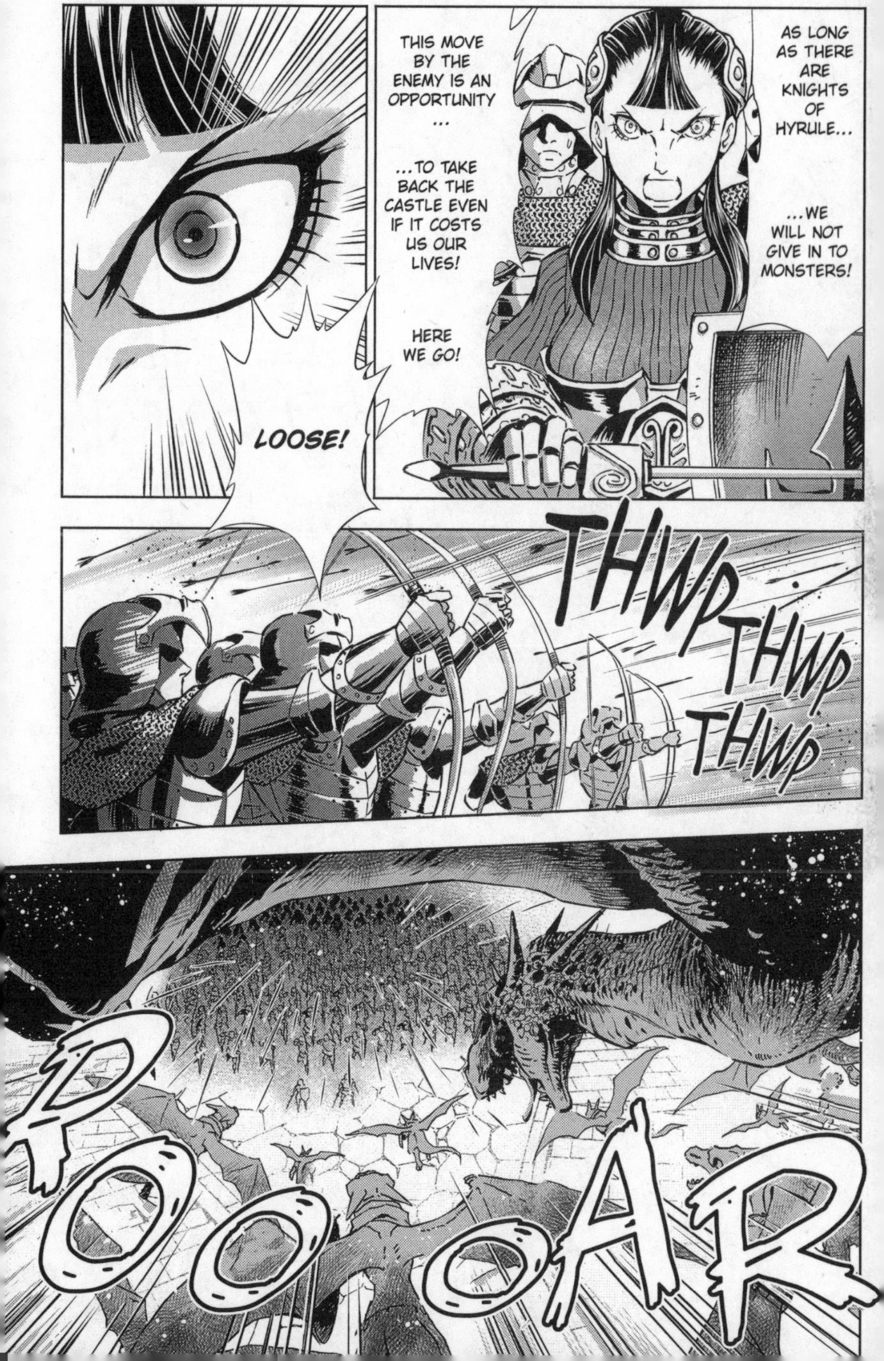
AS LONG AS THERE ARE KNIGHTS OF HYRULE...
...WE WILL NOT GIVE IN TO MONSTERS!
THIS MOVE BY THE ENEMY IS AN OPPORTUNITY...
...TO TAKE BACK THE CASTLE EVEN IF IT COSTS US OUR LIVES!
HERE WE GO!
LOOSE!
THWP THWP THWP
ROOOOAR

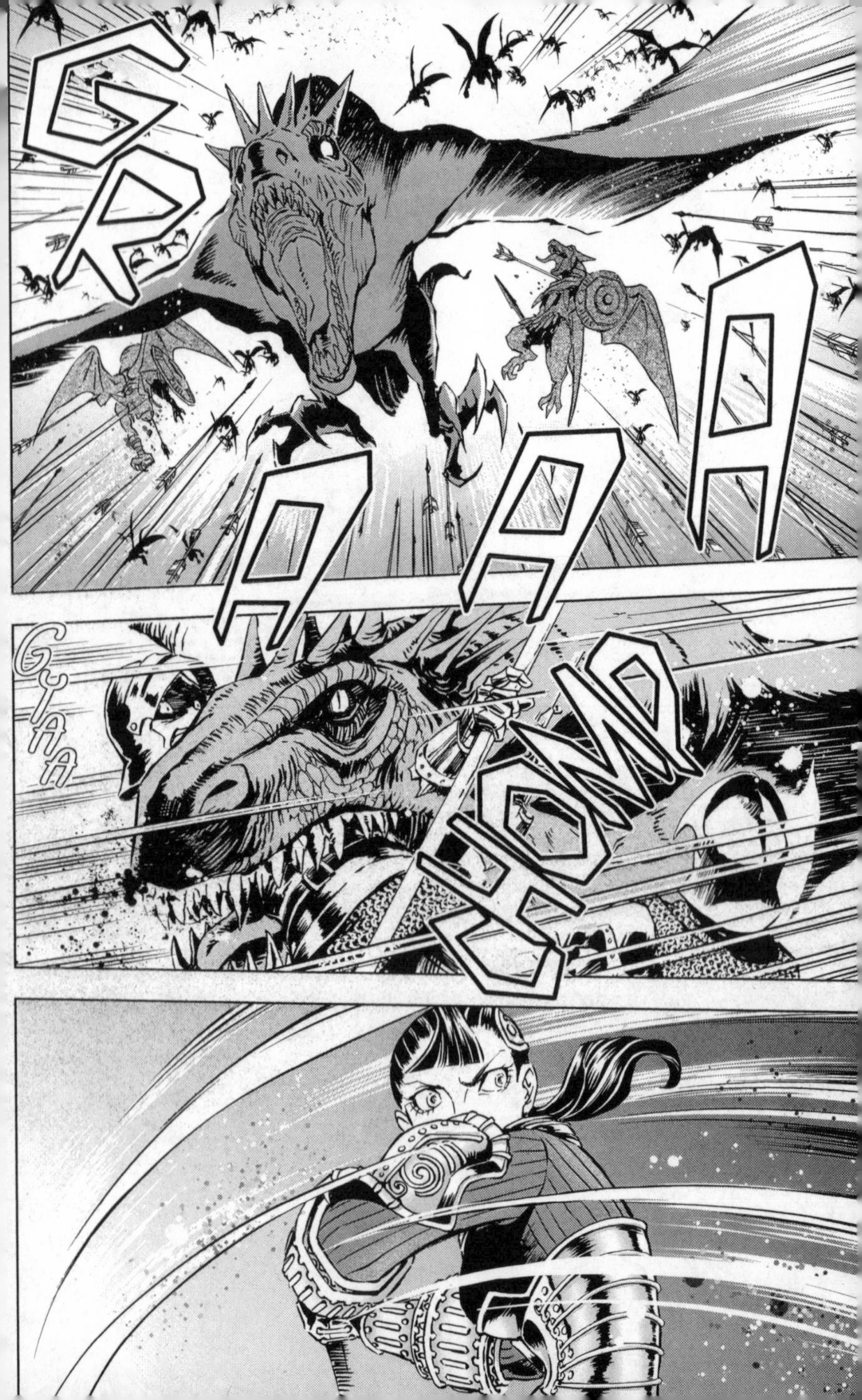
GRAAAA
GYAA
CHOMP

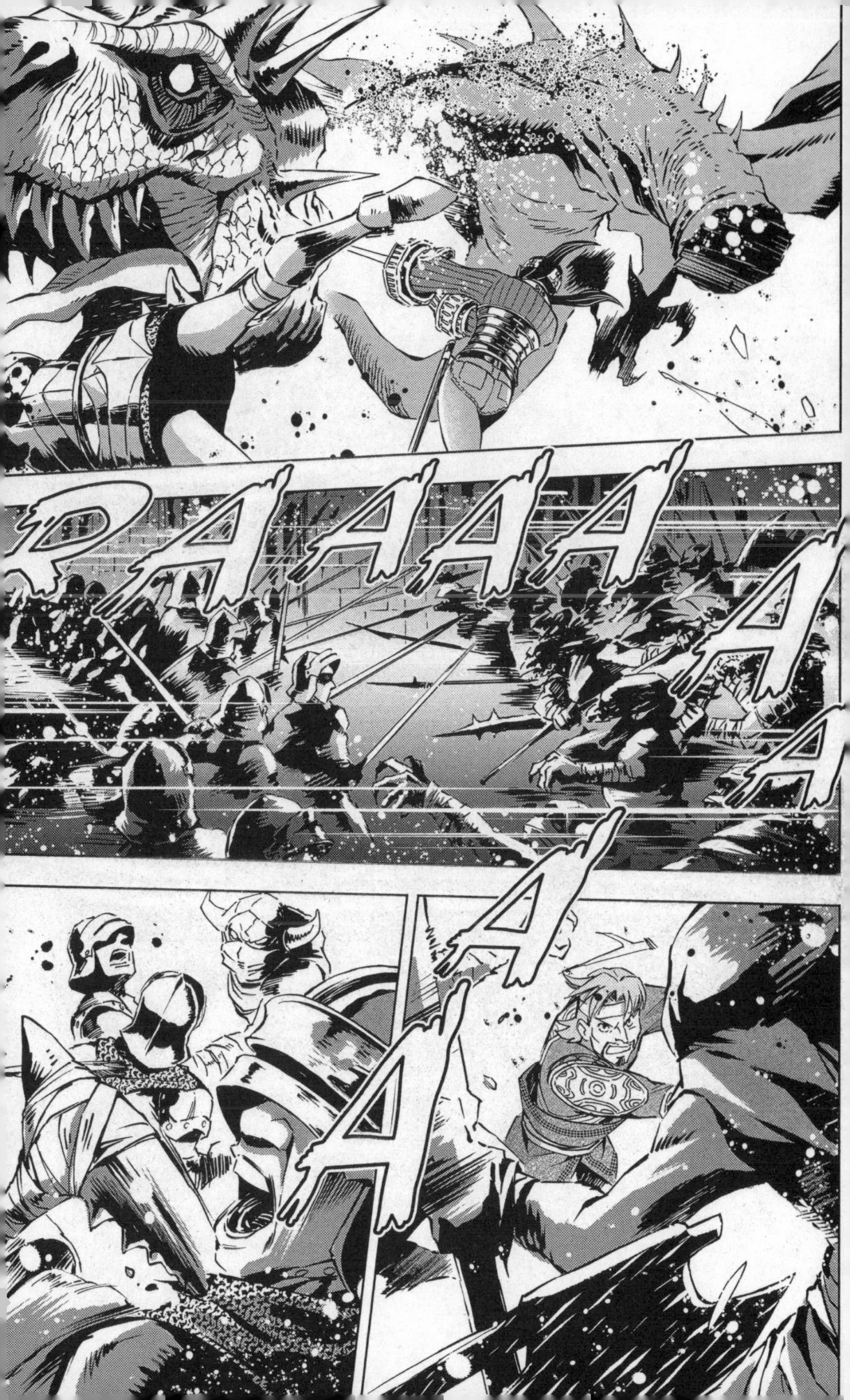
RAAAAAAAAAA

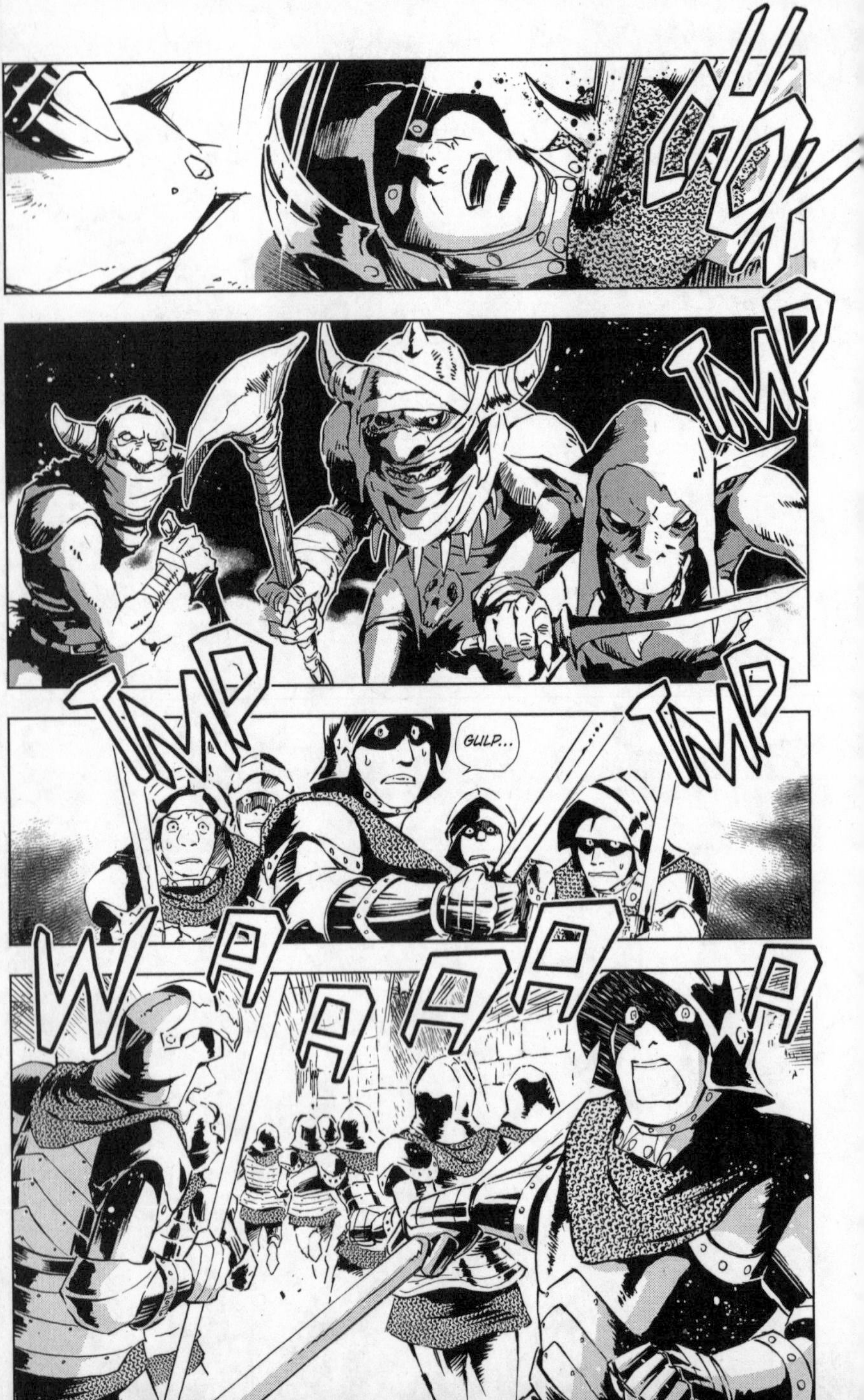
CHOK
TMP
TMP
GULP...
TMP
WAAAAA

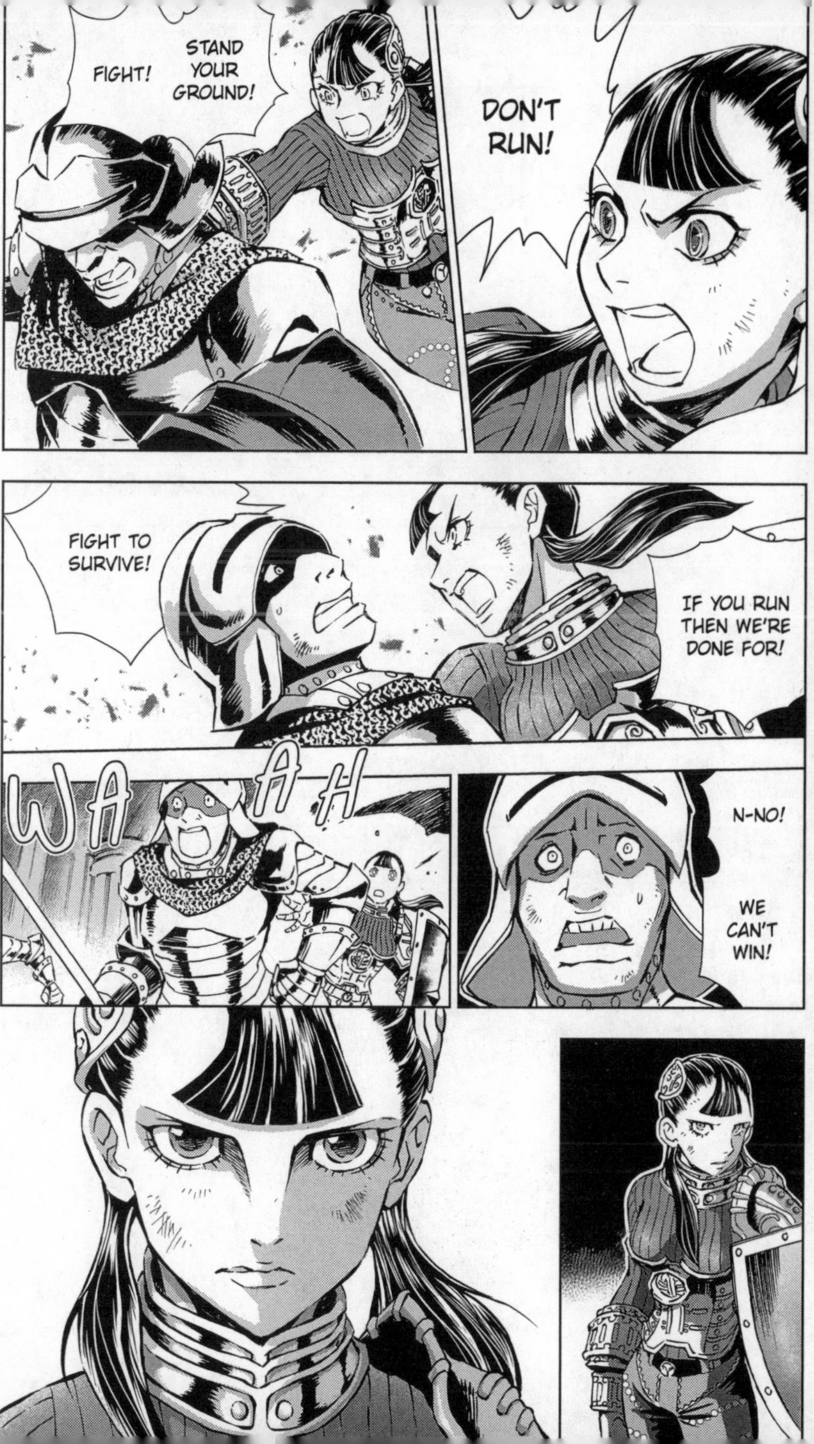
DON'T RUN!
FIGHT! STAND YOUR GROUND!
IF YOU RUN THEN WE'RE DONE FOR!
FIGHT TO SURVIVE!
N-NO!
WE CAN'T WIN!
WAAH

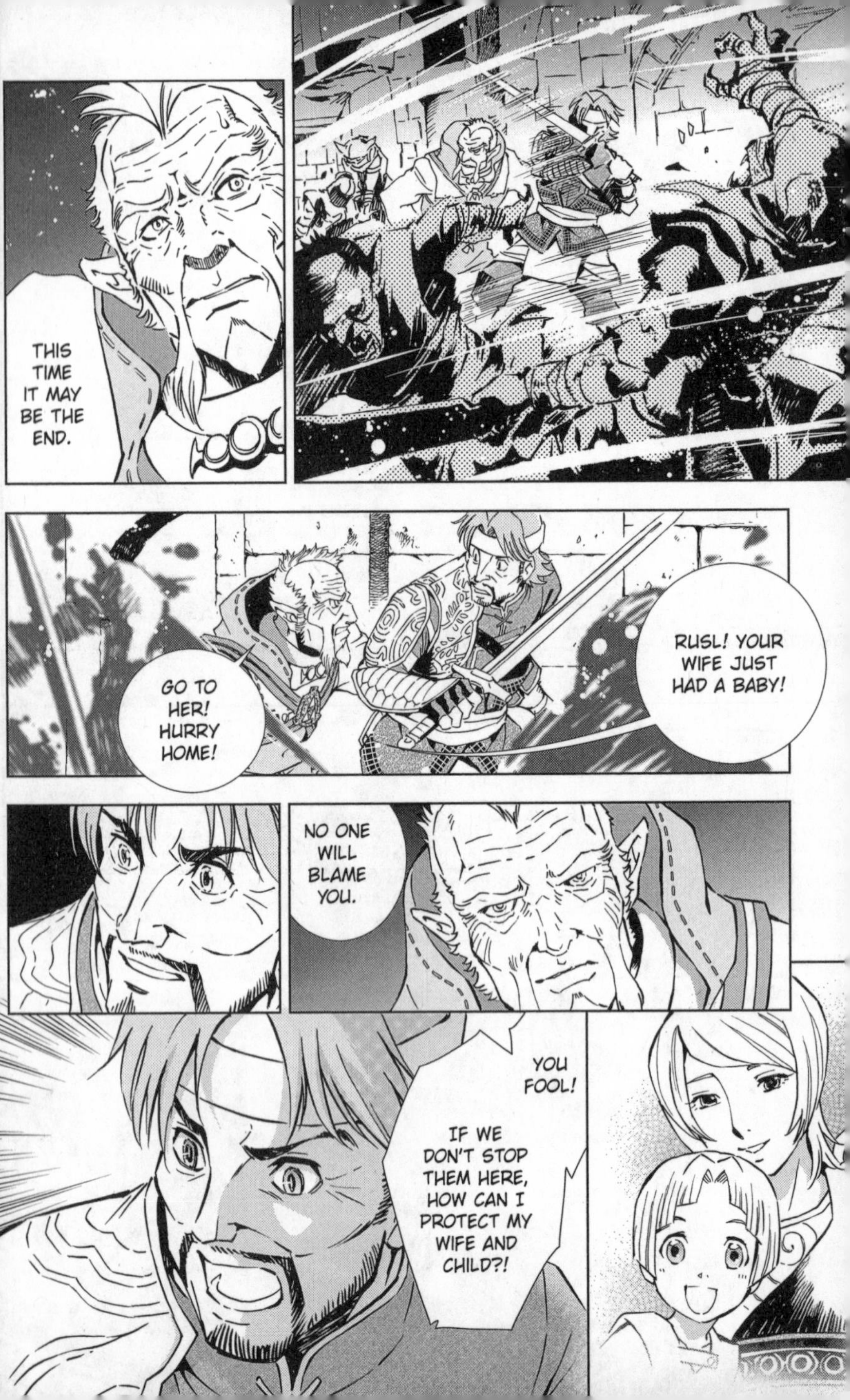
THIS TIME IT MAY BE THE END.
RUSL! YOUR WIFE JUST HAD A BABY!
GO TO HER! HURRY HOME!
NO ONE WILL BLAME YOU.
YOU FOOL!
IF WE DON'T STOP THEM HERE, HOW CAN I PROTECT MY WIFE AND CHILD?!

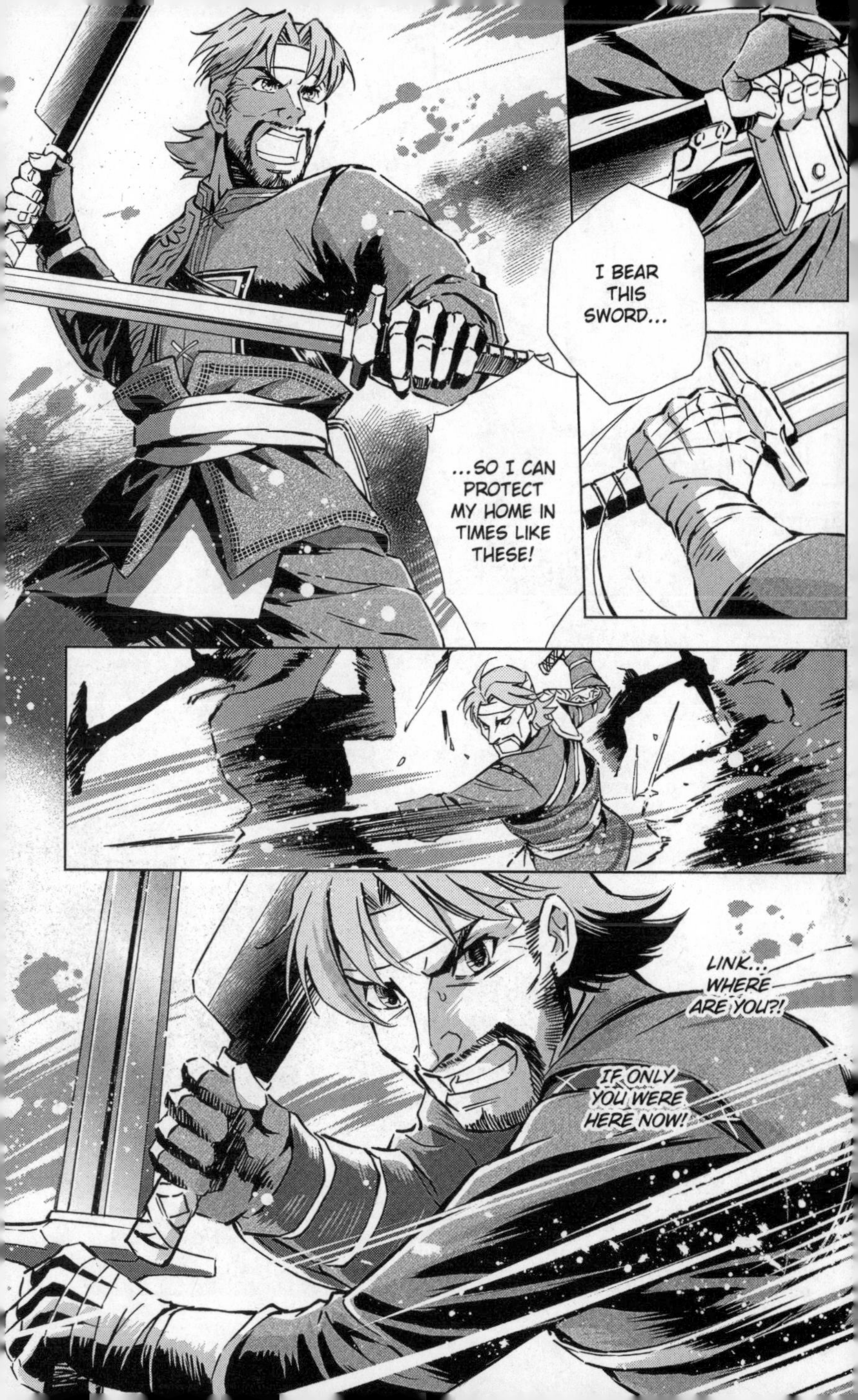
I BEAR THIS SWORD...
...SO I CAN PROTECT MY HOME IN TIMES LIKE THESE!
LINK... WHERE ARE YOU?!
IF ONLY YOU WERE HERE NOW!

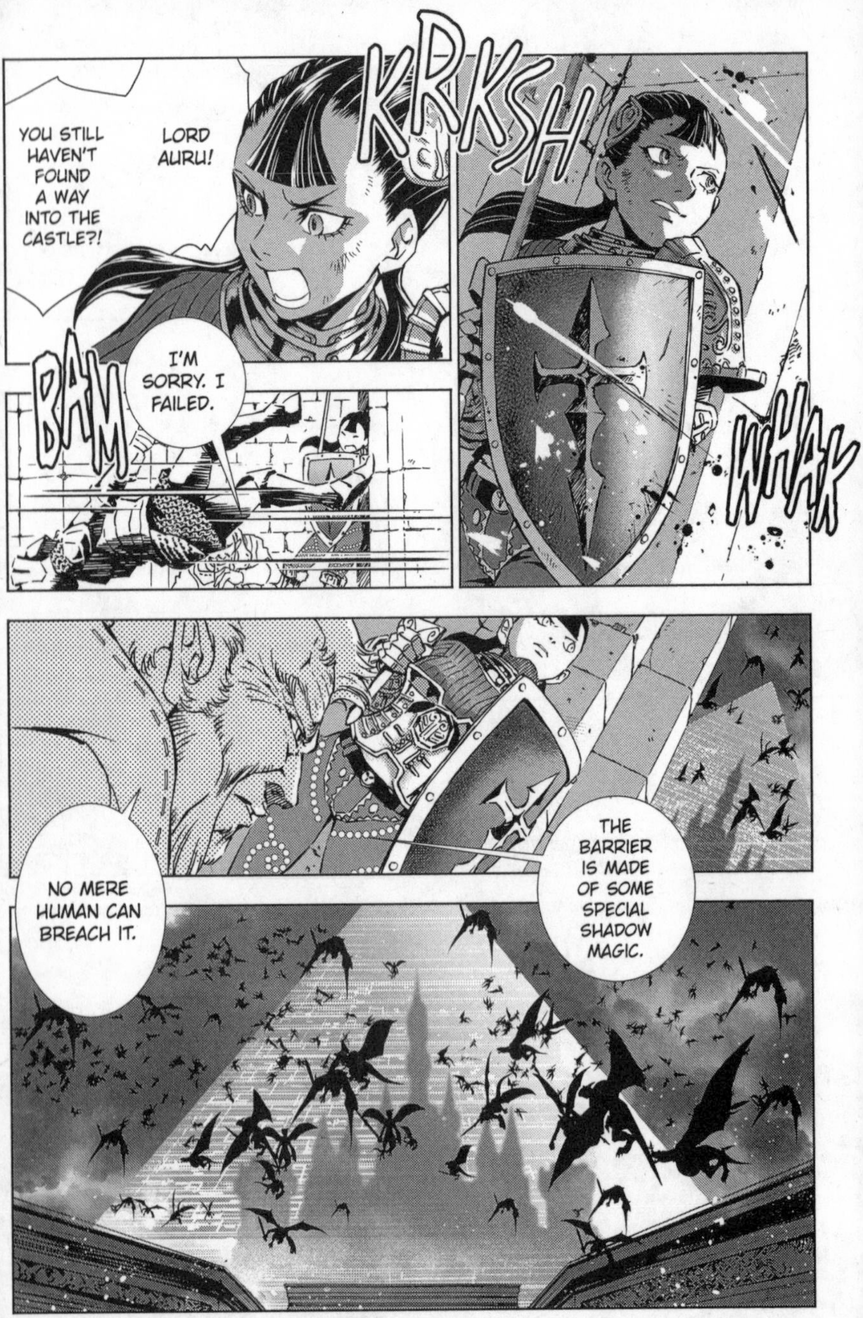
KRKSH
WHAK
LORD AURU!
YOU STILL HAVEN'T FOUND A WAY INTO THE CASTLE?!
I'M SORRY. I FAILED.
BAM
THE BARRIER IS MADE OF SOME SPECIAL SHADOW MAGIC.
NO MERE HUMAN CAN BREACH IT.

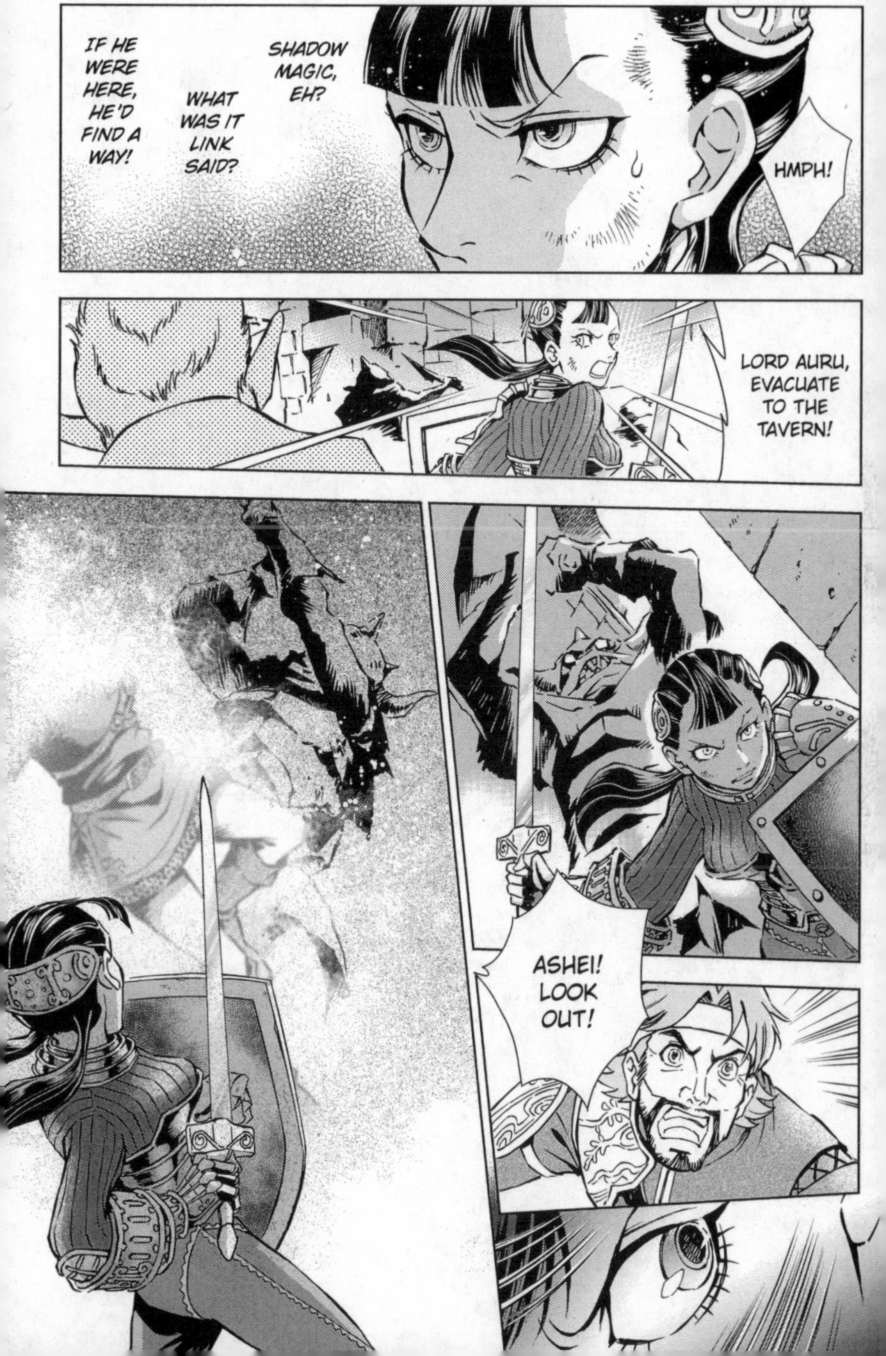
HMPH!
SHADOW MAGIC, EH?
WHAT WAS IT LINK SAID?
IF HE WERE HERE, HE'D FIND A WAY!
LORD AURU, EVACUATE TO THE TAVERN!
ASHEI! LOOK OUT!

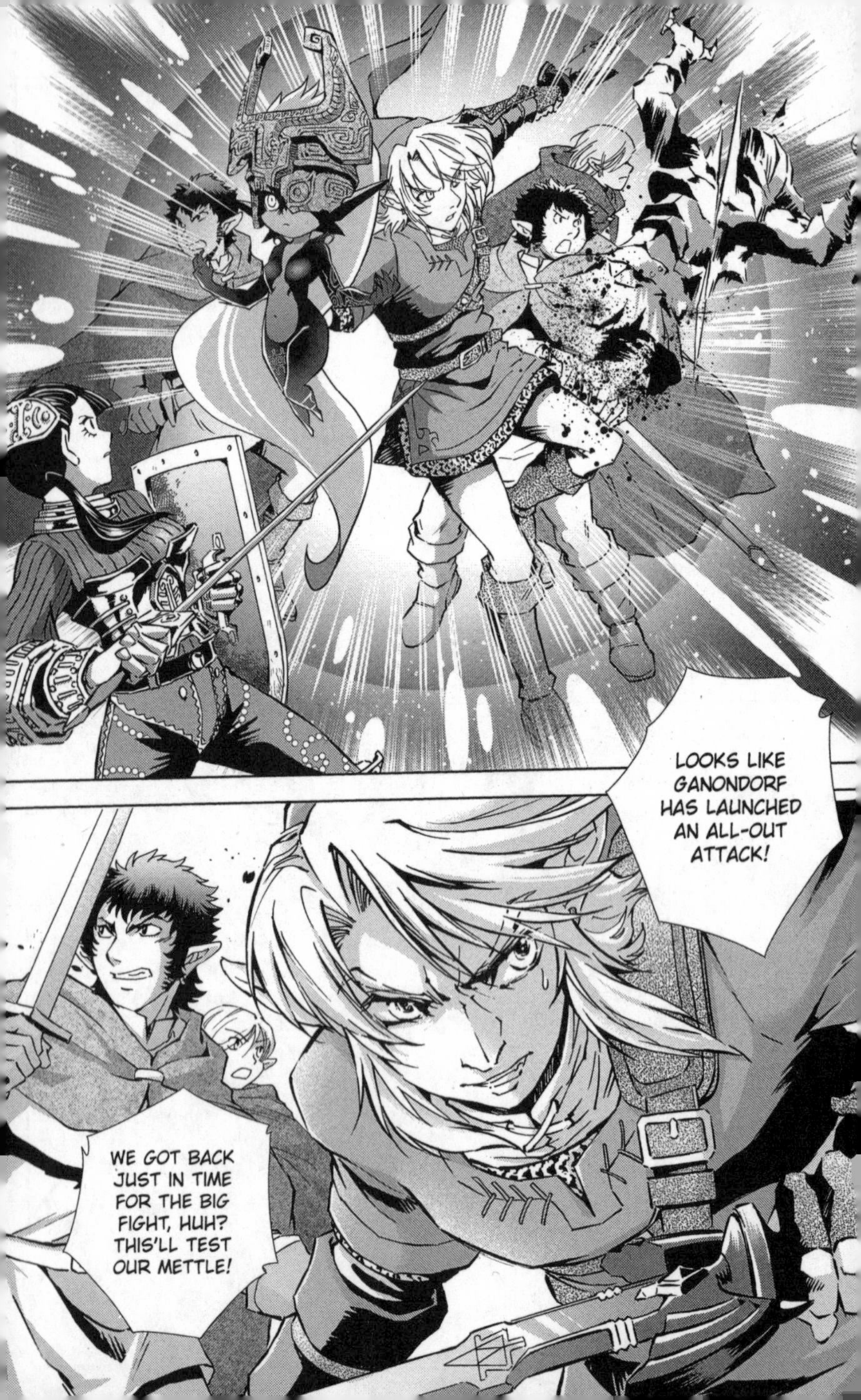
LOOKS LIKE GANONDORF HAS LAUNCHED AN ALL-OUT ATTACK!
WE GOT BACK JUST IN TIME FOR THE BIG FIGHT, HUH? THIS'LL TEST OUR METTLE!

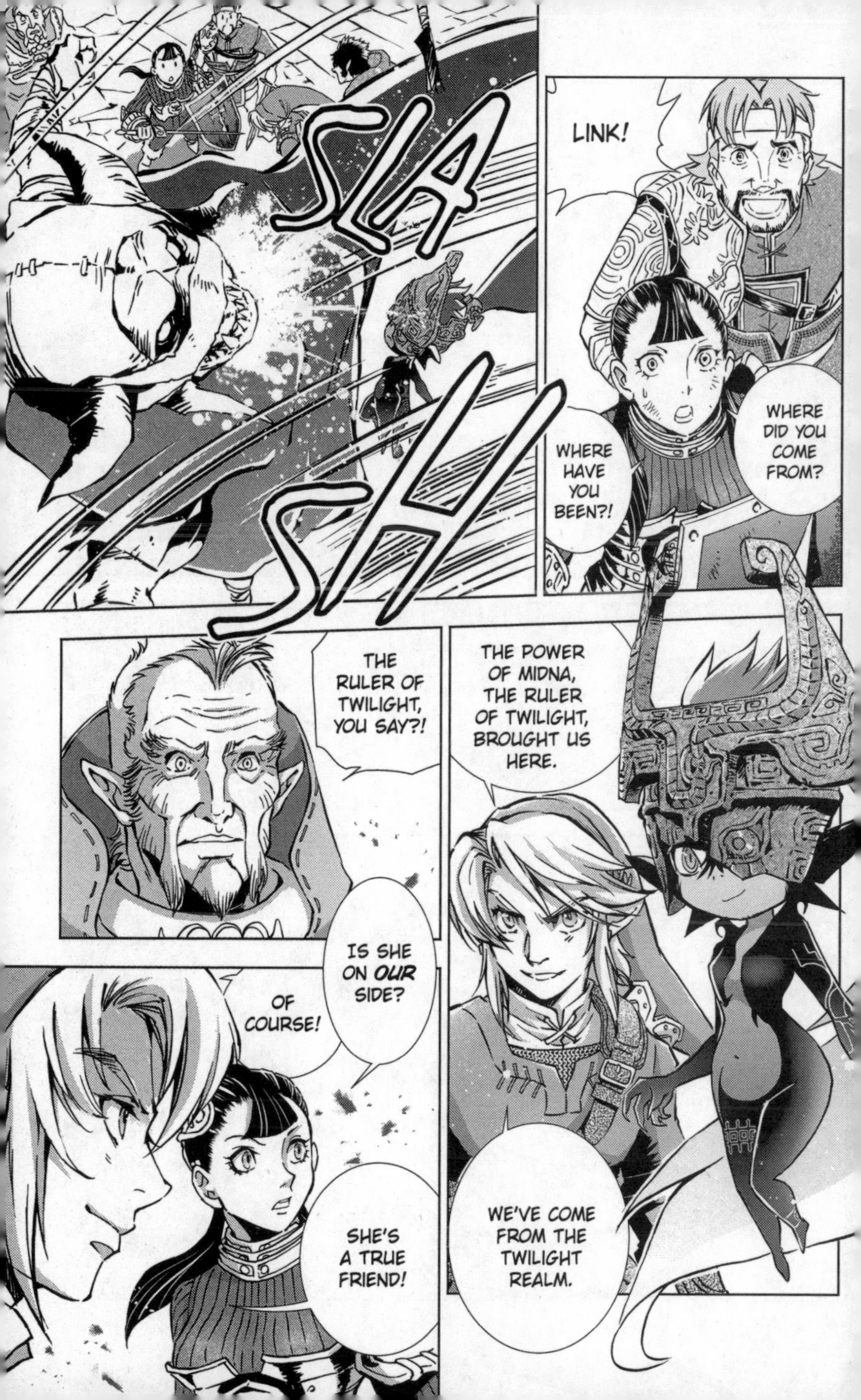
LINK!
WHERE DID YOU COME FROM?
WHERE HAVE YOU BEEN?!
SLASH
THE POWER OF MIDNA, THE RULER OF TWILIGHT, BROUGHT US HERE.
WE'VE COME FROM THE TWILIGHT REALM.
THE RULER OF TWILIGHT, YOU SAY?!
IS SHE ON *OUR* SIDE?
OF COURSE!
SHE'S A TRUE FRIEND!

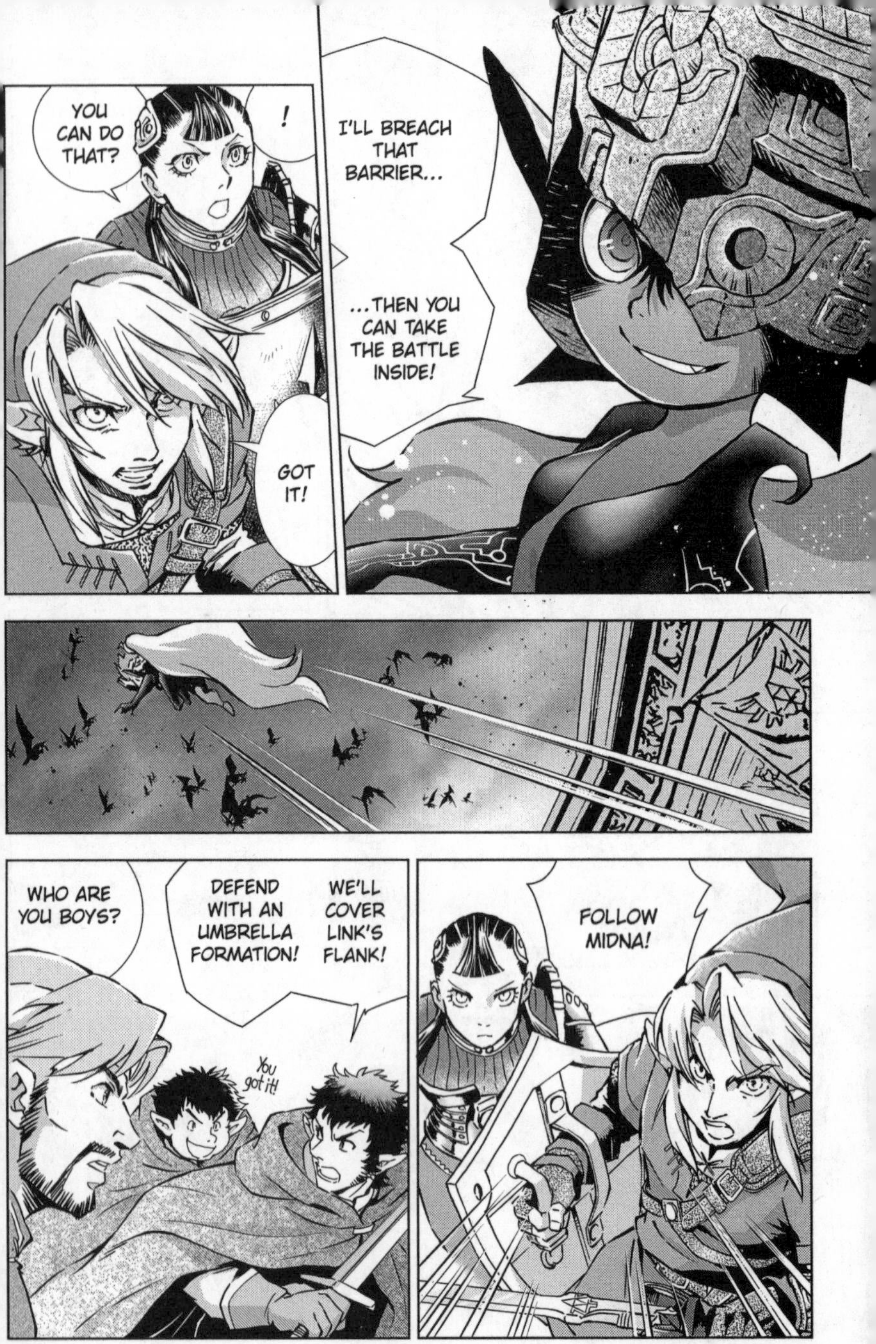
I'LL BREACH THAT BARRIER...
...THEN YOU CAN TAKE THE BATTLE INSIDE!
!
YOU CAN DO THAT?
GOT IT!
FOLLOW MIDNA!
WE'LL COVER LINK'S FLANK!
DEFEND WITH AN UMBRELLA FORMATION!
WHO ARE YOU BOYS?
You got it!

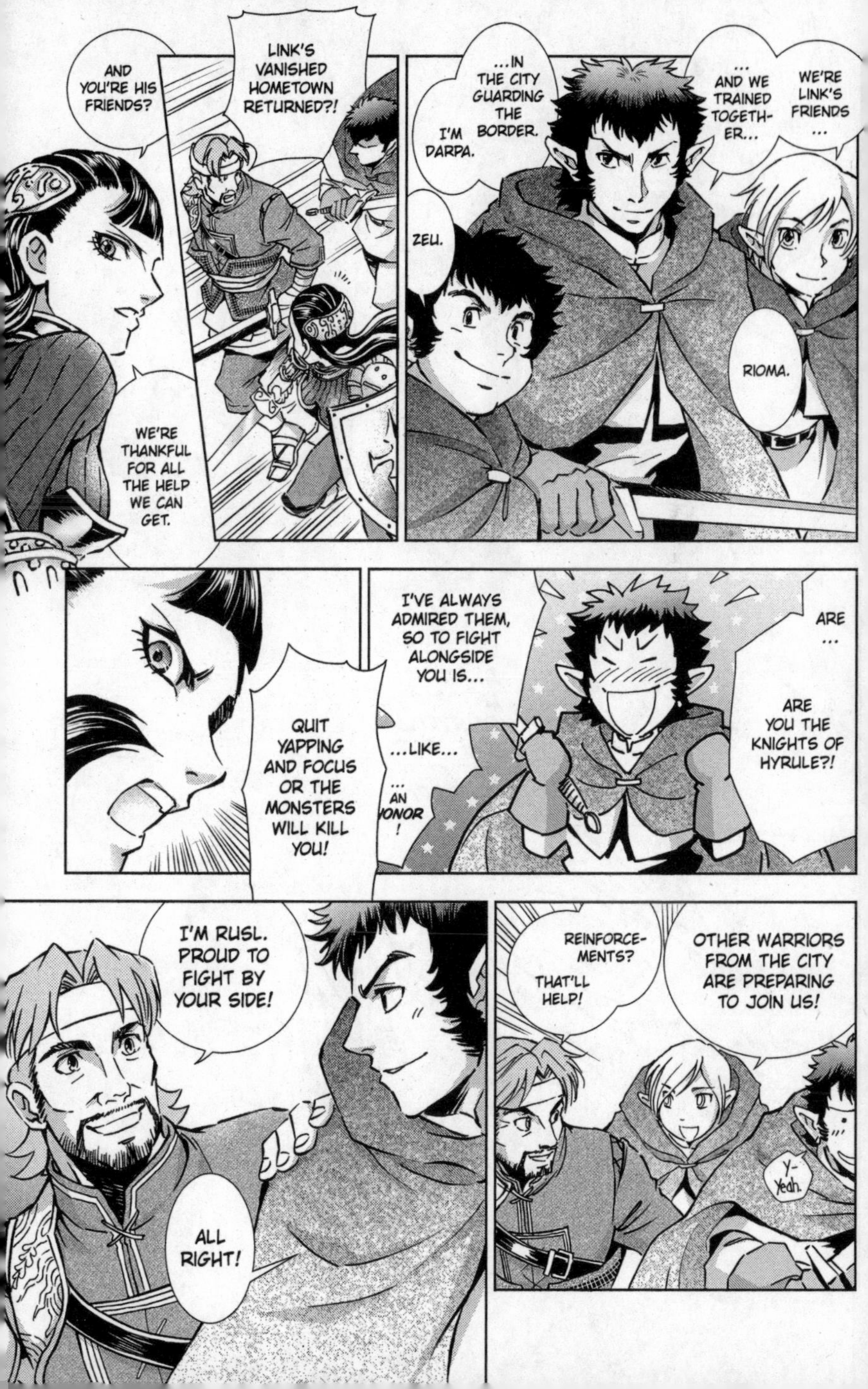
WE'RE LINK'S FRIENDS...
...AND WE TRAINED TOGETH-ER...
...IN THE CITY GUARDING THE BORDER.
I'M DARPA.
RIOMA.
ZEU.
LINK'S VANISHED HOMETOWN RETURNED?!
AND YOU'RE HIS FRIENDS?
WE'RE THANKFUL FOR ALL THE HELP WE CAN GET.
ARE...
ARE YOU THE KNIGHTS OF HYRULE?!
I'VE ALWAYS ADMIRED THEM, SO TO FIGHT ALONGSIDE YOU IS...
...LIKE...
...AN HONOR!
QUIT YAPPING AND FOCUS OR THE MONSTERS WILL KILL YOU!
OTHER WARRIORS FROM THE CITY ARE PREPARING TO JOIN US!
REINFORCE-MENTS?
THAT'LL HELP!
Y-Yeah.
I'M RUSL. PROUD TO FIGHT BY YOUR SIDE!
ALL RIGHT!

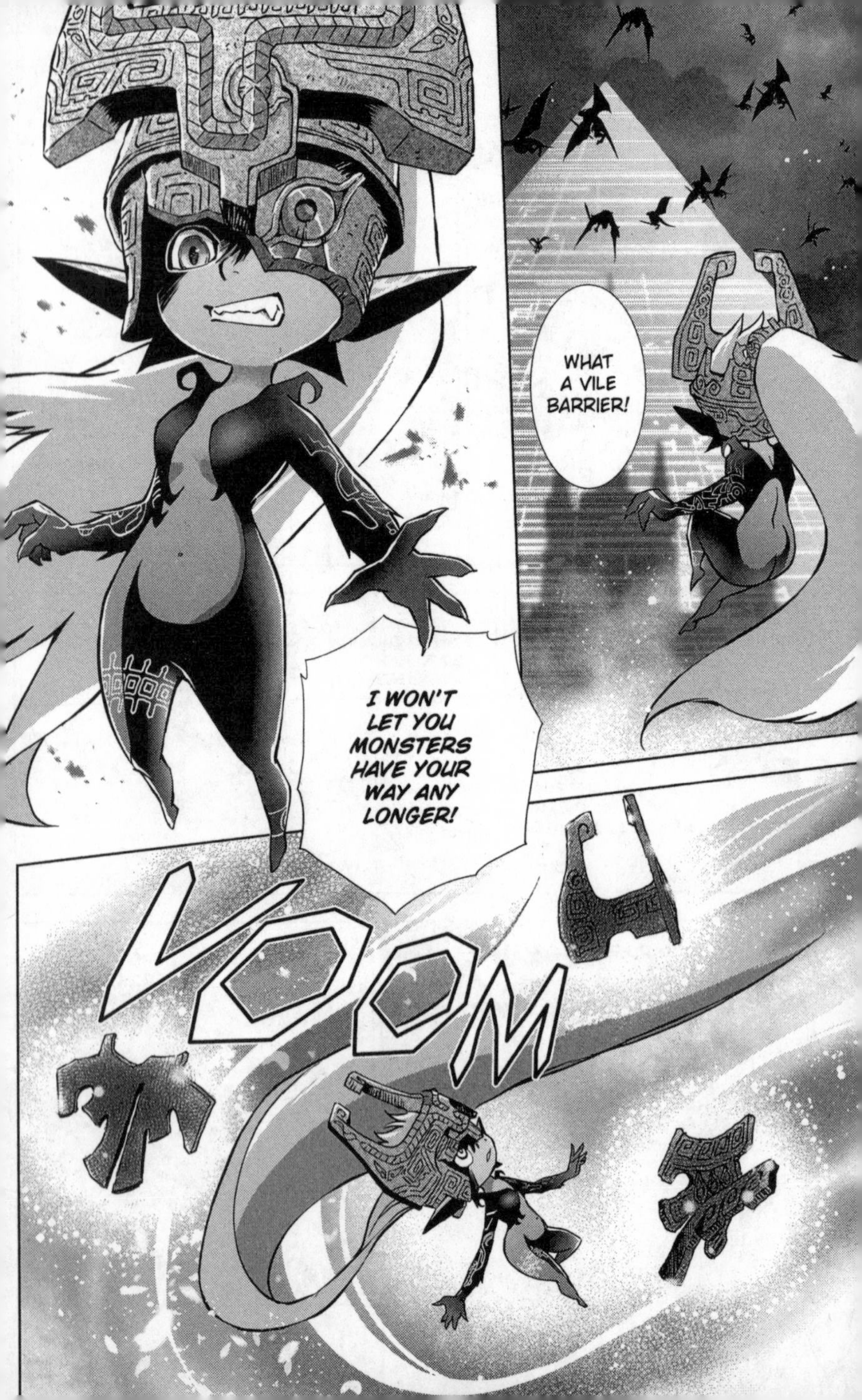
WHAT A VILE BARRIER!
I WON'T LET YOU MONSTERS HAVE YOUR WAY ANY LONGER!
VOOM

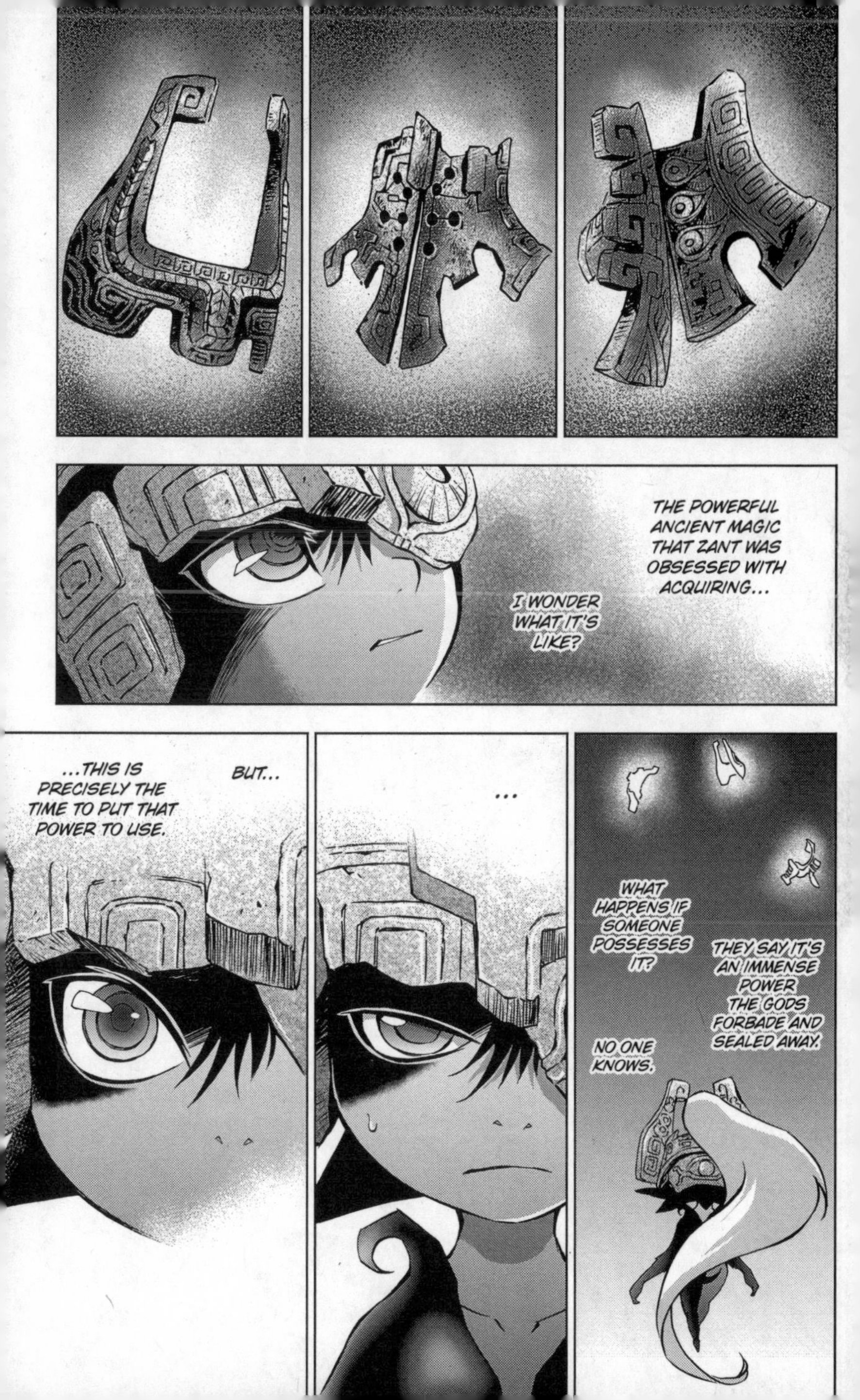
THE POWERFUL ANCIENT MAGIC THAT ZANT WAS OBSESSED WITH ACQUIRING...
I WONDER WHAT IT'S LIKE?
THEY SAY IT'S AN IMMENSE POWER THE GODS FORBADE AND SEALED AWAY.
WHAT HAPPENS IF SOMEONE POSSESSES IT?
NO ONE KNOWS.
...
BUT...
...THIS IS PRECISELY THE TIME TO PUT THAT POWER TO USE.

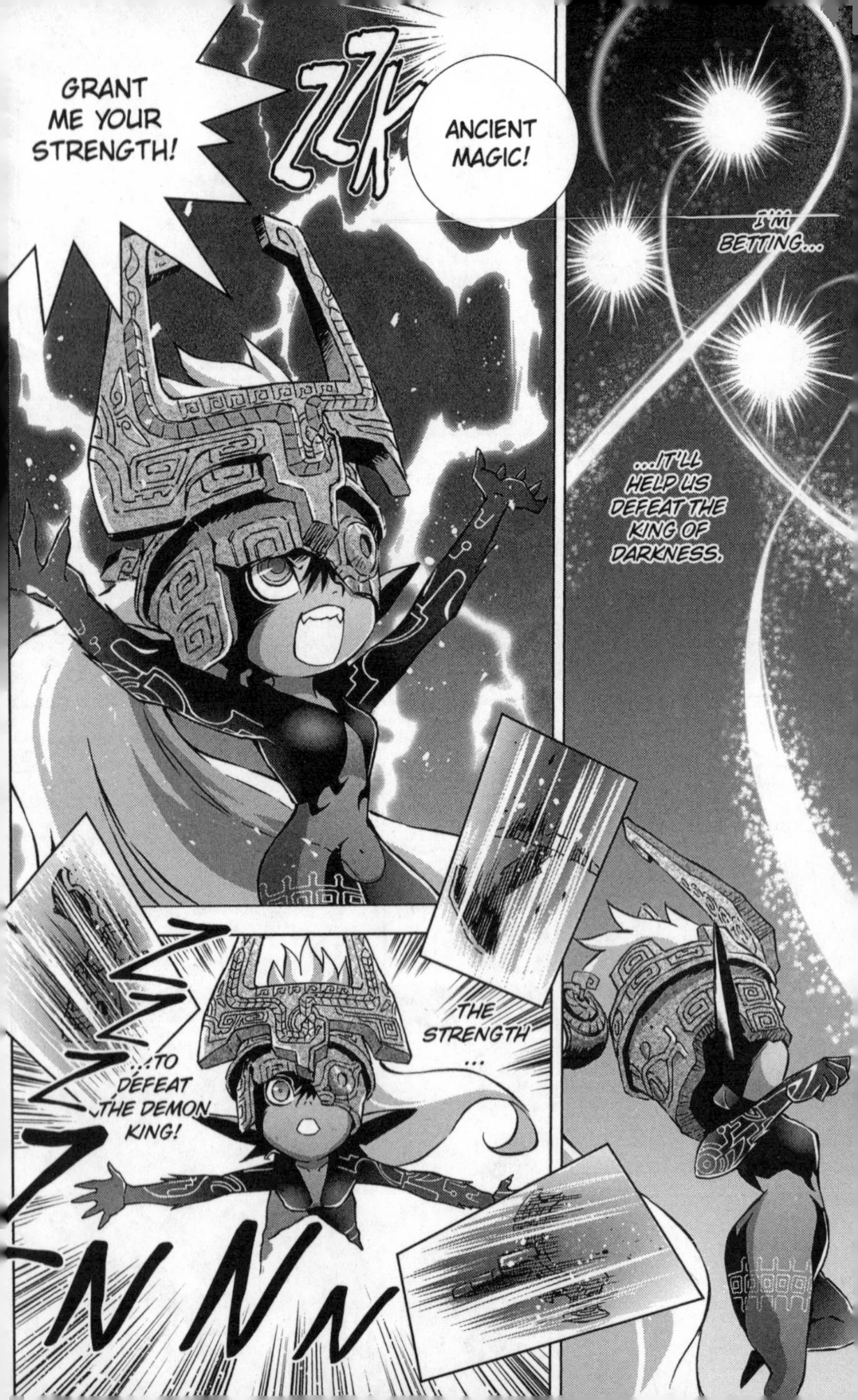
I'M BETTING...
...IT'LL HELP US DEFEAT THE KING OF DARKNESS.
ZZK
ANCIENT MAGIC!
GRANT ME YOUR STRENGTH!
THE STRENGTH...
...TO DEFEAT THE DEMON KING!
NNN

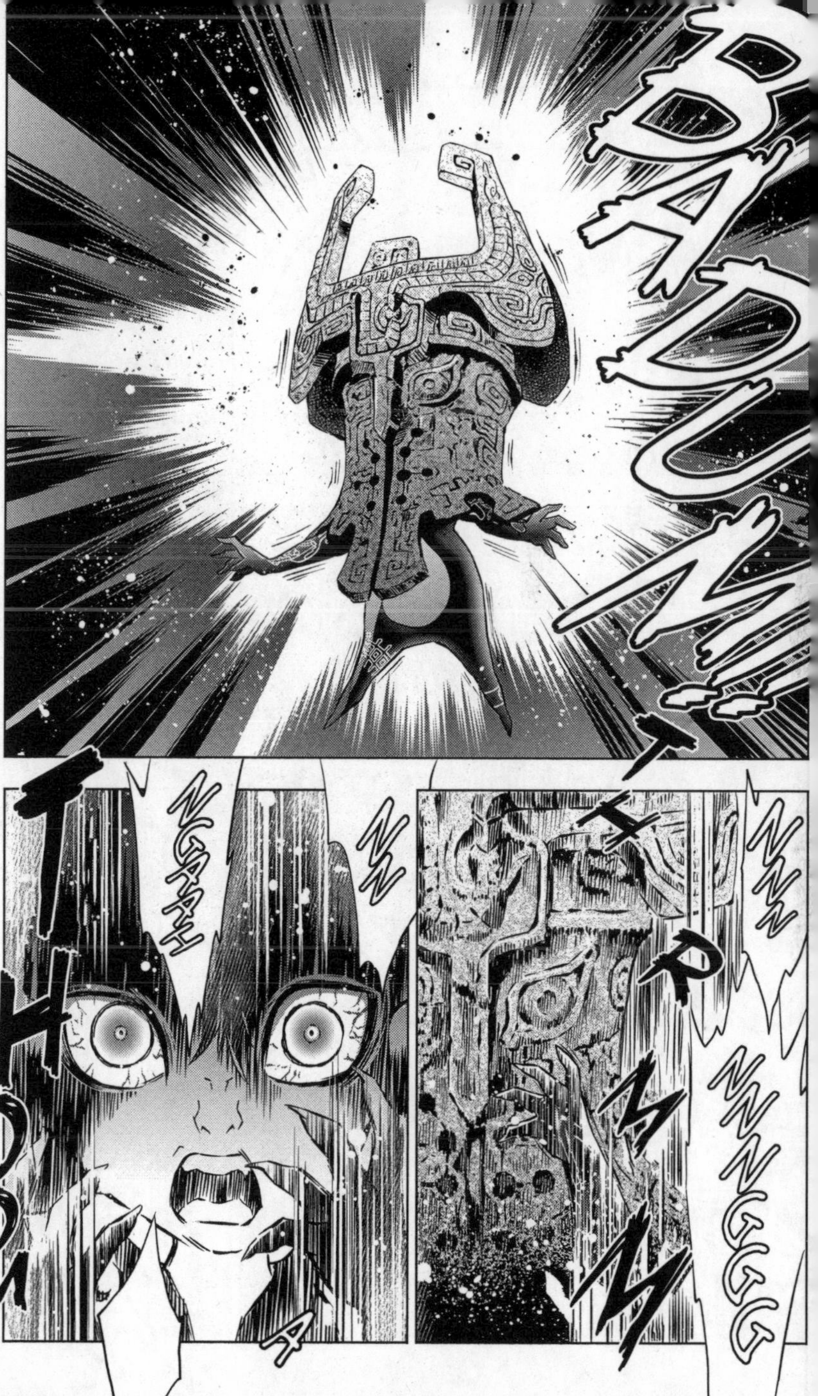
BADUM!!
THRMMM
NNN NNNNGGG
NN NGAAAH
THOOOM
A

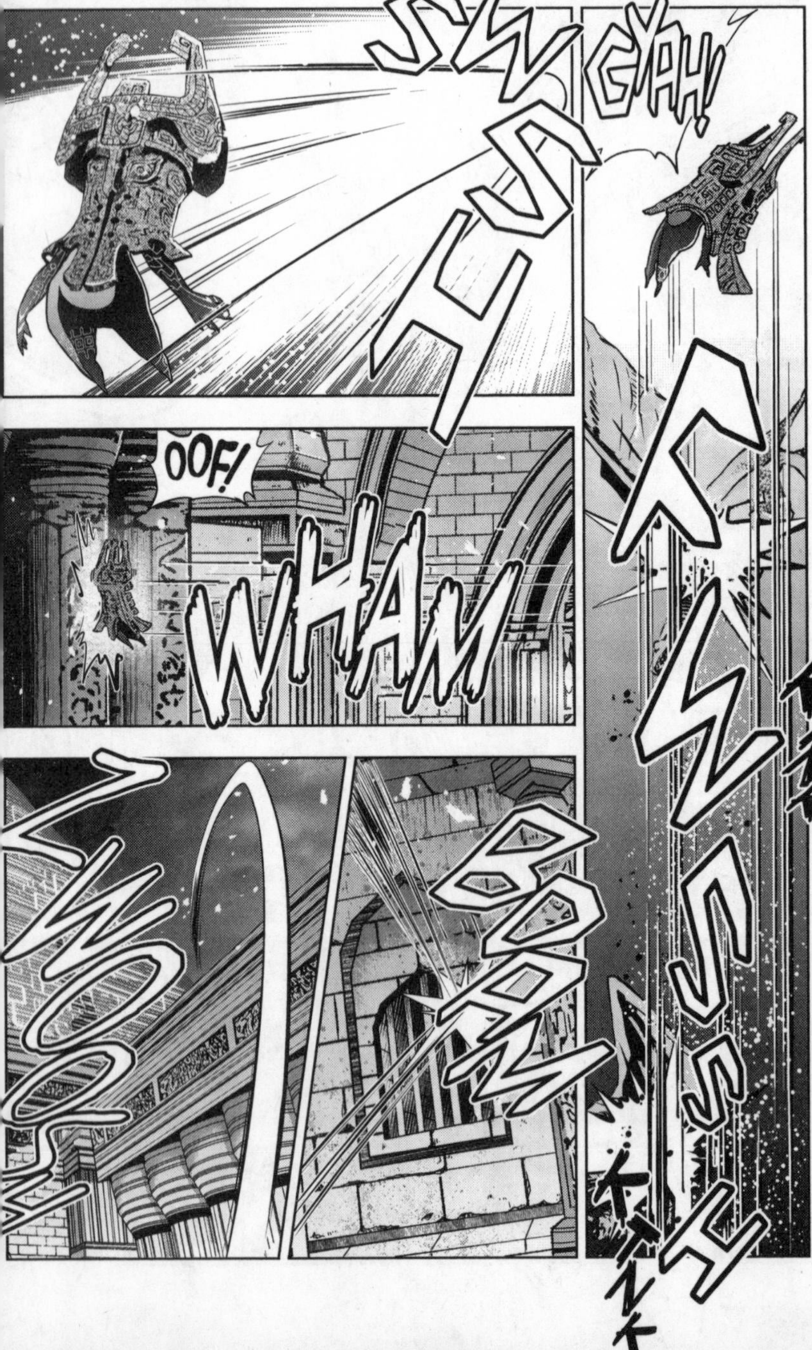
GYAH!
KINK
KINK
OOF!
WHAM

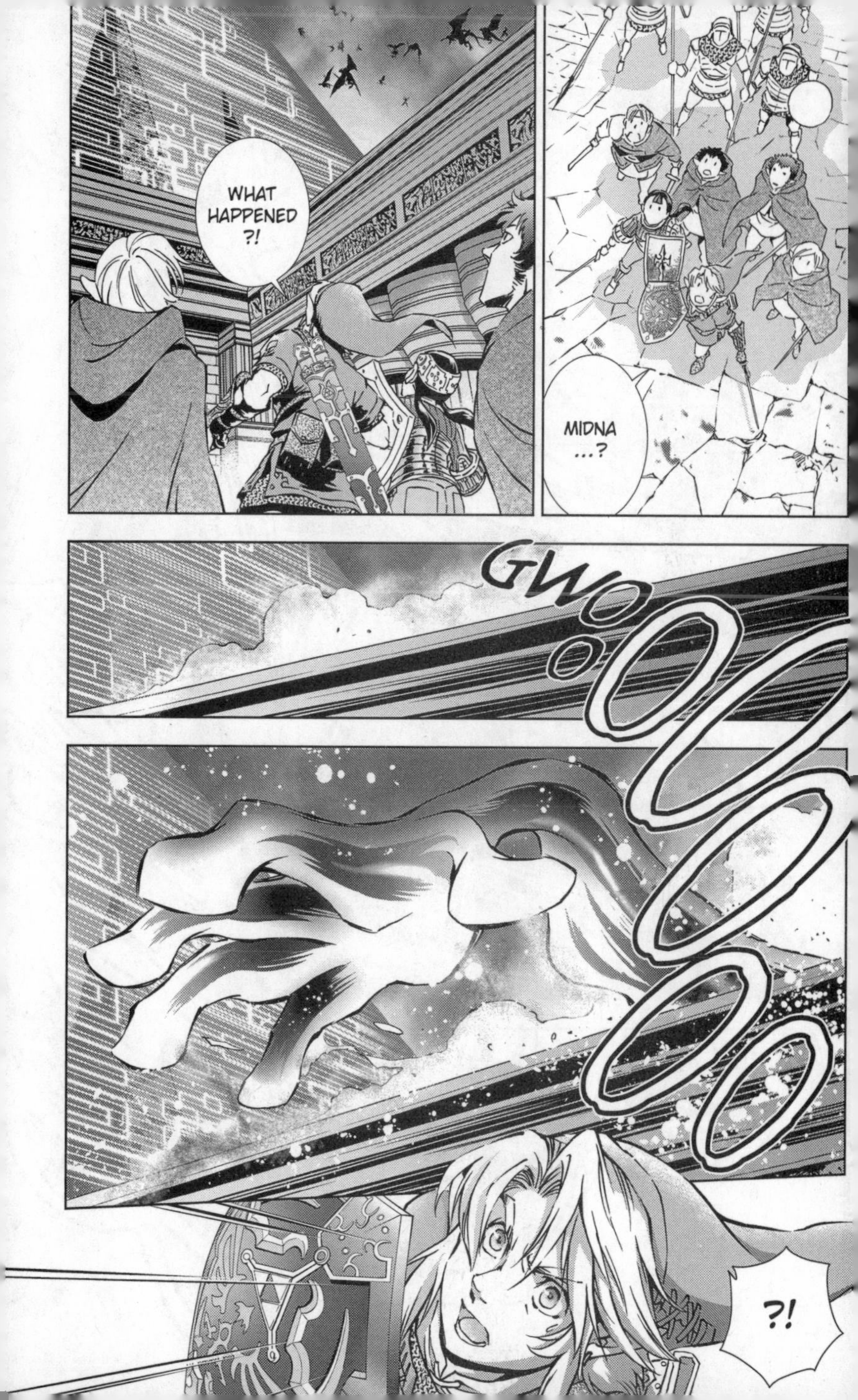
MIDNA ...?
WHAT HAPPENED ?!
GWOOOOOOOO
?!

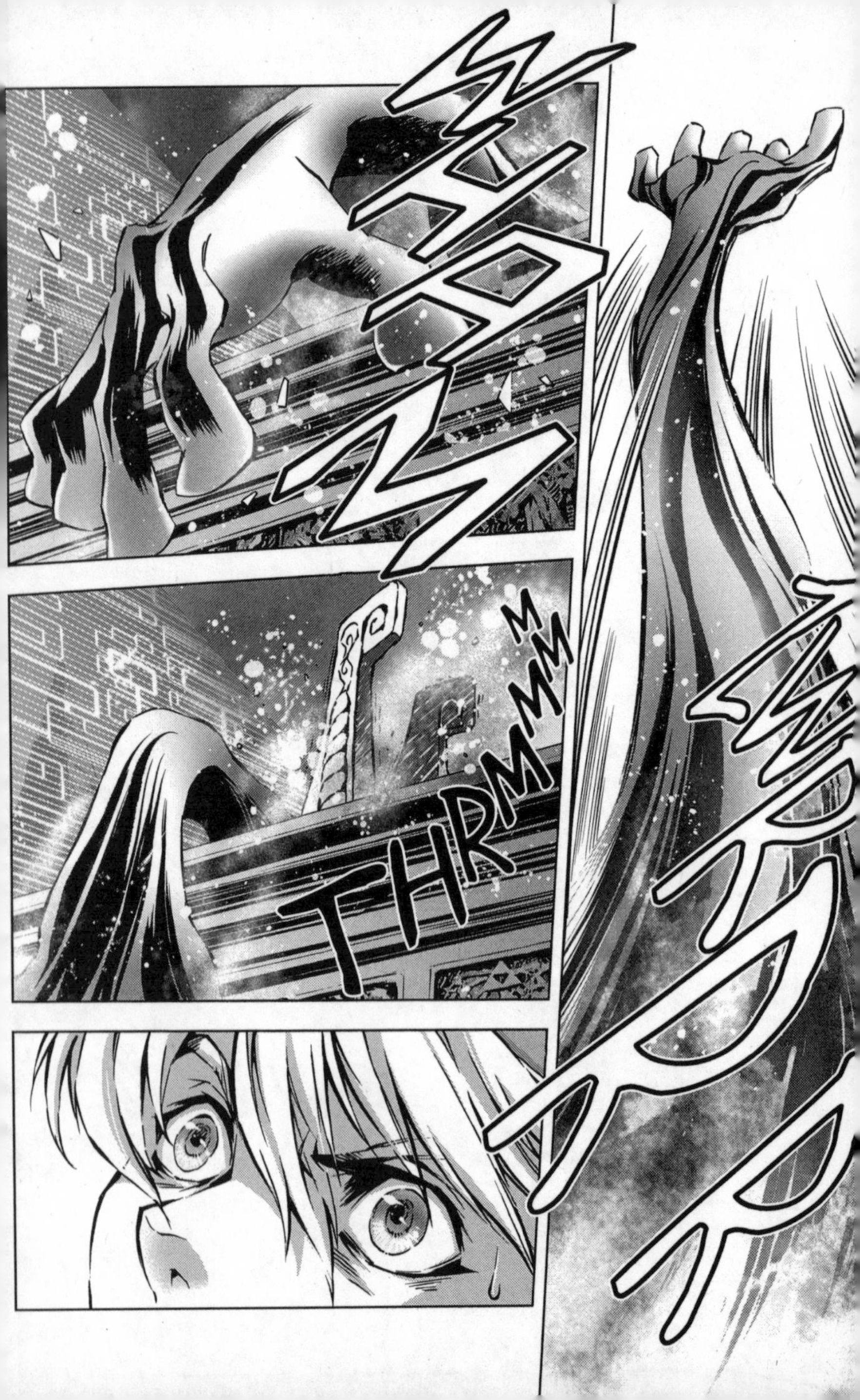
THRMMMM

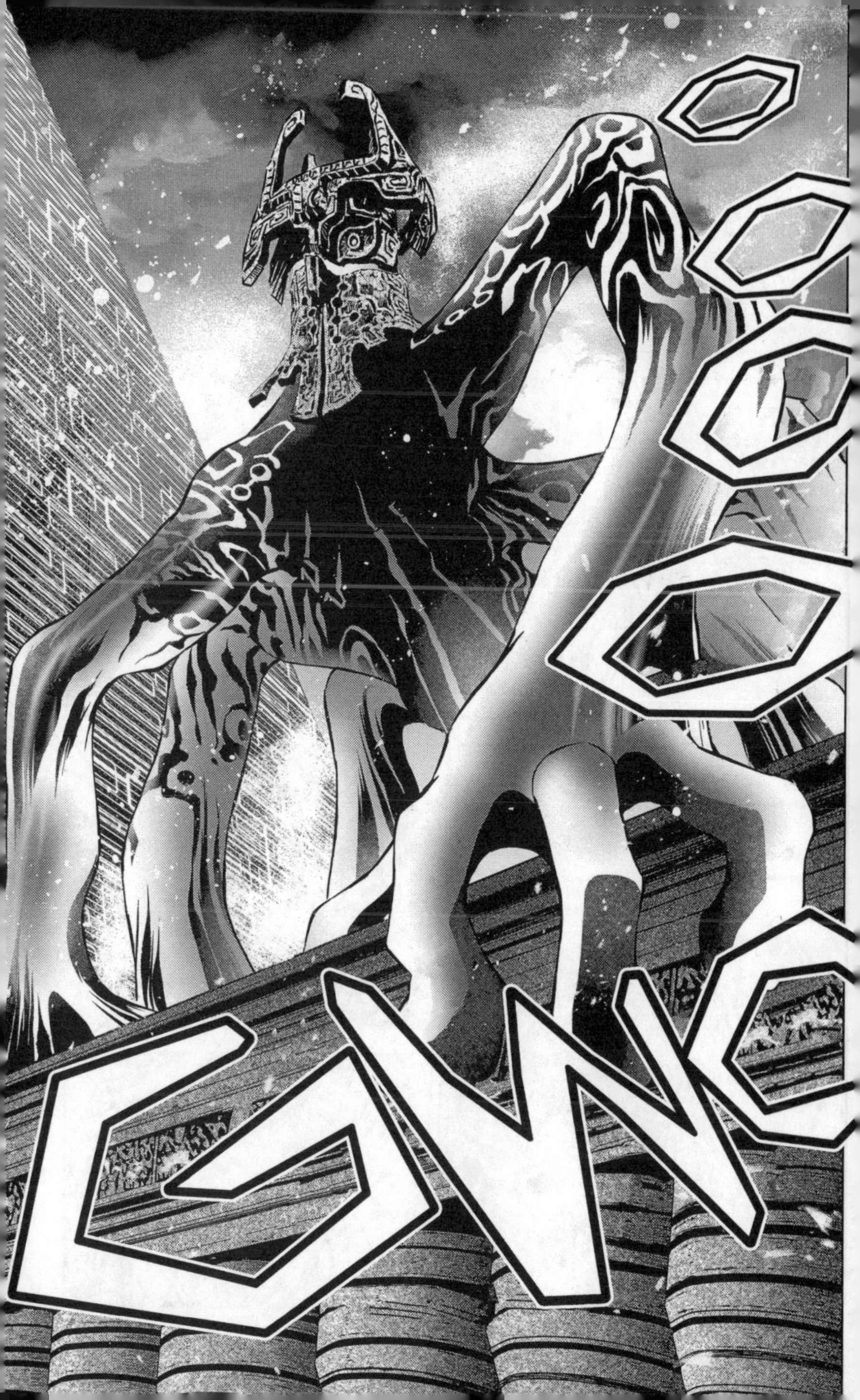
GWOOOOO

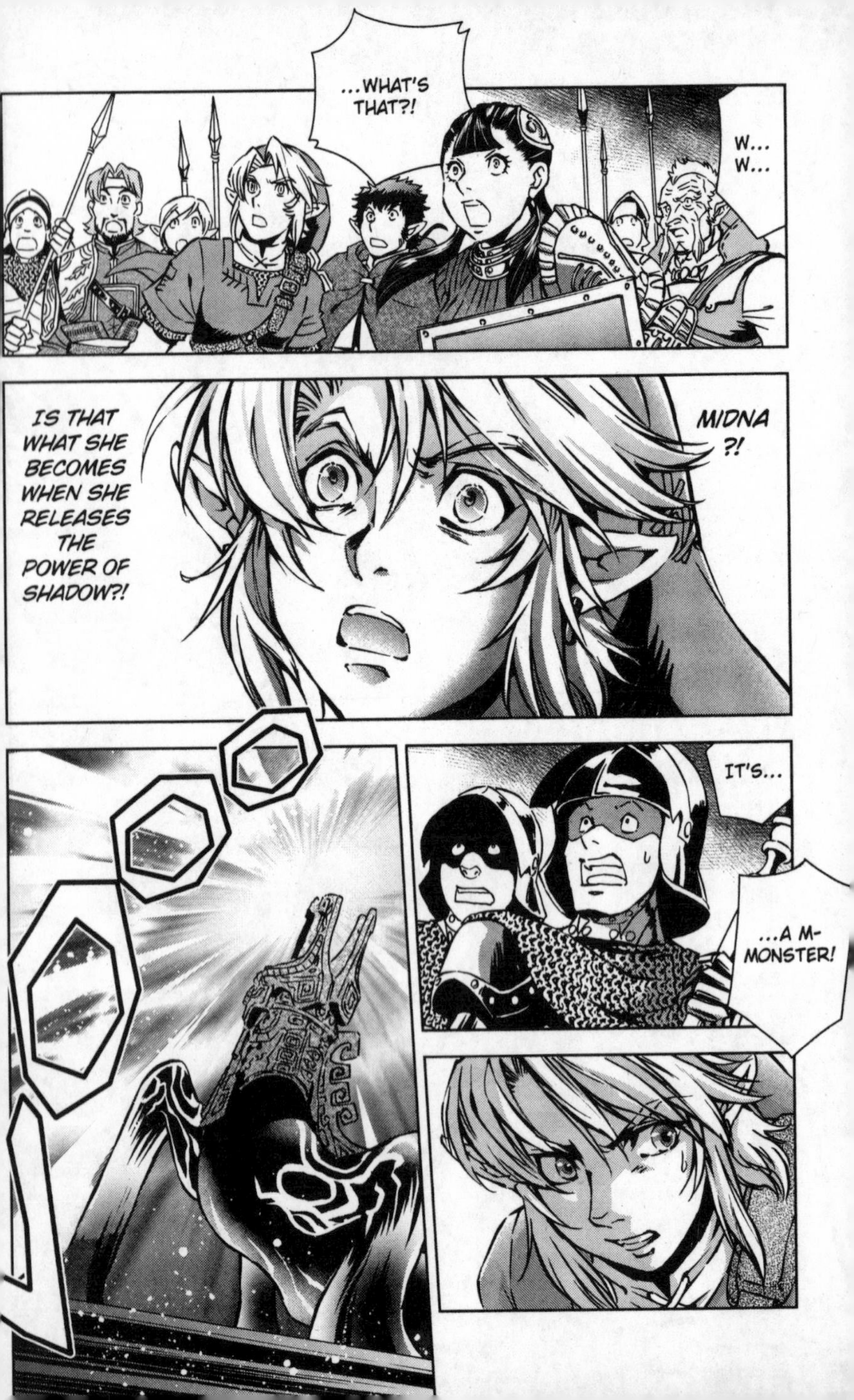
W... W...
...WHAT'S THAT?!
MIDNA ?!
IS THAT WHAT SHE BECOMES WHEN SHE RELEASES THE POWER OF SHADOW?!
IT'S...
...A M-MONSTER!

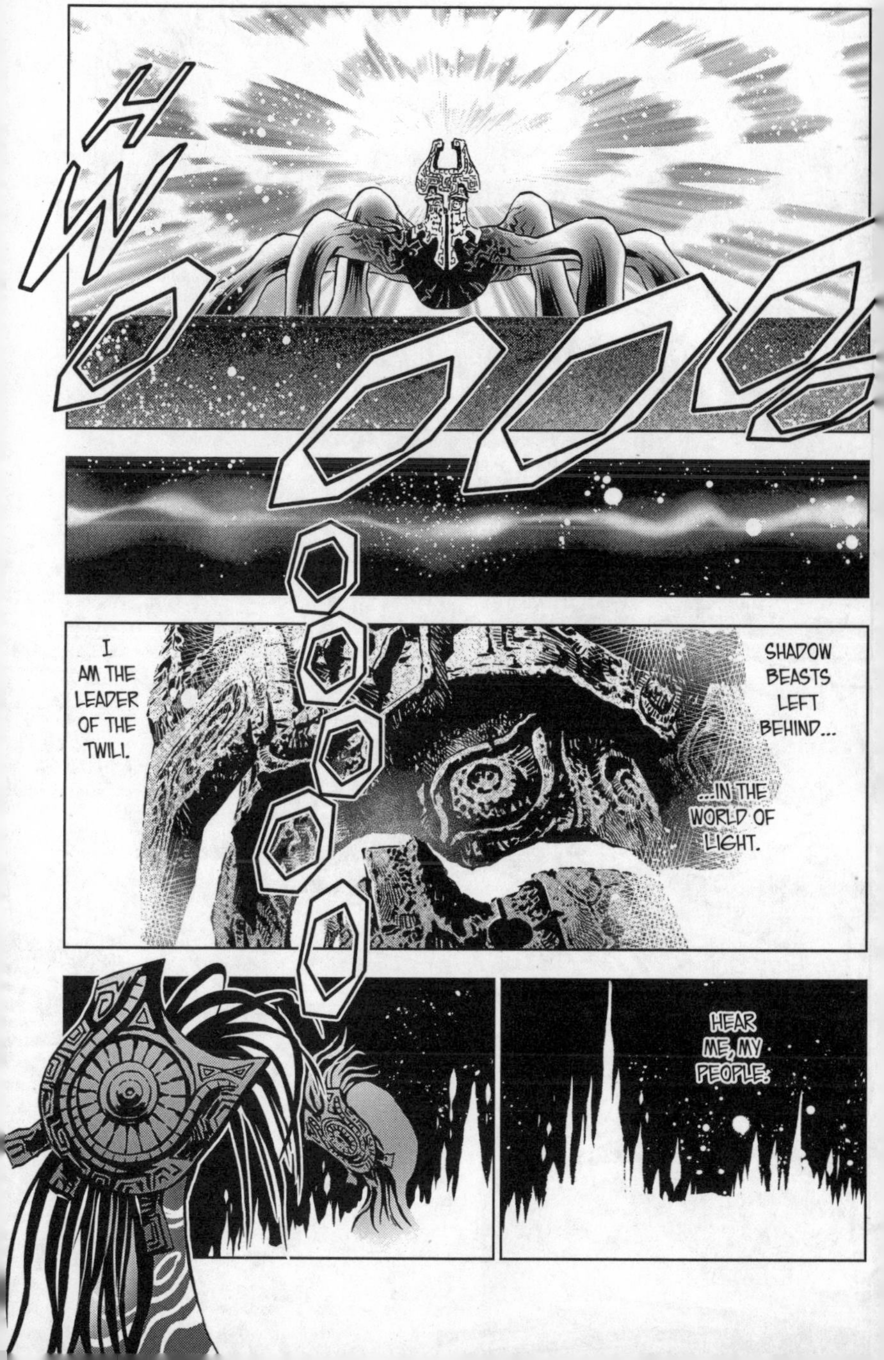
SHADOW BEASTS LEFT BEHIND...
...IN THE WORLD OF LIGHT.
I AM THE LEADER OF THE TWILI.
HEAR ME, MY PEOPLE.

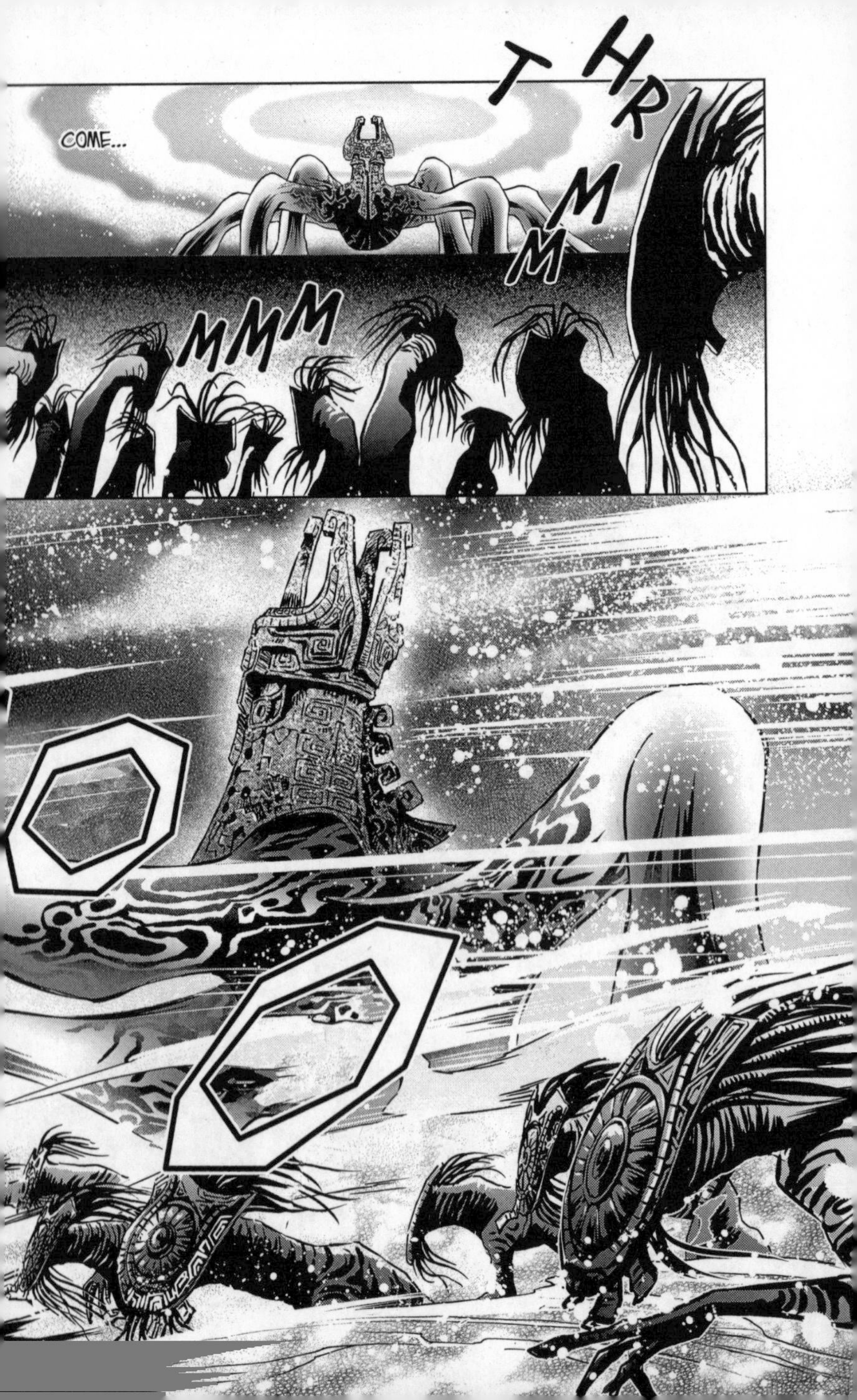

HRMMM
COME...
MMM

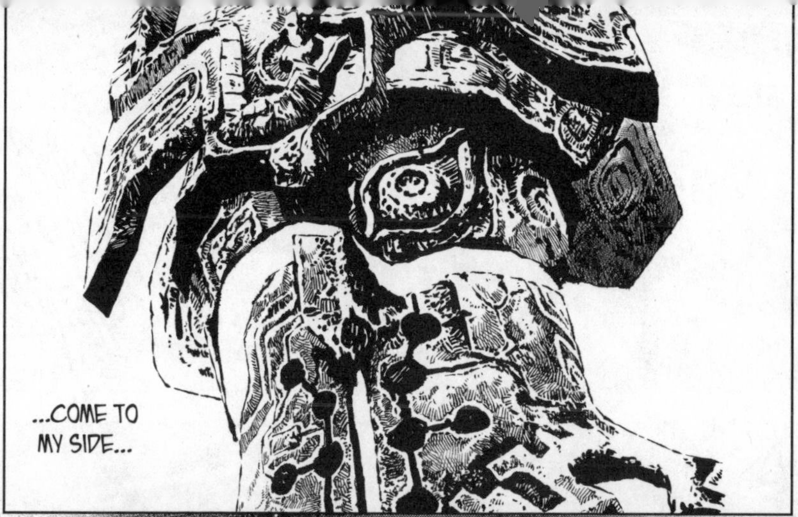
...COME TO MY SIDE...

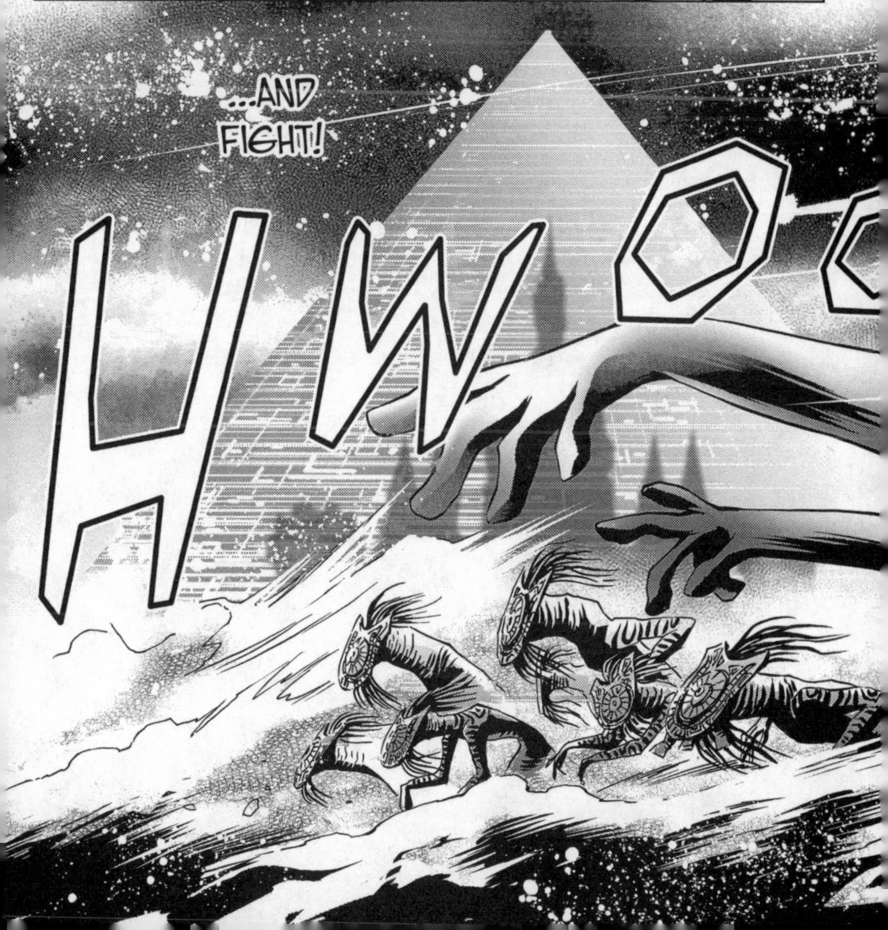
...AND FIGHT!
HWO

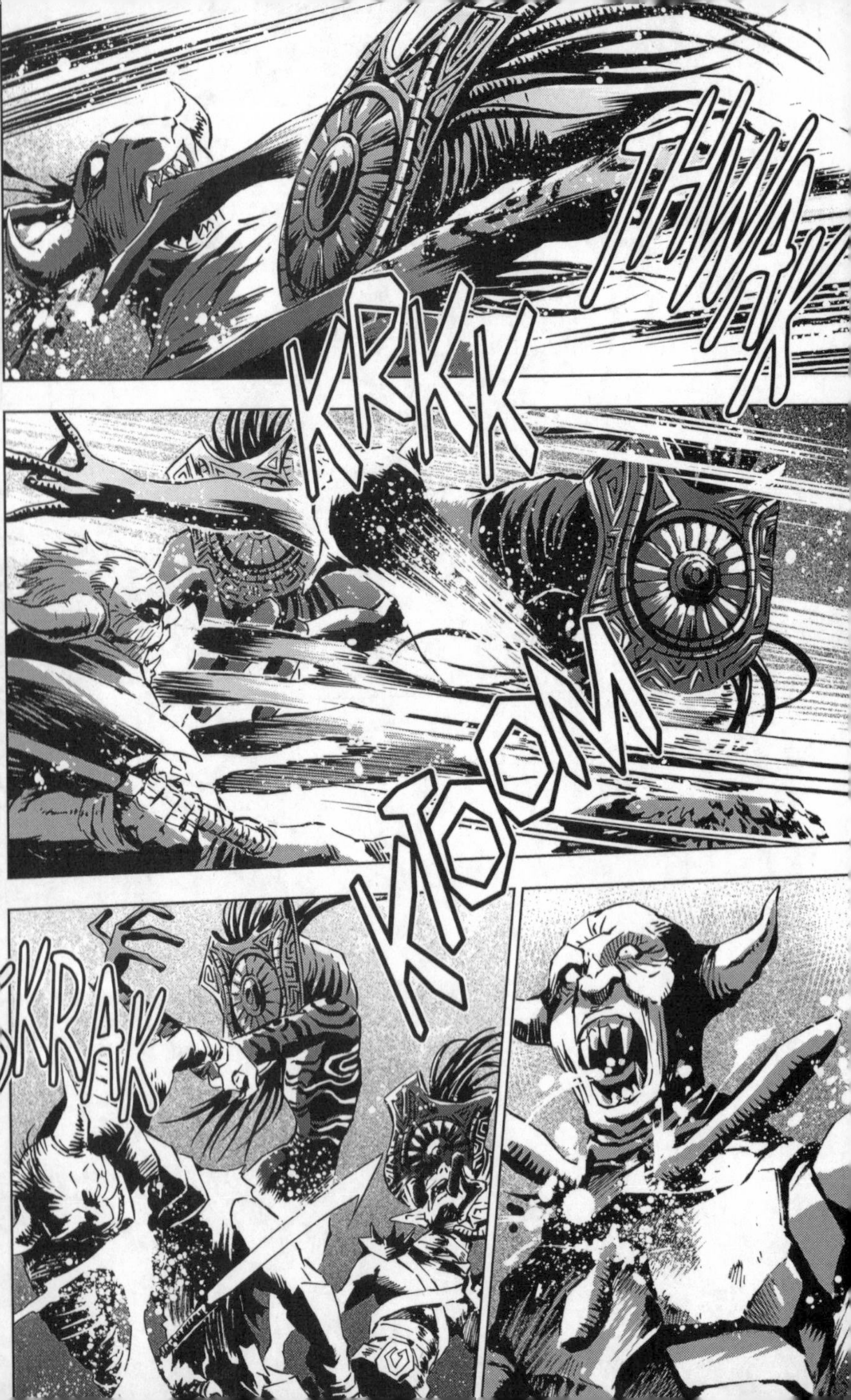
THWAK
KRKK
KTOOM
SKRAK

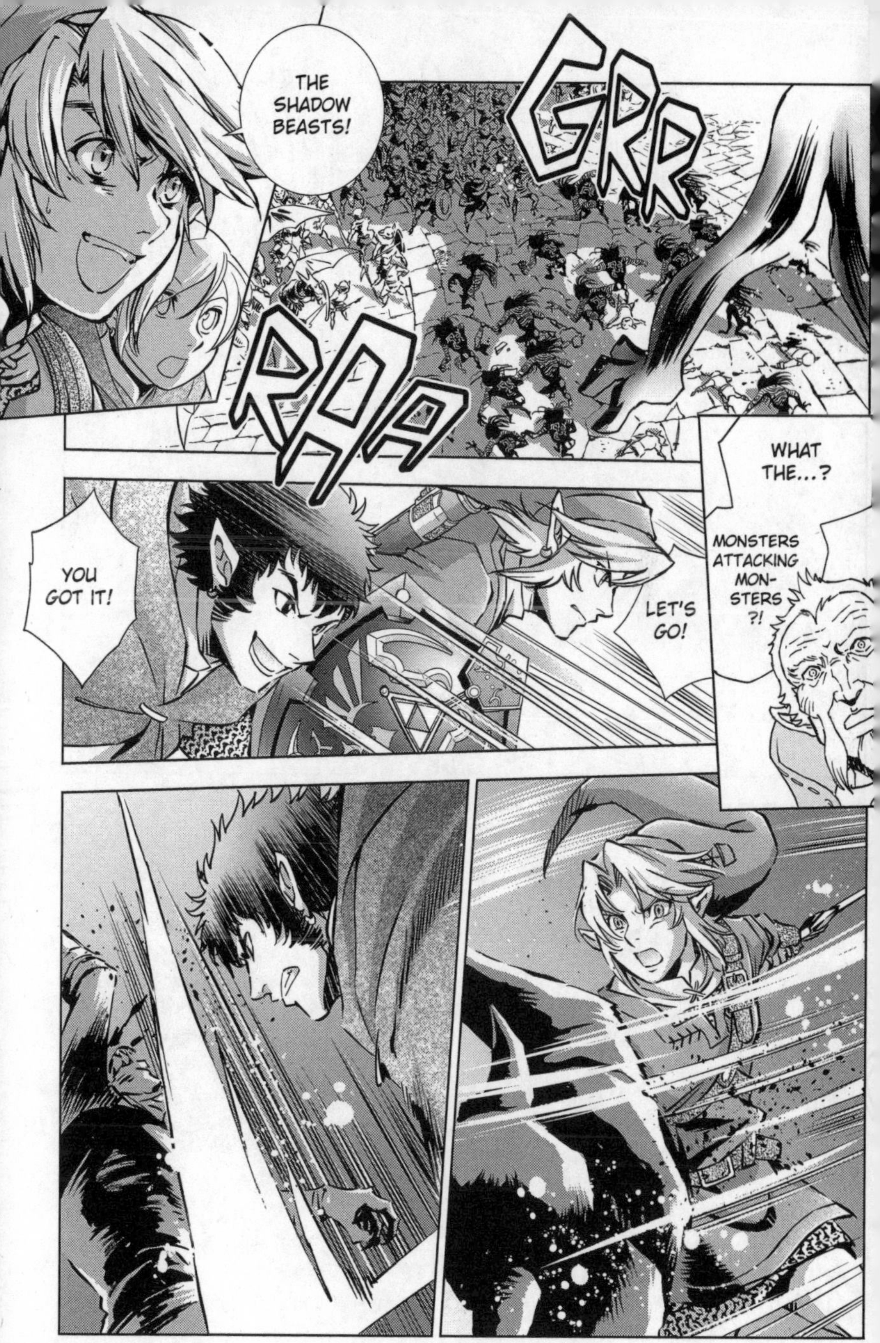
GRR
RAA
THE SHADOW BEASTS!
WHAT THE...?
MONSTERS ATTACKING MON-STERS?!
LET'S GO!
YOU GOT IT!

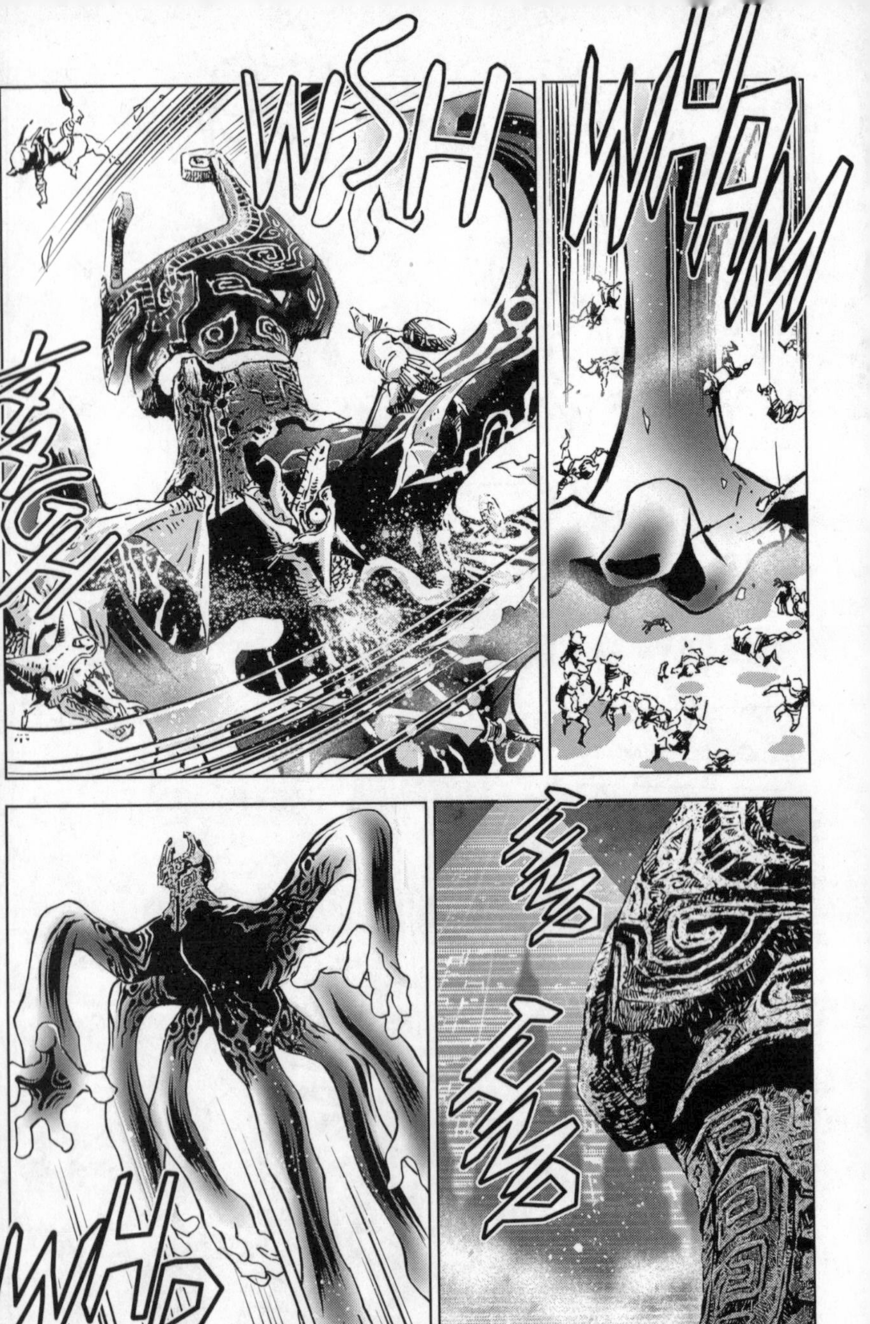
WHAM
WSH
THMP
THMP
WHP

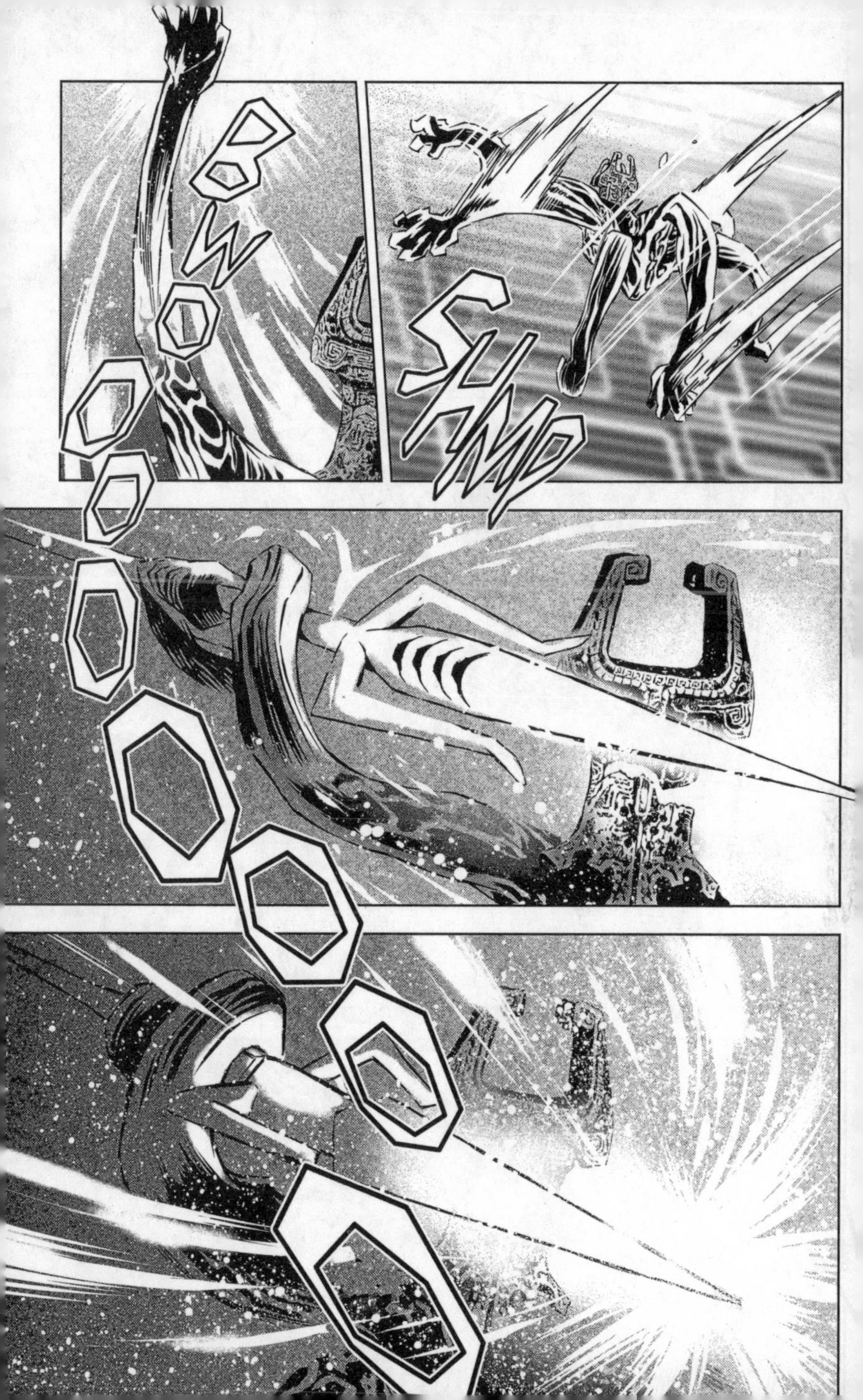
SHMP
BWOOOOOOOO

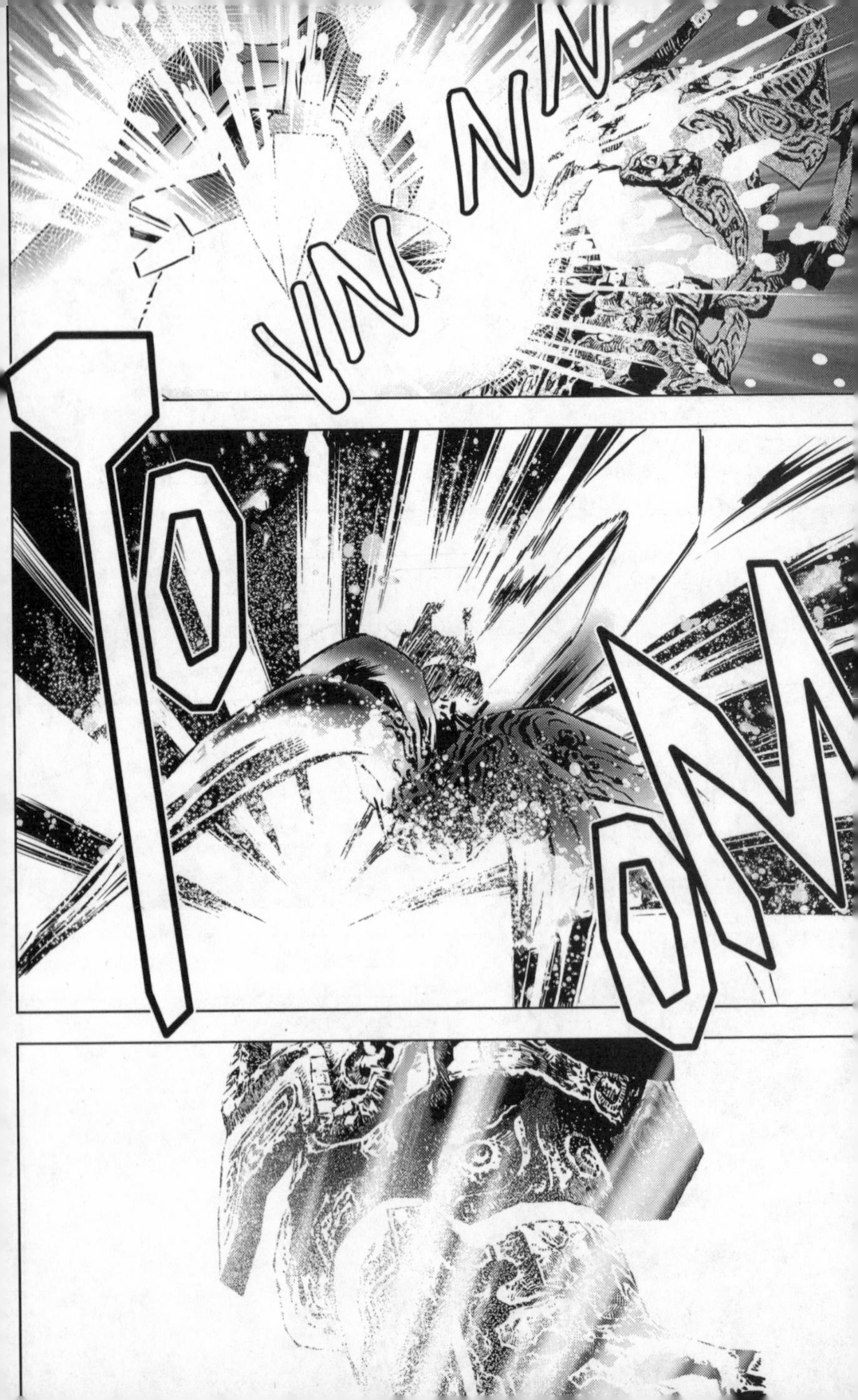
VNNN
FOOM

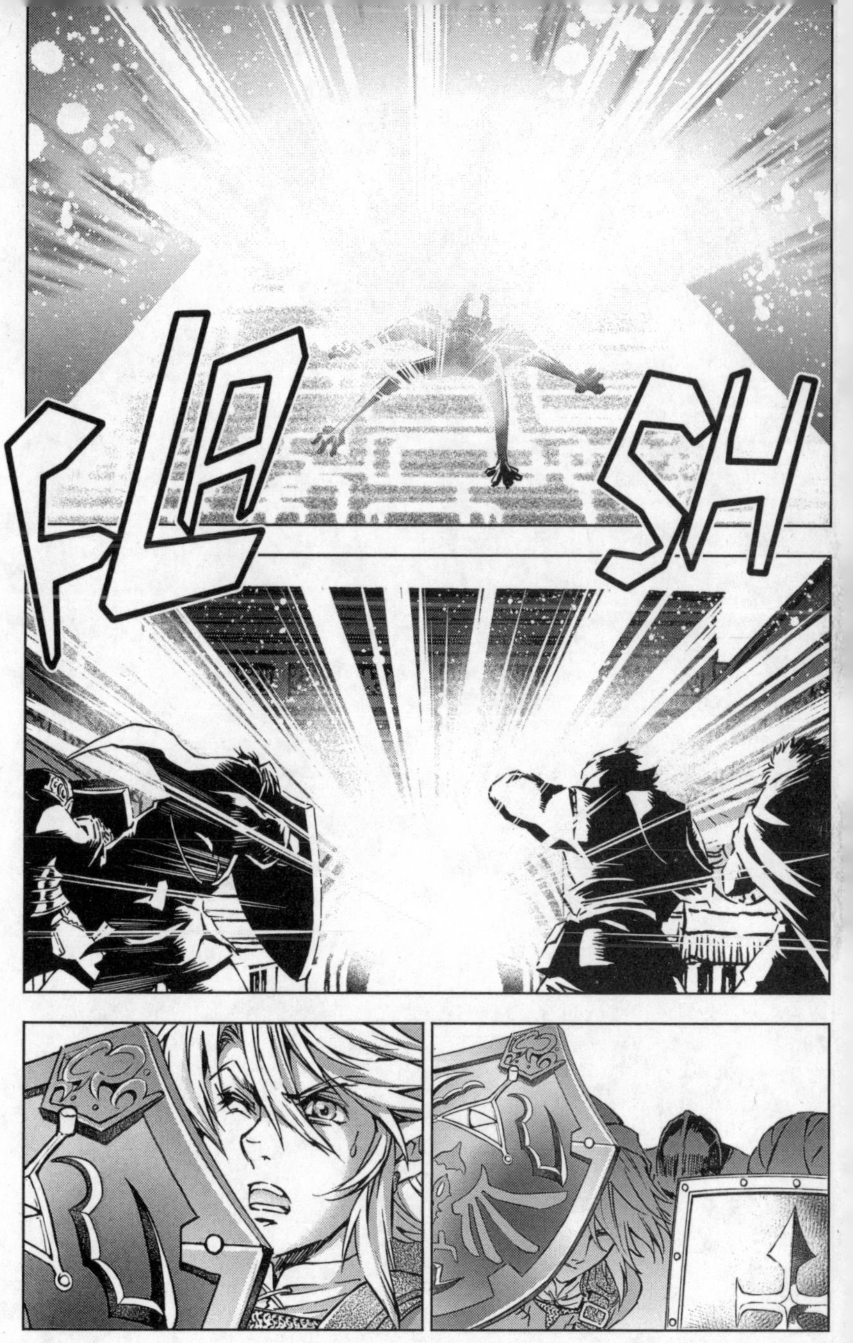
FLASH

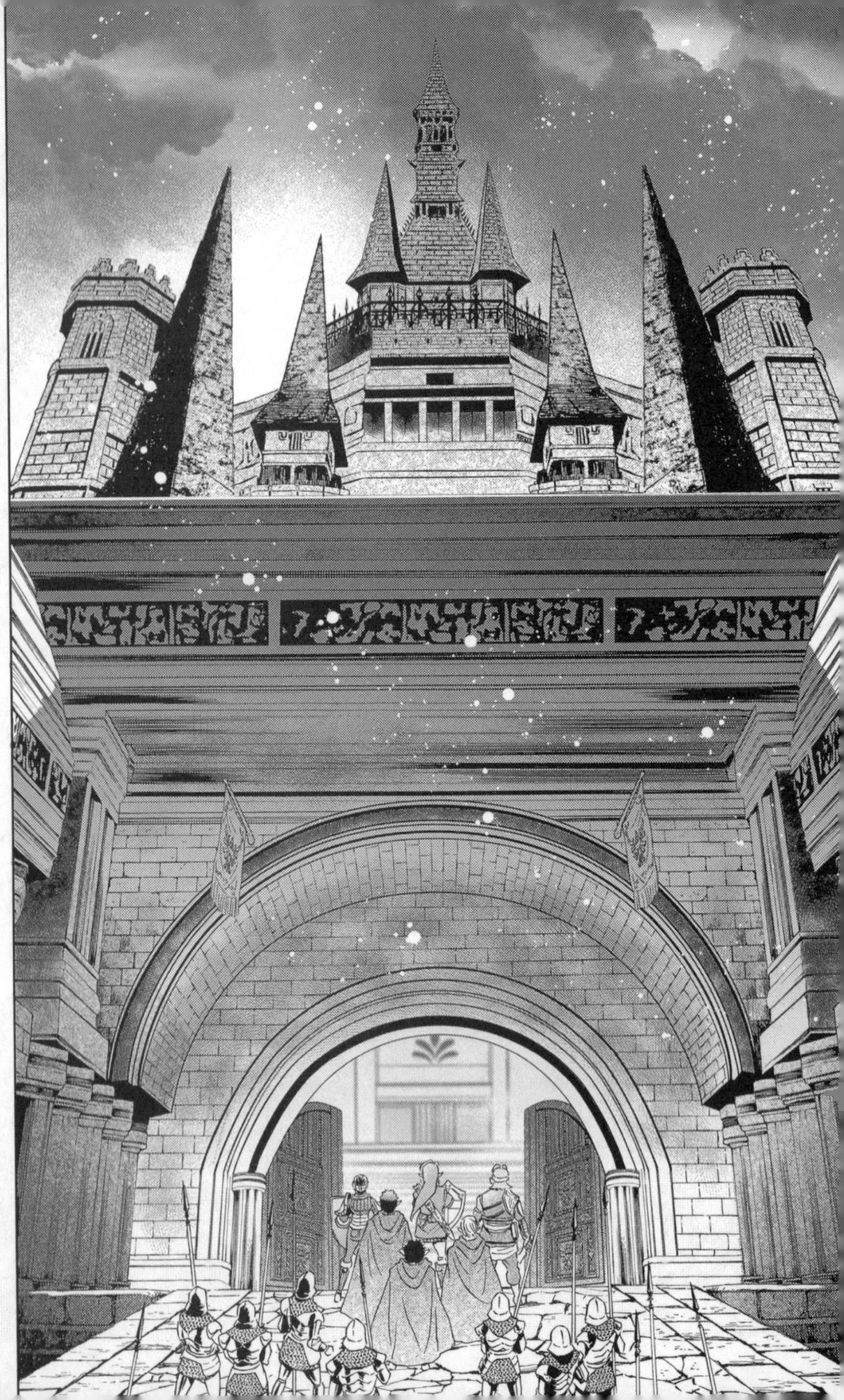

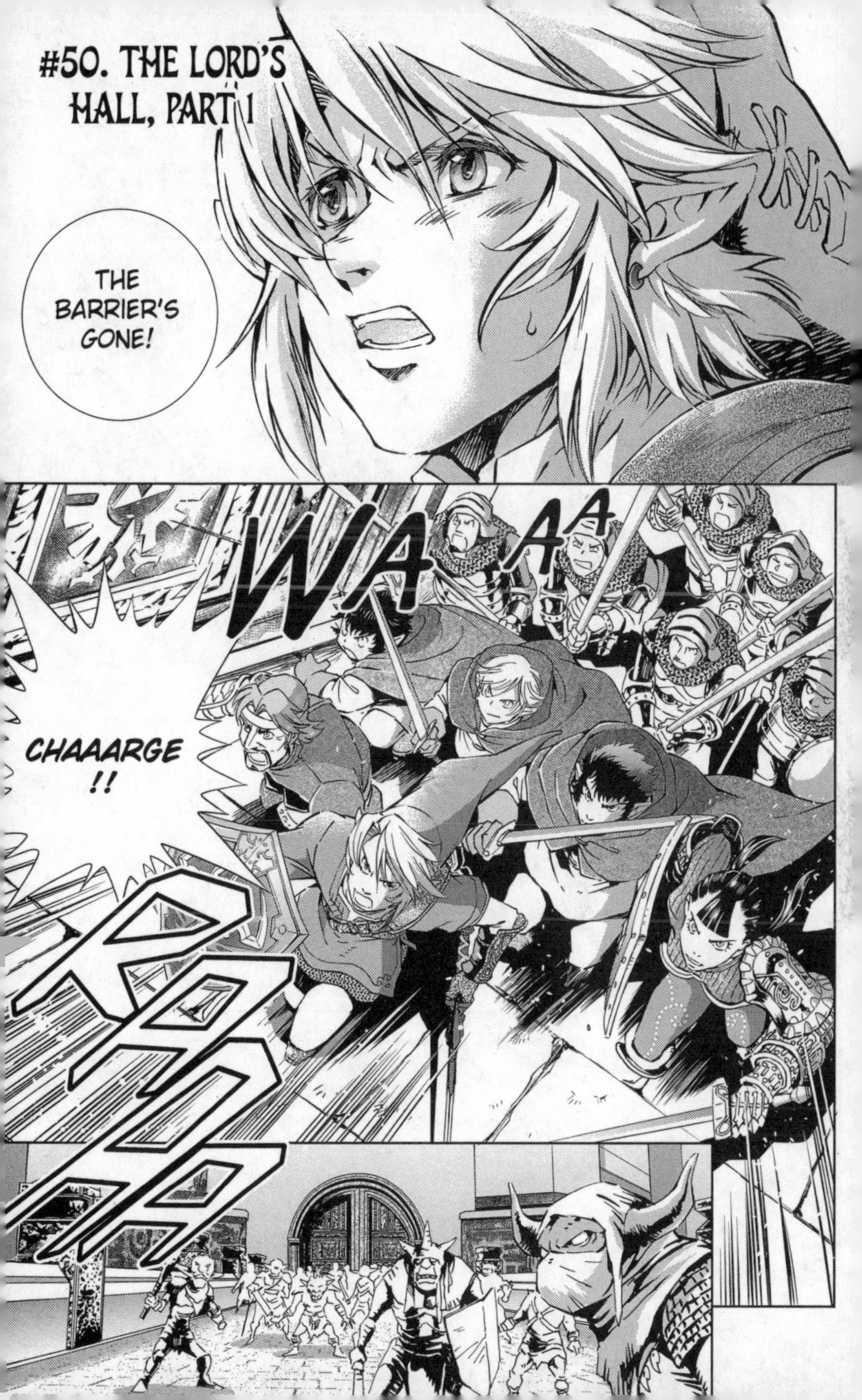
#50. THE LORD'S HALL, PART 1
THE BARRIER'S GONE!
WAAA
CHAAARGE !!

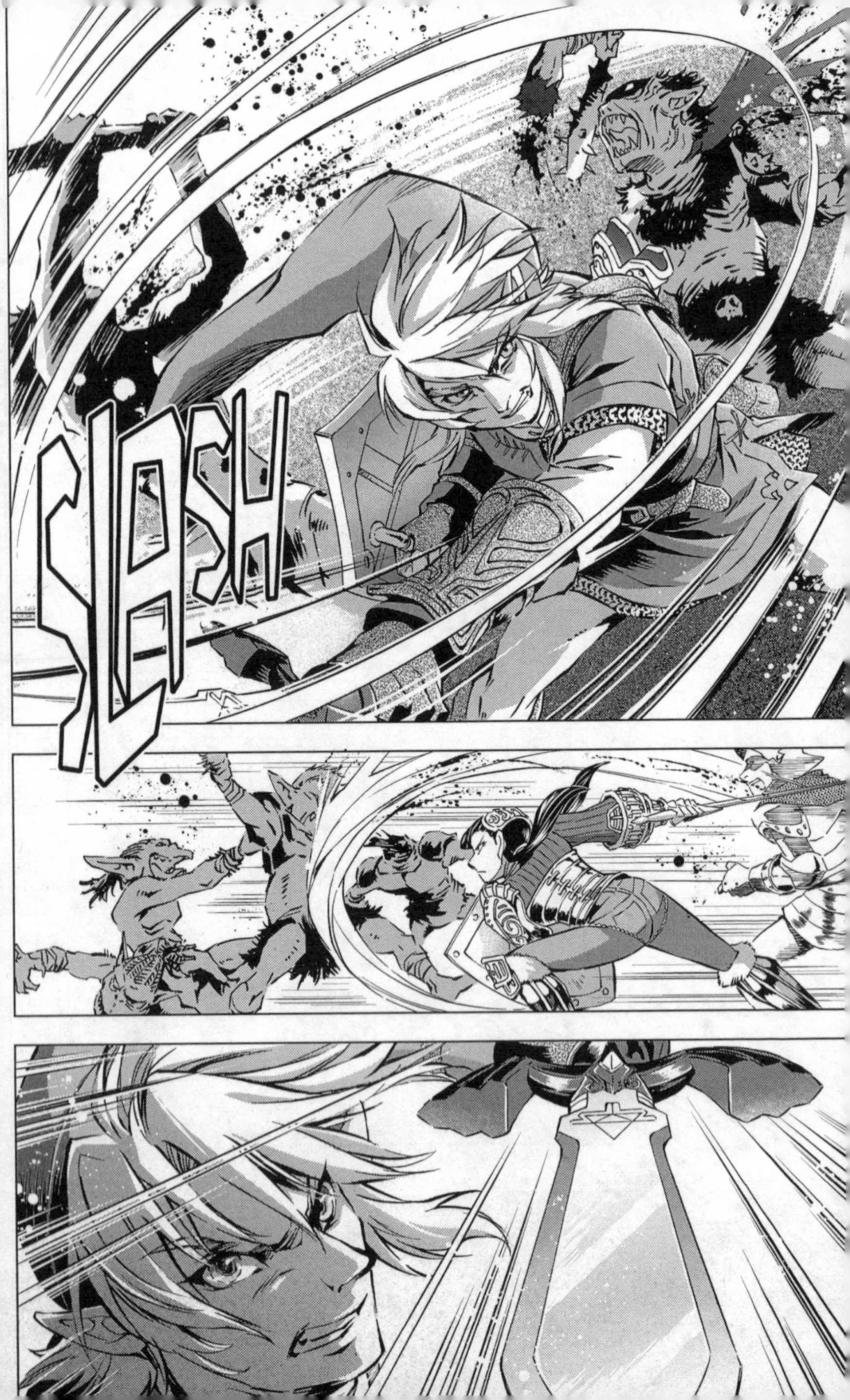
SLASH

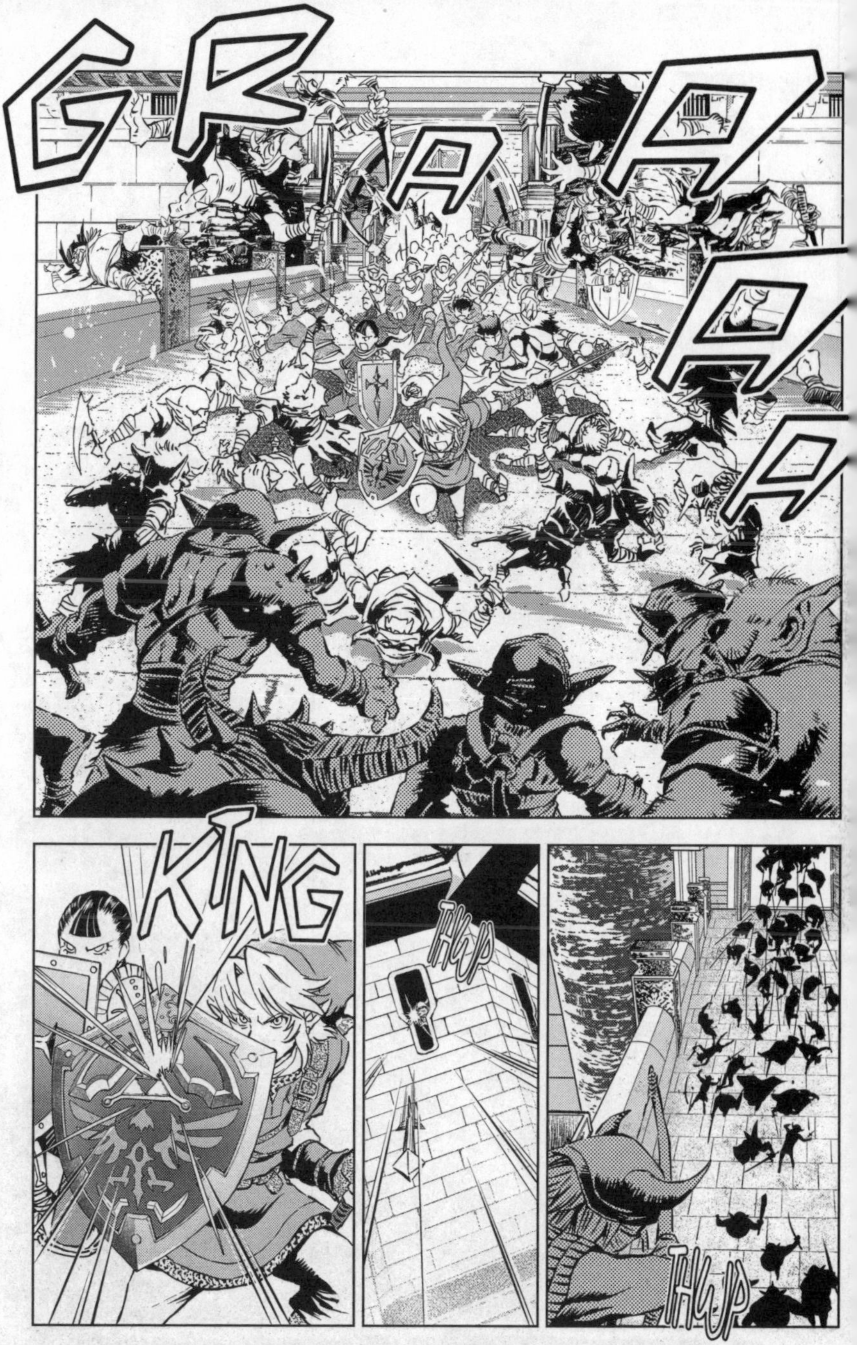
GRAAAA
THUP
THUP
KING

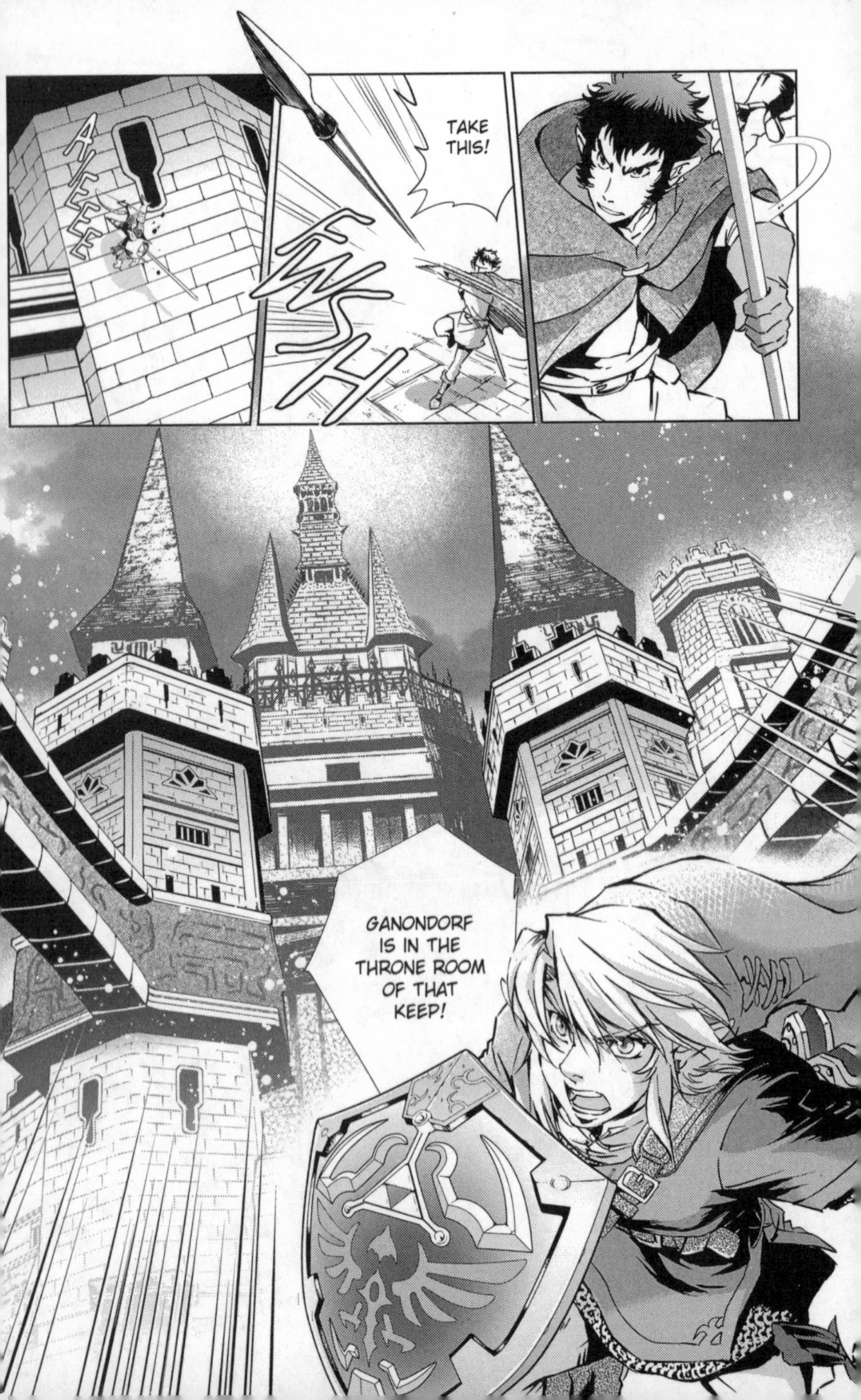
TAKE THIS!
FWSH
AIEEEE
YAH
GANONDORF IS IN THE THRONE ROOM OF THAT KEEP!

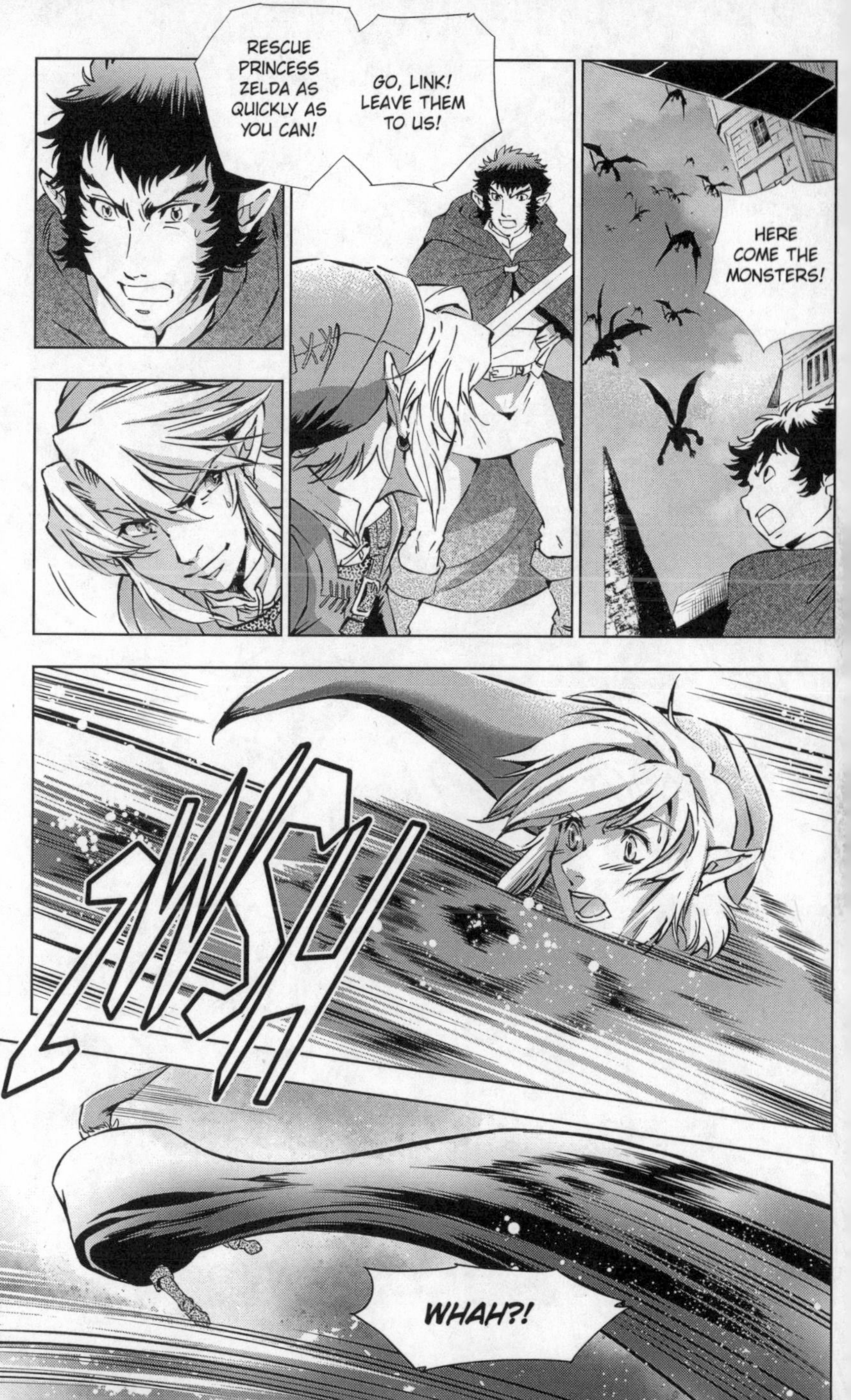
HERE COME THE MONSTERS!
GO, LINK! LEAVE THEM TO US!
RESCUE PRINCESS ZELDA AS QUICKLY AS YOU CAN!
WHAH?!

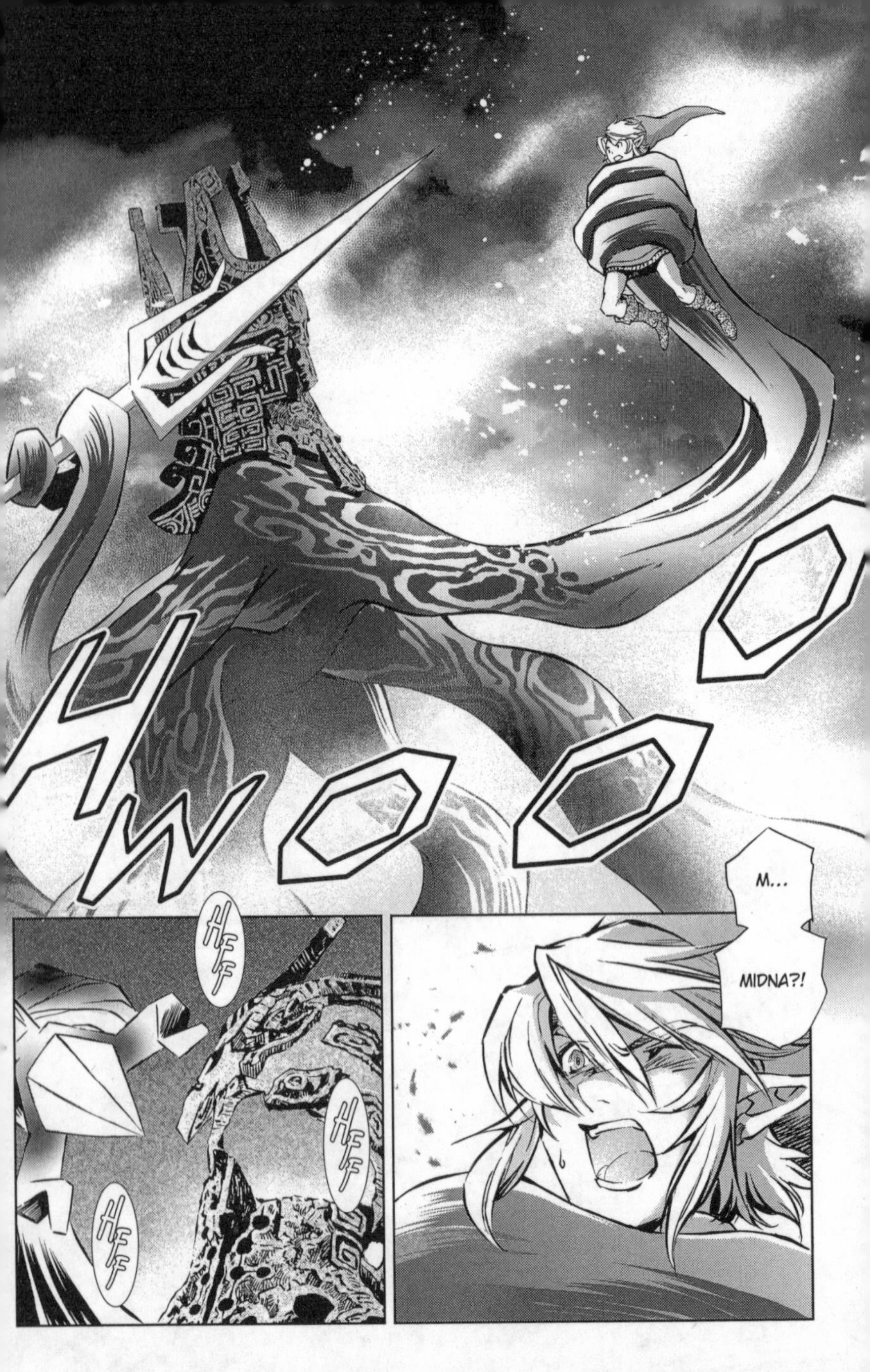
HWOOOO
M...
MIDNA?!
HEFF
HEFF
HEFF

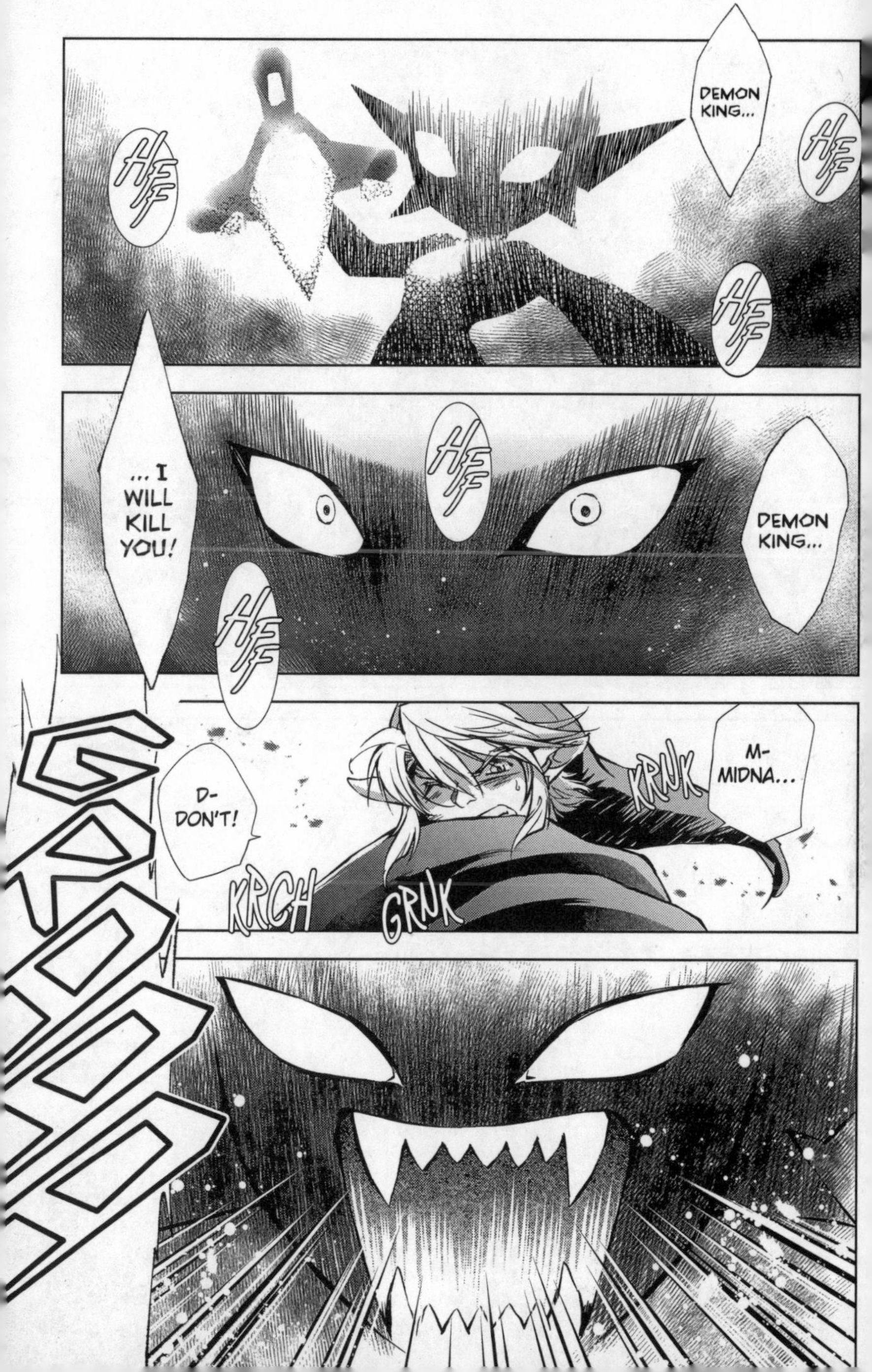
DEMON KING...
HFF
HFF
HFF
DEMON KING...
HFF
HFF
...I WILL KILL YOU!
M-MIDNA...
KRNK
GRNK
KRCH
D-DON'T!

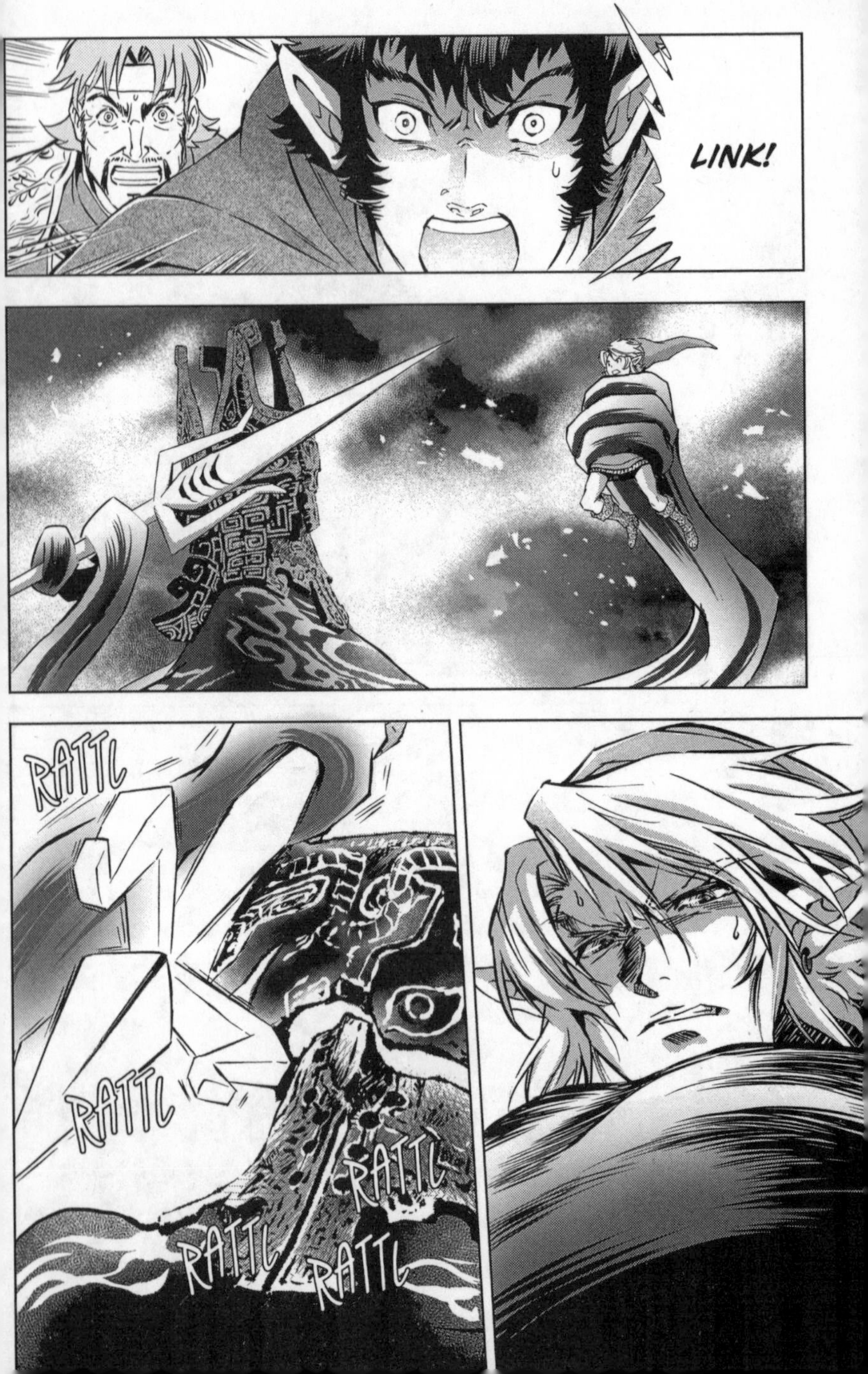
LINK!
RATTL
RATTL
RATTL
RATTL
RATTL

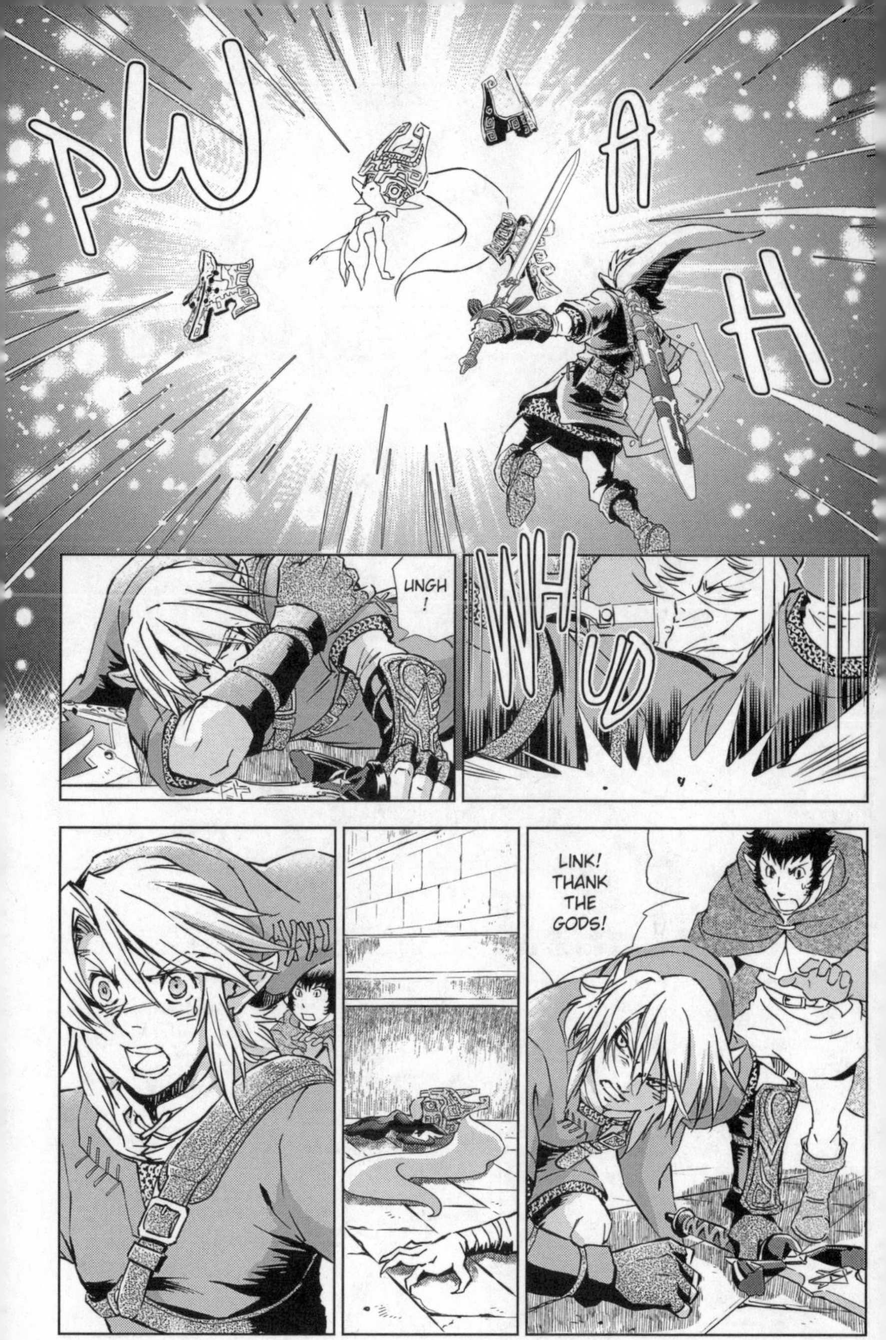
PWAH
WHUD
UNGH!
LINK! THANK THE GODS!

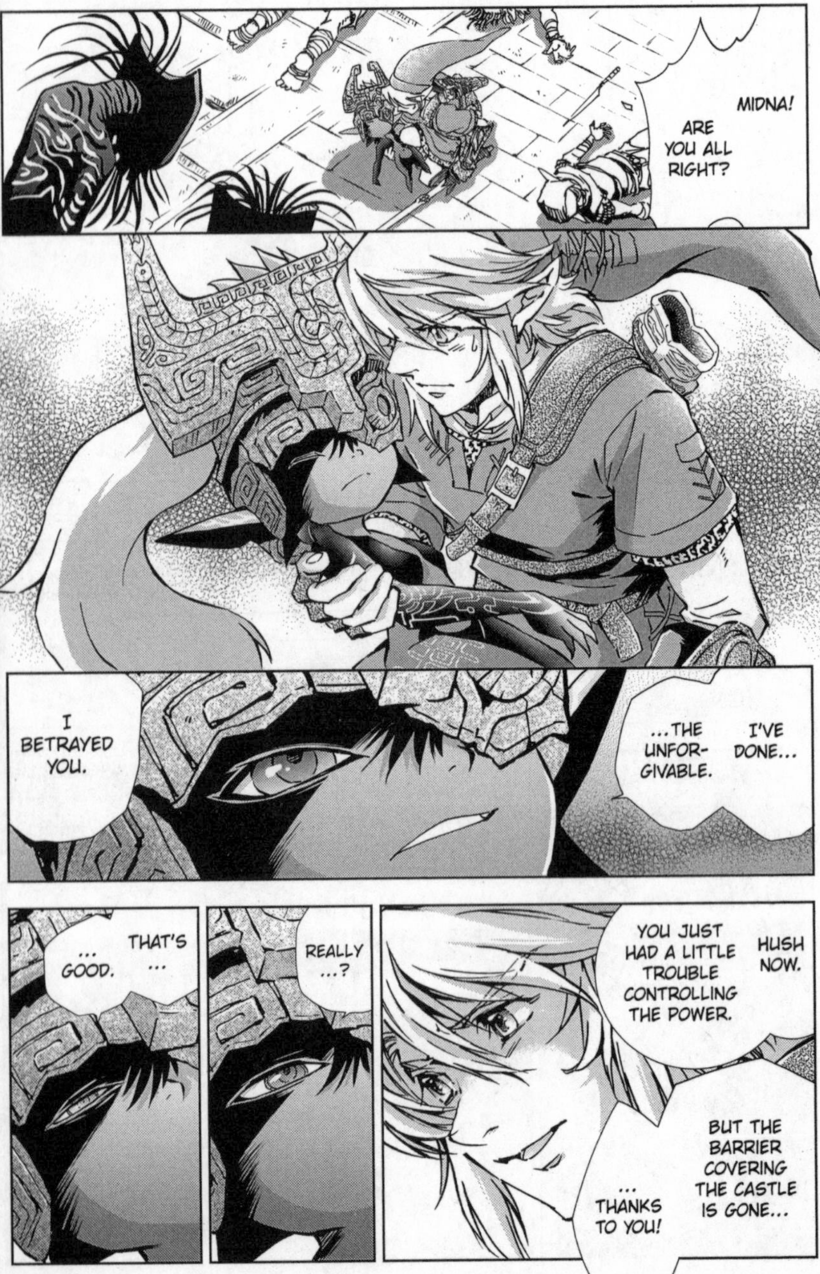
MIDNA!
ARE YOU ALL RIGHT?
I'VE DONE...
...THE UNFORGIVABLE.
I BETRAYED YOU.
HUSH NOW.
YOU JUST HAD A LITTLE TROUBLE CONTROLLING THE POWER.
BUT THE BARRIER COVERING THE CASTLE IS GONE...
...THANKS TO YOU!
REALLY ...?
THAT'S ...
... GOOD.

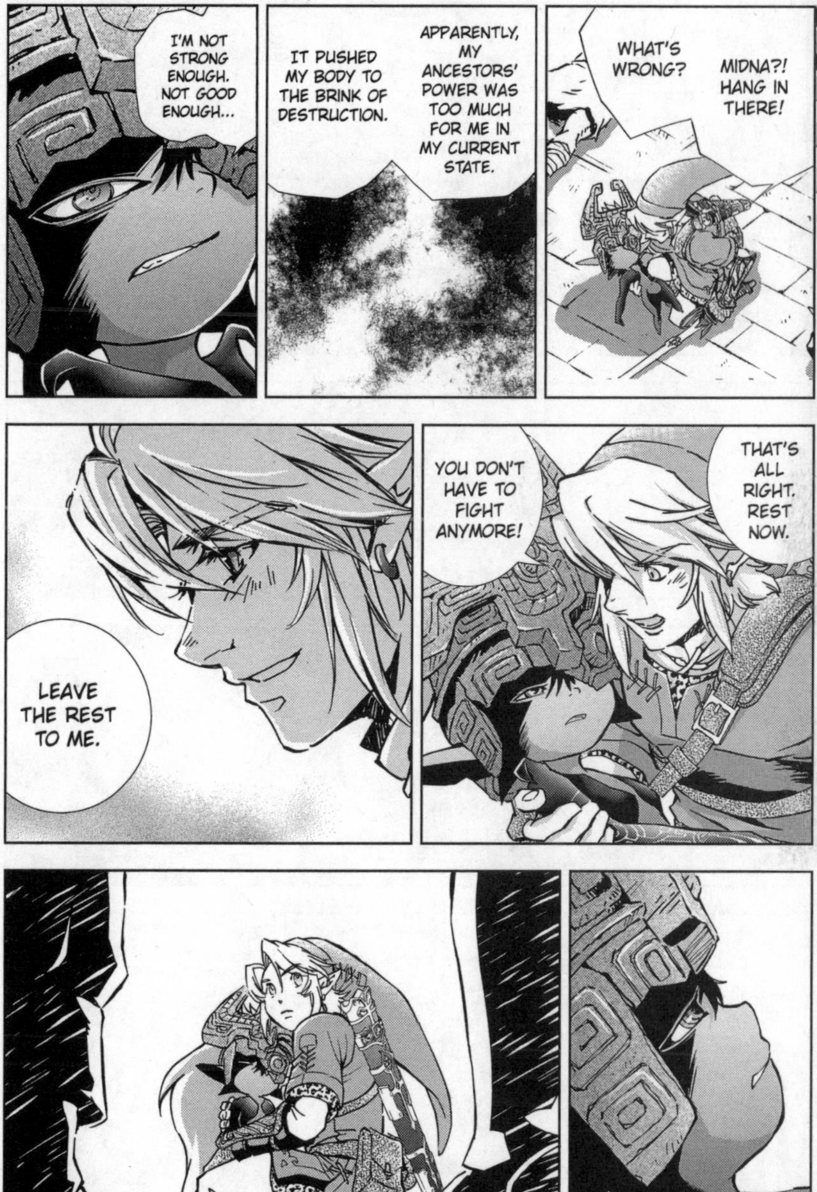
MIDNA?! HANG IN THERE!
WHAT'S WRONG?
APPARENTLY, MY ANCESTORS' POWER WAS TOO MUCH FOR ME IN MY CURRENT STATE.
IT PUSHED MY BODY TO THE BRINK OF DESTRUCTION.
I'M NOT STRONG ENOUGH. NOT GOOD ENOUGH...
THAT'S ALL RIGHT. REST NOW.
YOU DON'T HAVE TO FIGHT ANYMORE!
LEAVE THE REST TO ME.

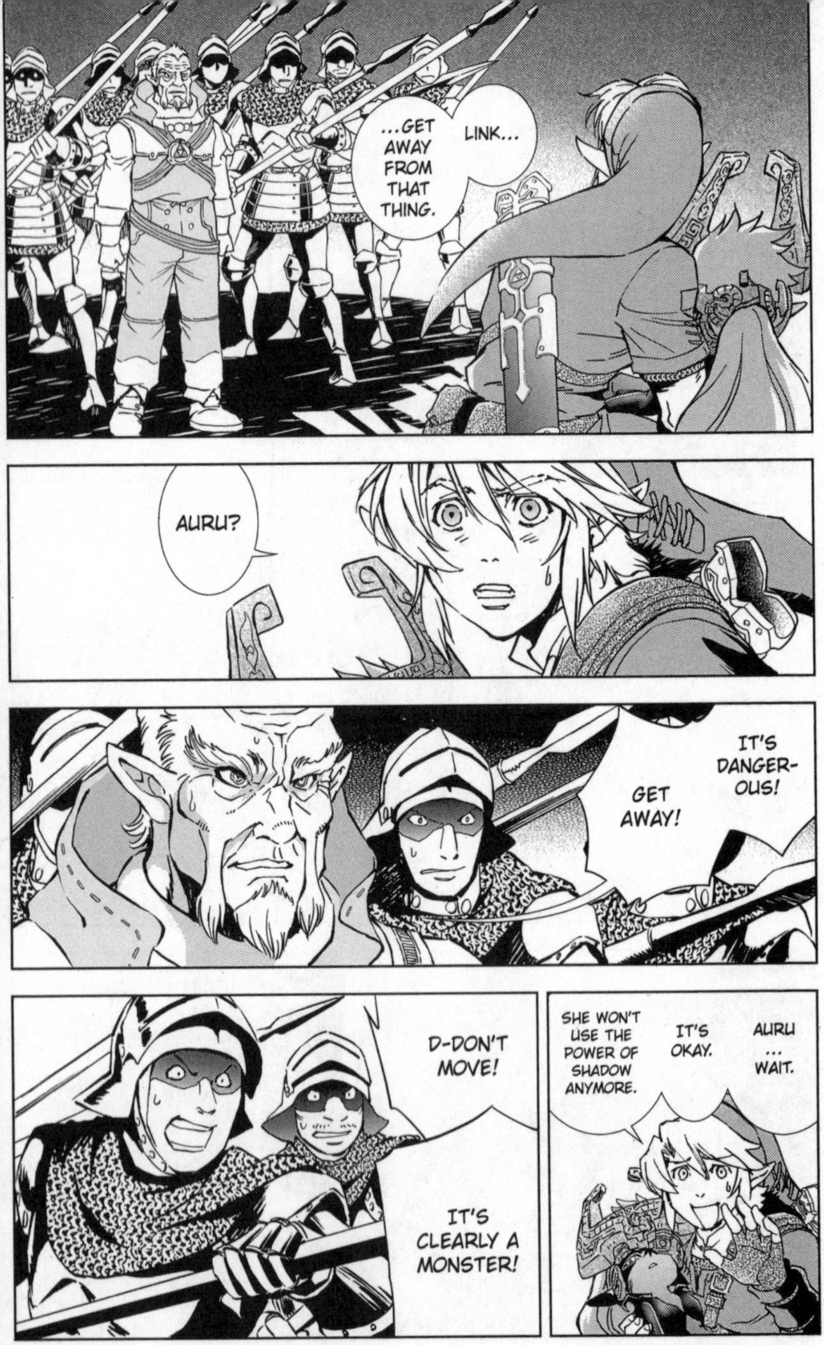
LINK...
...GET AWAY FROM THAT THING.
AURU?
IT'S DANGER-OUS!
GET AWAY!
AURU ... WAIT.
IT'S OKAY.
SHE WON'T USE THE POWER OF SHADOW ANYMORE.
D-DON'T MOVE!
IT'S CLEARLY A MONSTER!

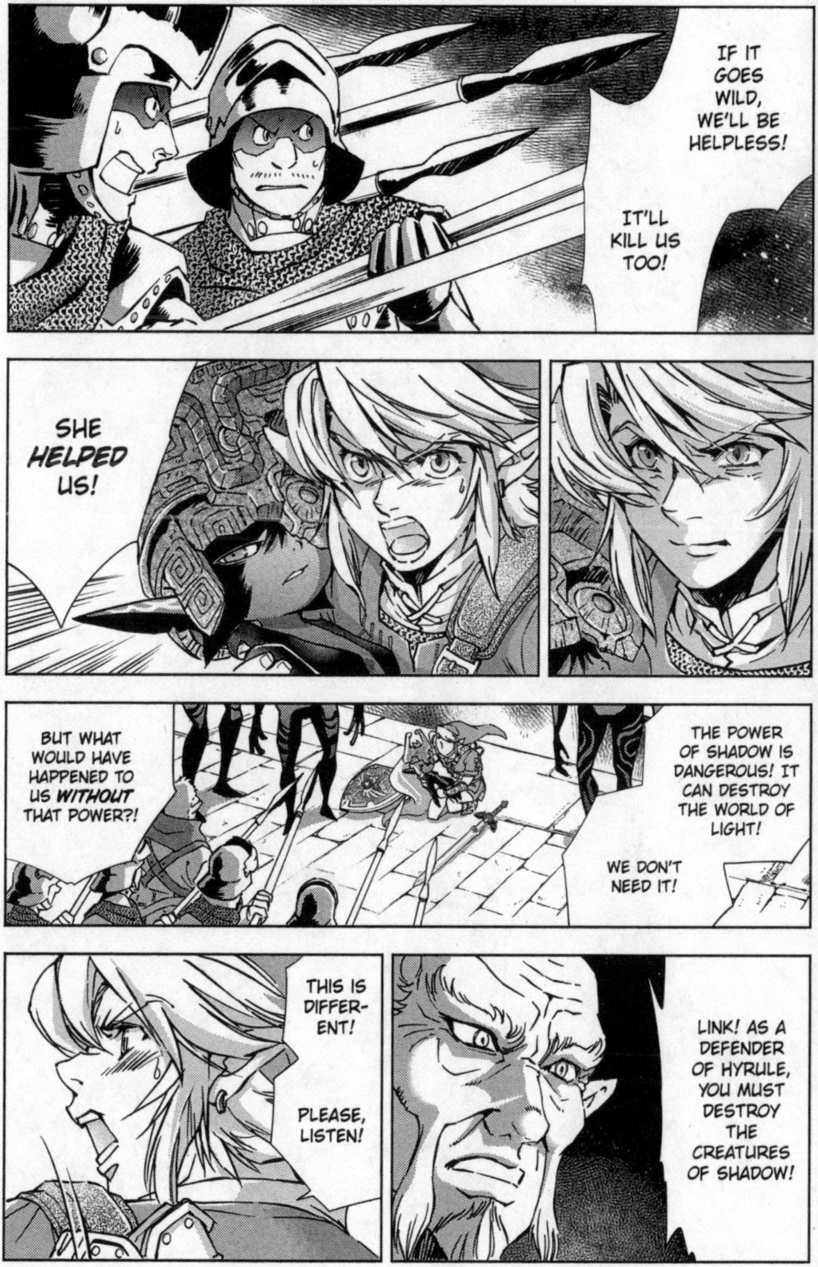
IF IT GOES WILD, WE'LL BE HELPLESS!
IT'LL KILL US TOO!
SHE *HELPED* US!
THE POWER OF SHADOW IS DANGEROUS! IT CAN DESTROY THE WORLD OF LIGHT!
WE DON'T NEED IT!
BUT WHAT WOULD HAVE HAPPENED TO US *WITHOUT* THAT POWER?!
LINK! AS A DEFENDER OF HYRULE, YOU MUST DESTROY THE CREATURES OF SHADOW!
THIS IS DIFFER-ENT!
PLEASE, LISTEN!

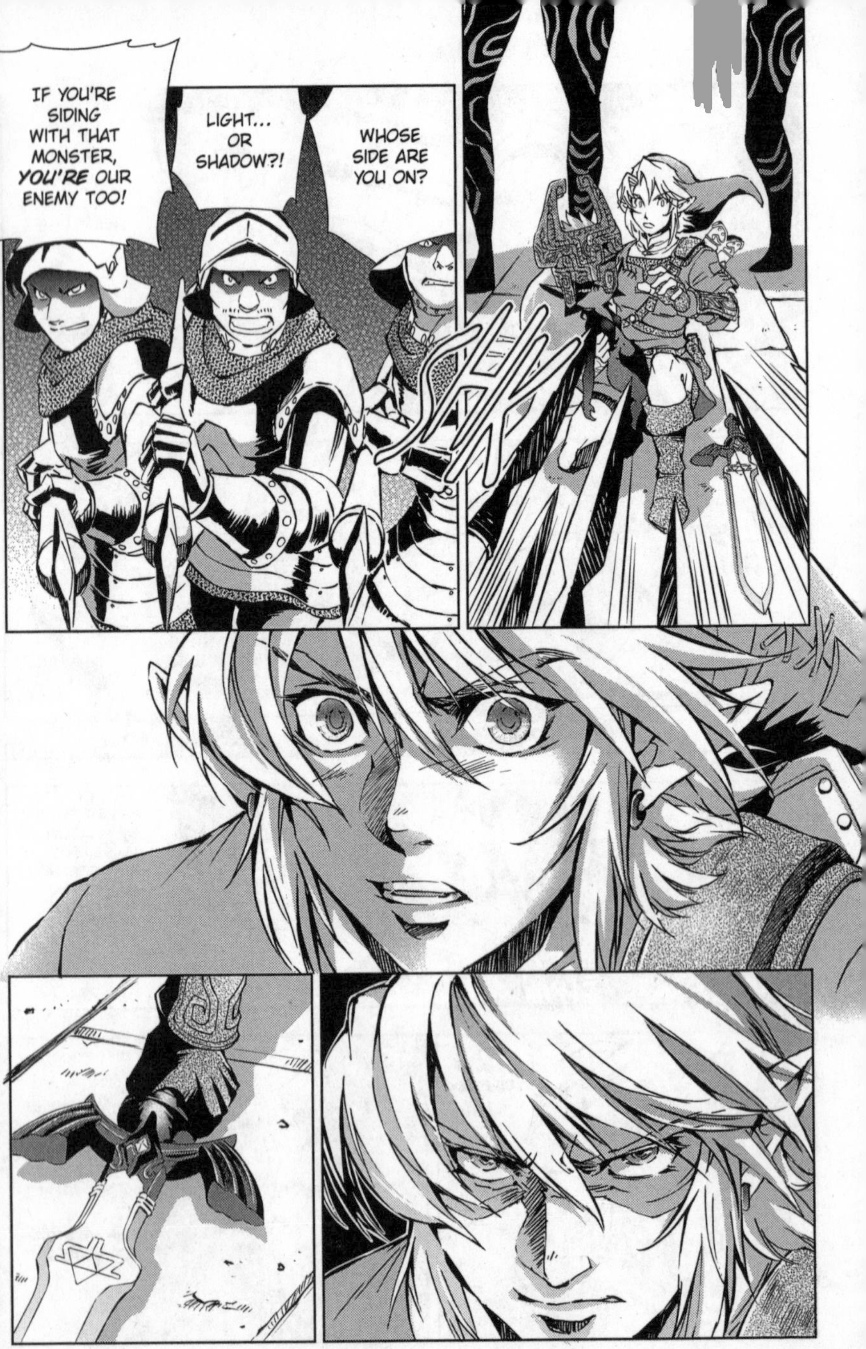
SHK
WHOSE SIDE ARE YOU ON?
LIGHT... OR SHADOW?!
IF YOU'RE SIDING WITH THAT MONSTER, *YOU'RE* OUR ENEMY TOO!

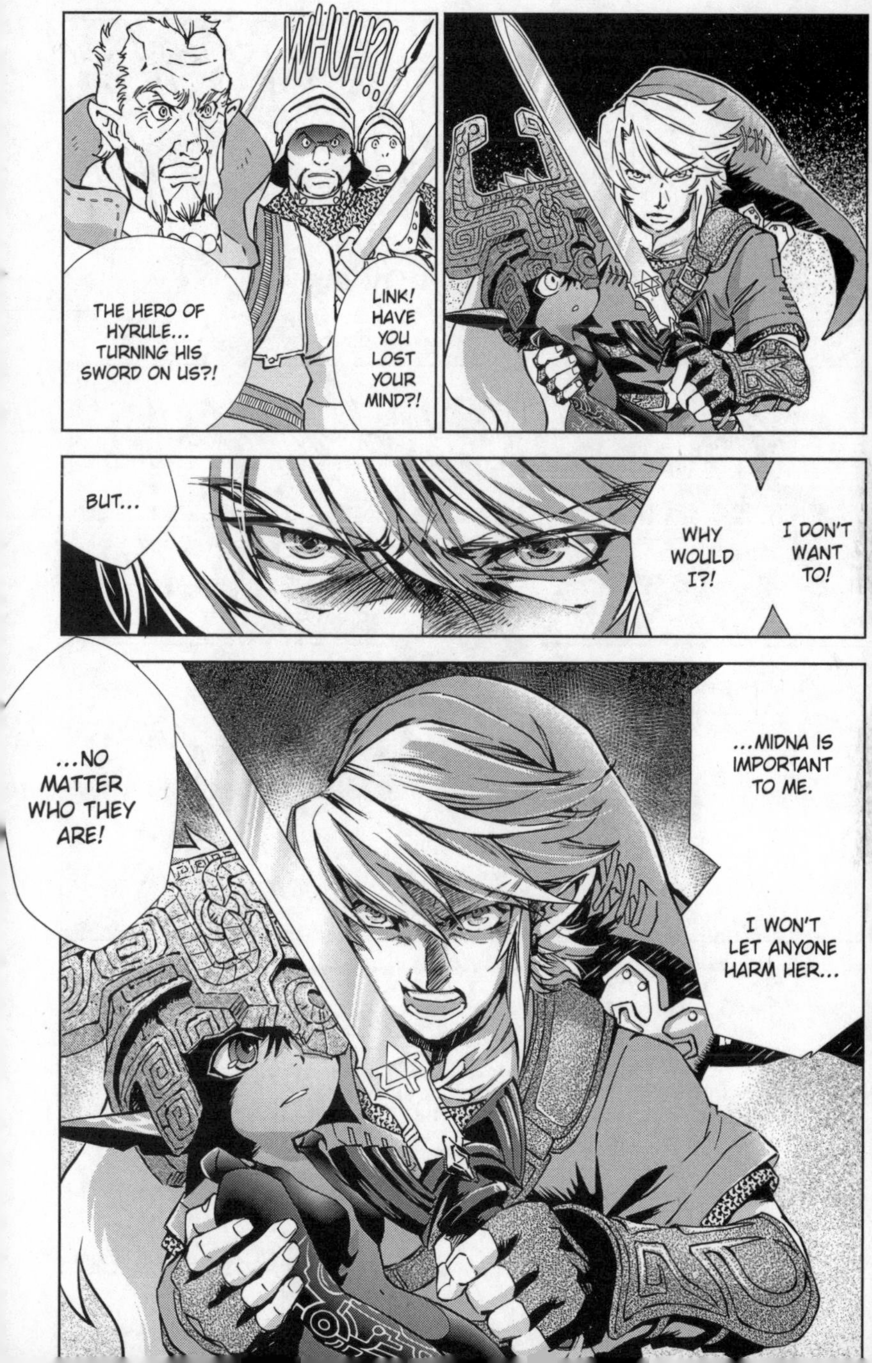
WHUH?!
LINK! HAVE YOU LOST YOUR MIND?!
THE HERO OF HYRULE... TURNING HIS SWORD ON US?!
I DON'T WANT TO!
WHY WOULD I?!
BUT...
...MIDNA IS IMPORTANT TO ME.
I WON'T LET ANYONE HARM HER...
...NO MATTER WHO THEY ARE!

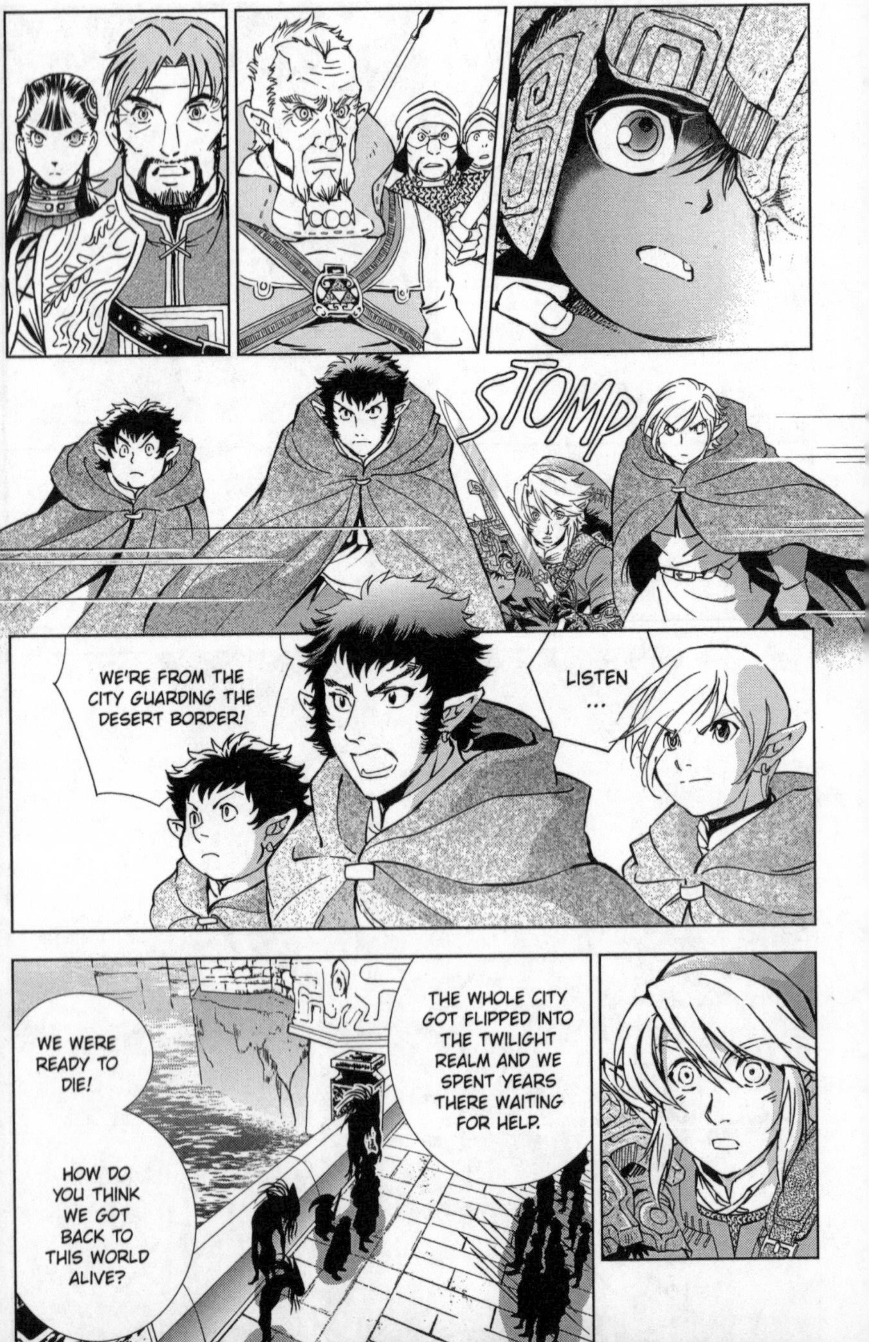
STOMP
LISTEN ...
WE'RE FROM THE CITY GUARDING THE DESERT BORDER!
THE WHOLE CITY GOT FLIPPED INTO THE TWILIGHT REALM AND WE SPENT YEARS THERE WAITING FOR HELP.
WE WERE READY TO DIE!
HOW DO YOU THINK WE GOT BACK TO THIS WORLD ALIVE?

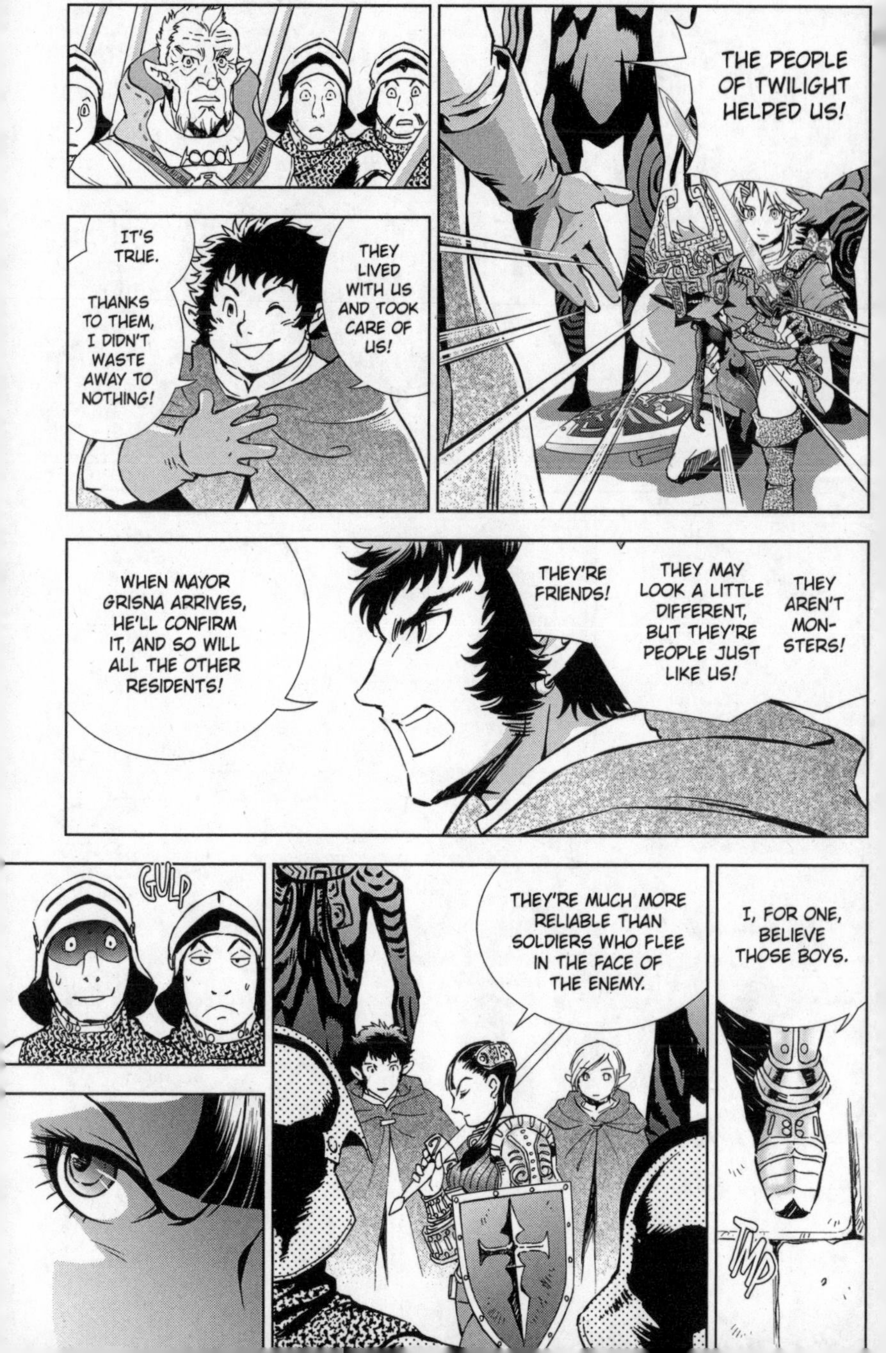
THE PEOPLE OF TWILIGHT HELPED US!
THEY LIVED WITH US AND TOOK CARE OF US!
IT'S TRUE.
THANKS TO THEM, I DIDN'T WASTE AWAY TO NOTHING!
THEY AREN'T MON-STERS!
THEY MAY LOOK A LITTLE DIFFERENT, BUT THEY'RE PEOPLE JUST LIKE US!
THEY'RE FRIENDS!
WHEN MAYOR GRISNA ARRIVES, HE'LL CONFIRM IT, AND SO WILL ALL THE OTHER RESIDENTS!
I, FOR ONE, BELIEVE THOSE BOYS.
TMP
THEY'RE MUCH MORE RELIABLE THAN SOLDIERS WHO FLEE IN THE FACE OF THE ENEMY.
GULP

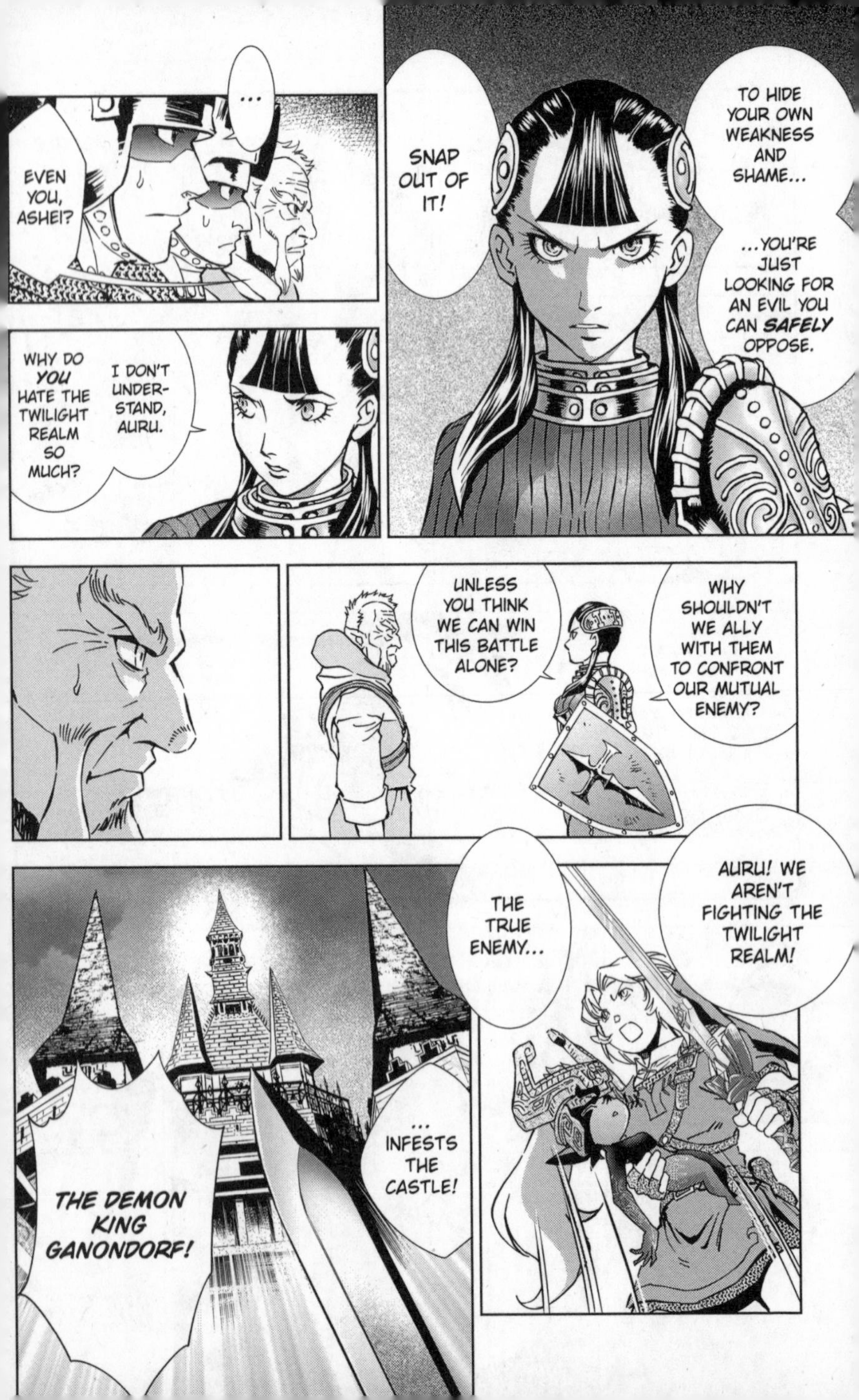
TO HIDE YOUR OWN WEAKNESS AND SHAME...
...YOU'RE JUST LOOKING FOR AN EVIL YOU CAN *SAFELY* OPPOSE.
SNAP OUT OF IT!
...
EVEN YOU, ASHEI?
I DON'T UNDER-STAND, AURU.
WHY DO *YOU* HATE THE TWILIGHT REALM SO MUCH?
WHY SHOULDN'T WE ALLY WITH THEM TO CONFRONT OUR MUTUAL ENEMY?
UNLESS YOU THINK WE CAN WIN THIS BATTLE ALONE?
AURU! WE AREN'T FIGHTING THE TWILIGHT REALM!
THE TRUE ENEMY...
...INFESTS THE CASTLE!
THE DEMON KING GANONDORF!

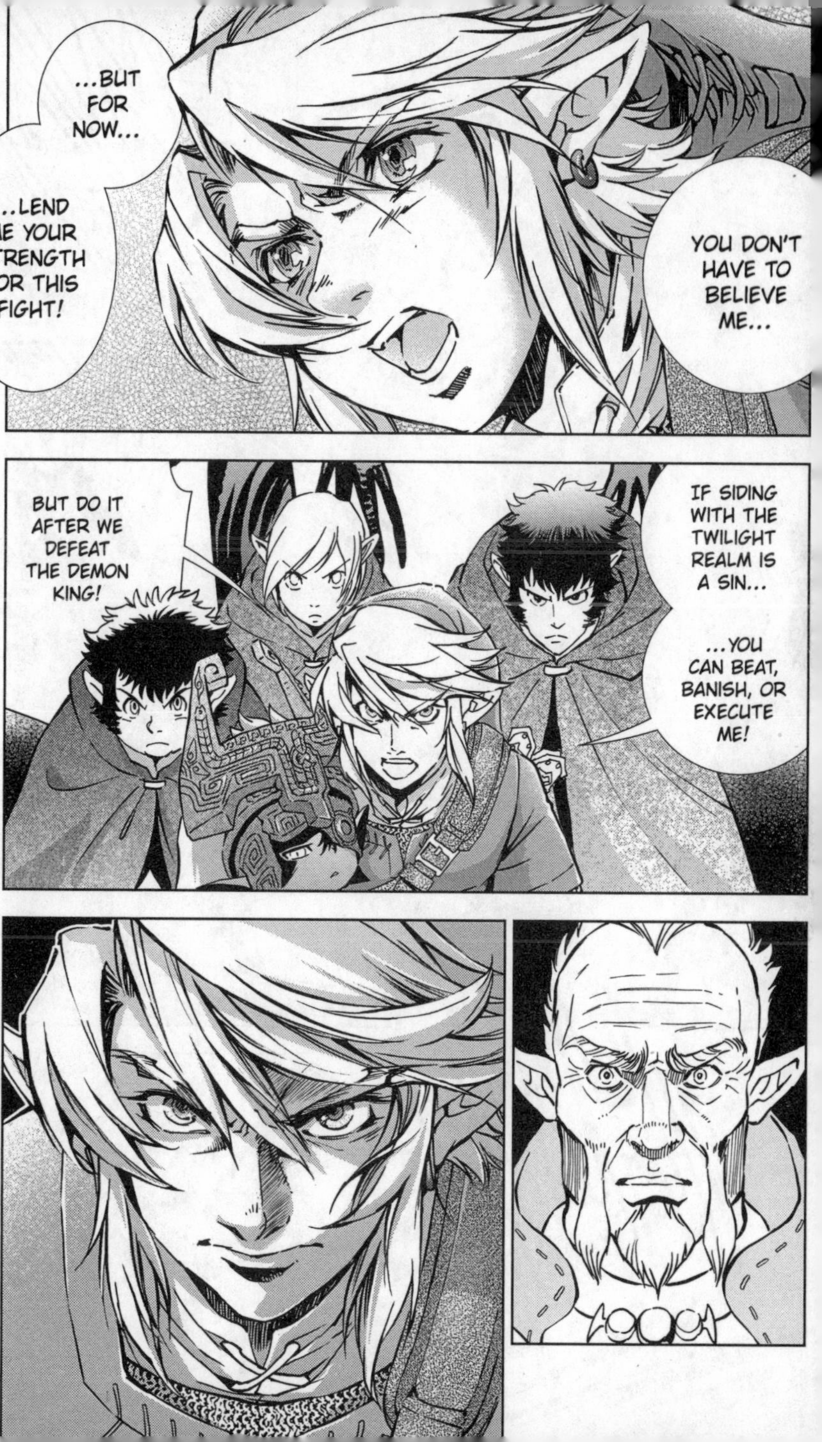
YOU DON'T HAVE TO BELIEVE ME...
...BUT FOR NOW...
...LEND ME YOUR STRENGTH FOR THIS FIGHT!
IF SIDING WITH THE TWILIGHT REALM IS A SIN...
...YOU CAN BEAT, BANISH, OR EXECUTE ME!
BUT DO IT AFTER WE DEFEAT THE DEMON KING!

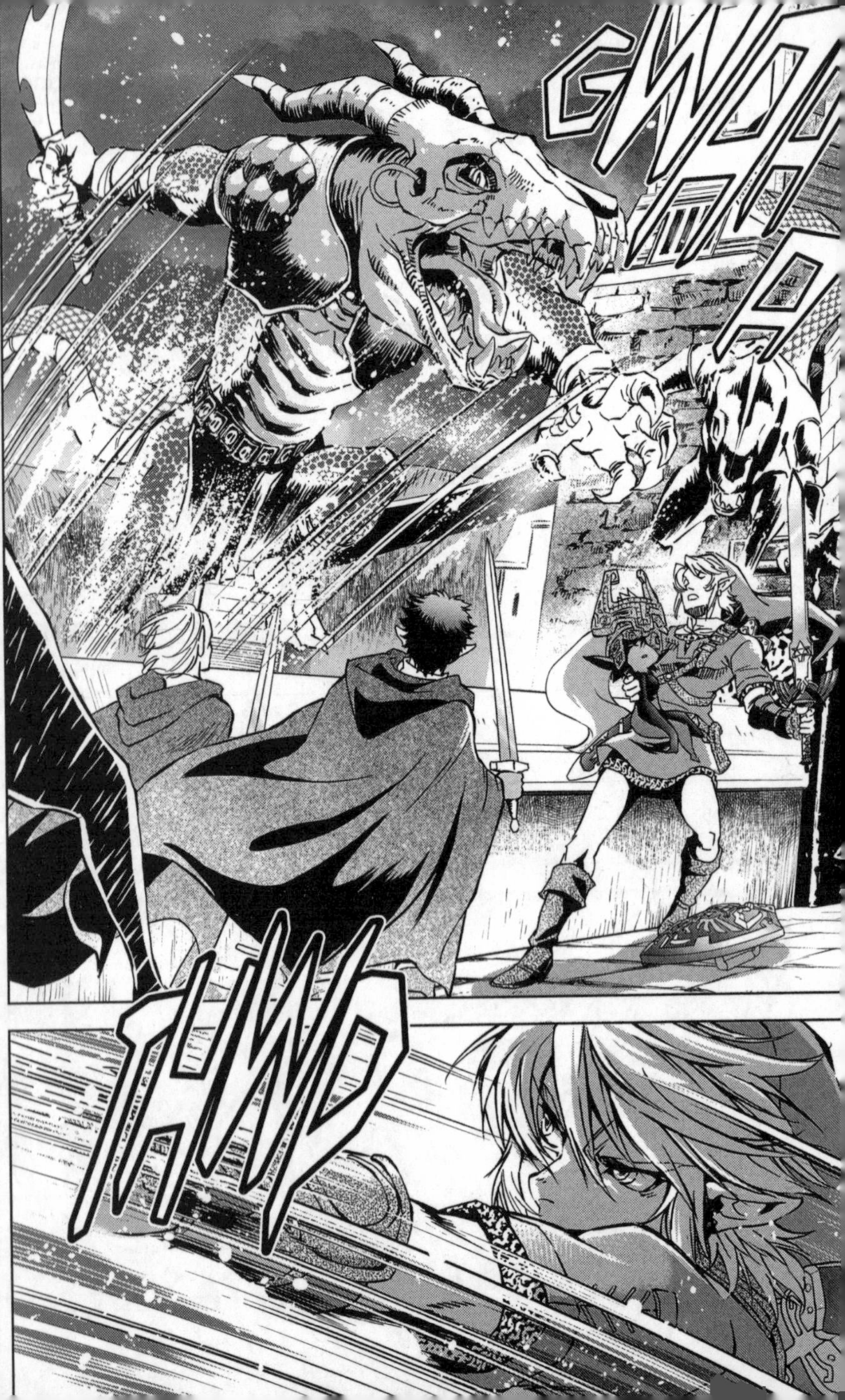
GWAHA
THWP

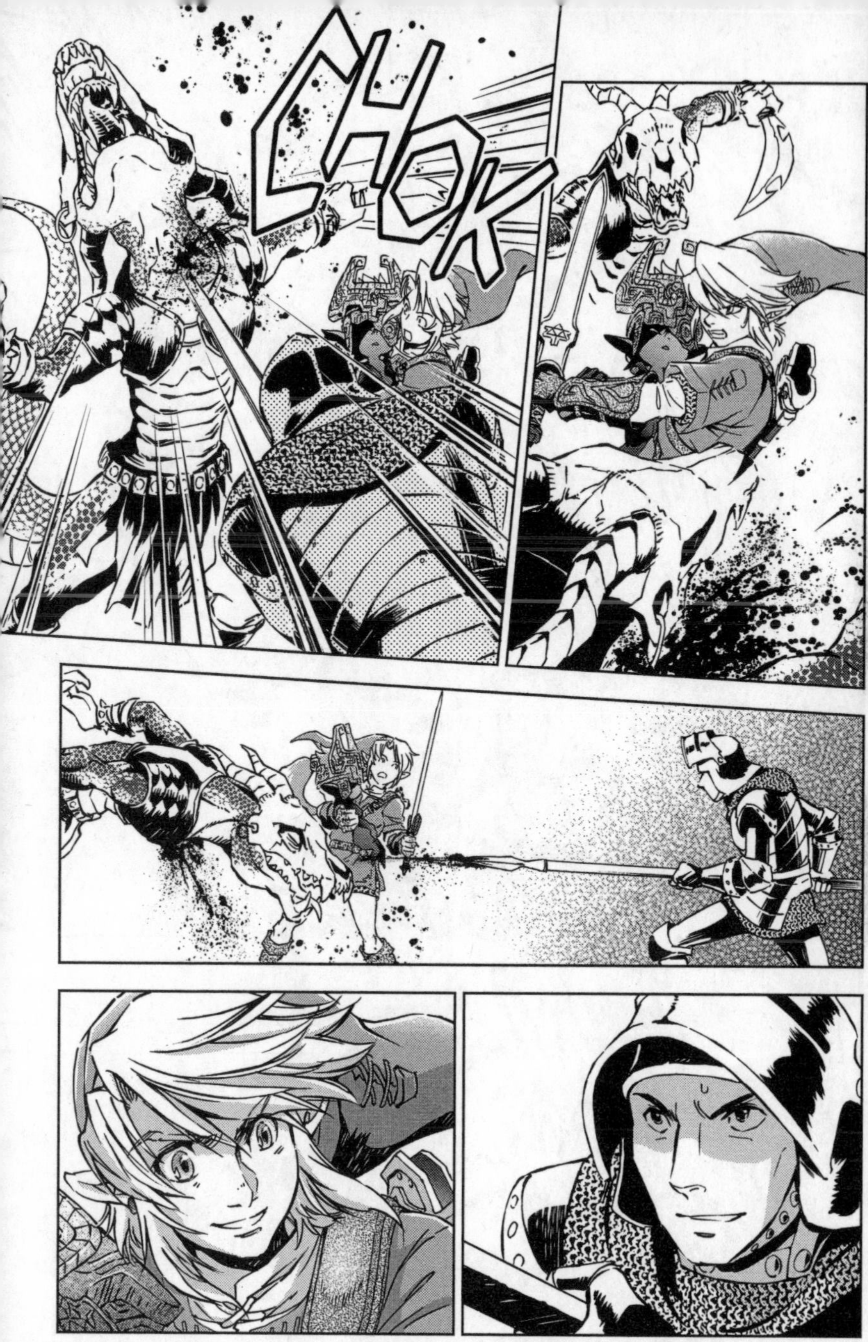
CHOK

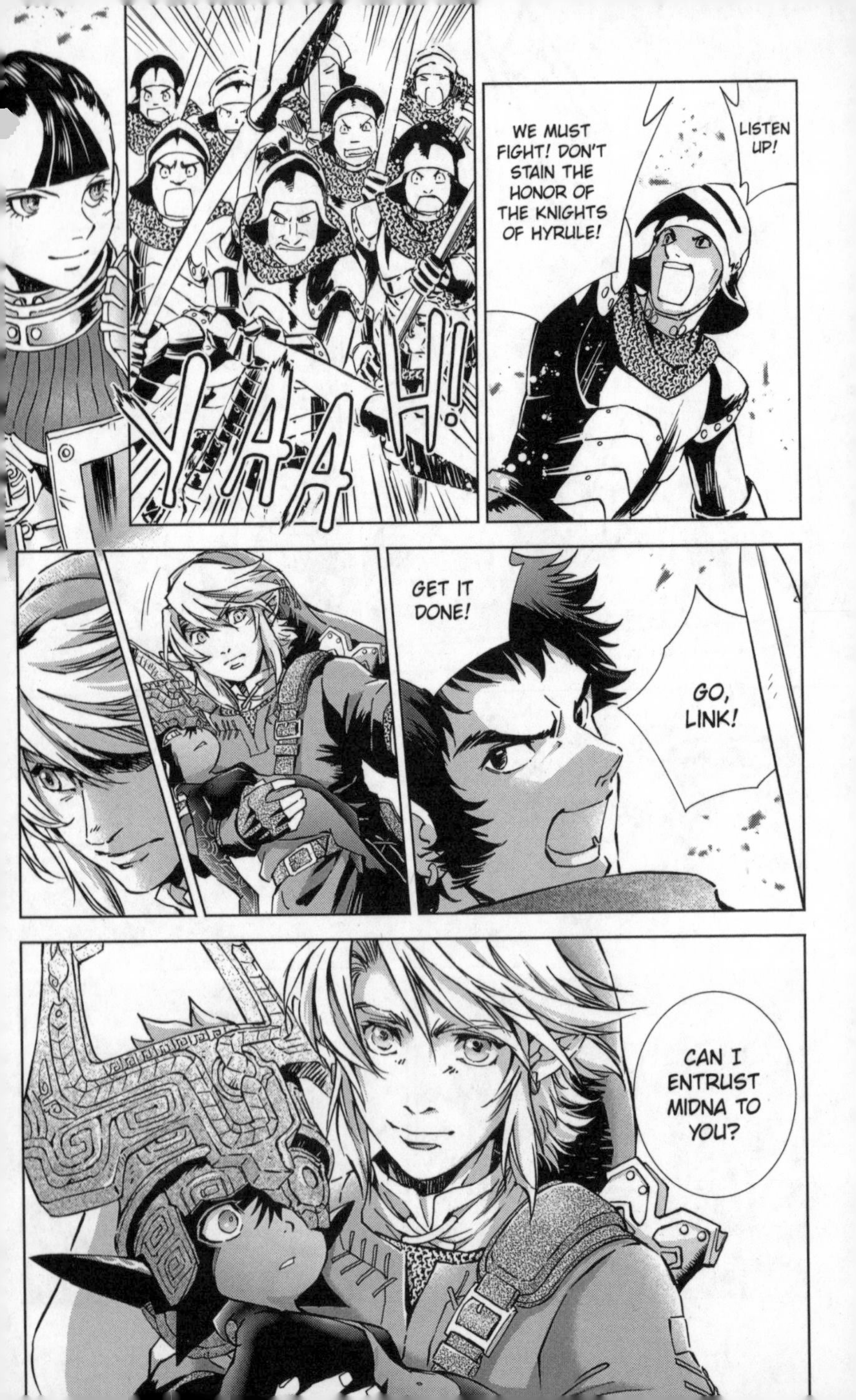
LISTEN UP!
WE MUST FIGHT! DON'T STAIN THE HONOR OF THE KNIGHTS OF HYRULE!
YAAH!
GO, LINK!
GET IT DONE!
CAN I ENTRUST MIDNA TO YOU?

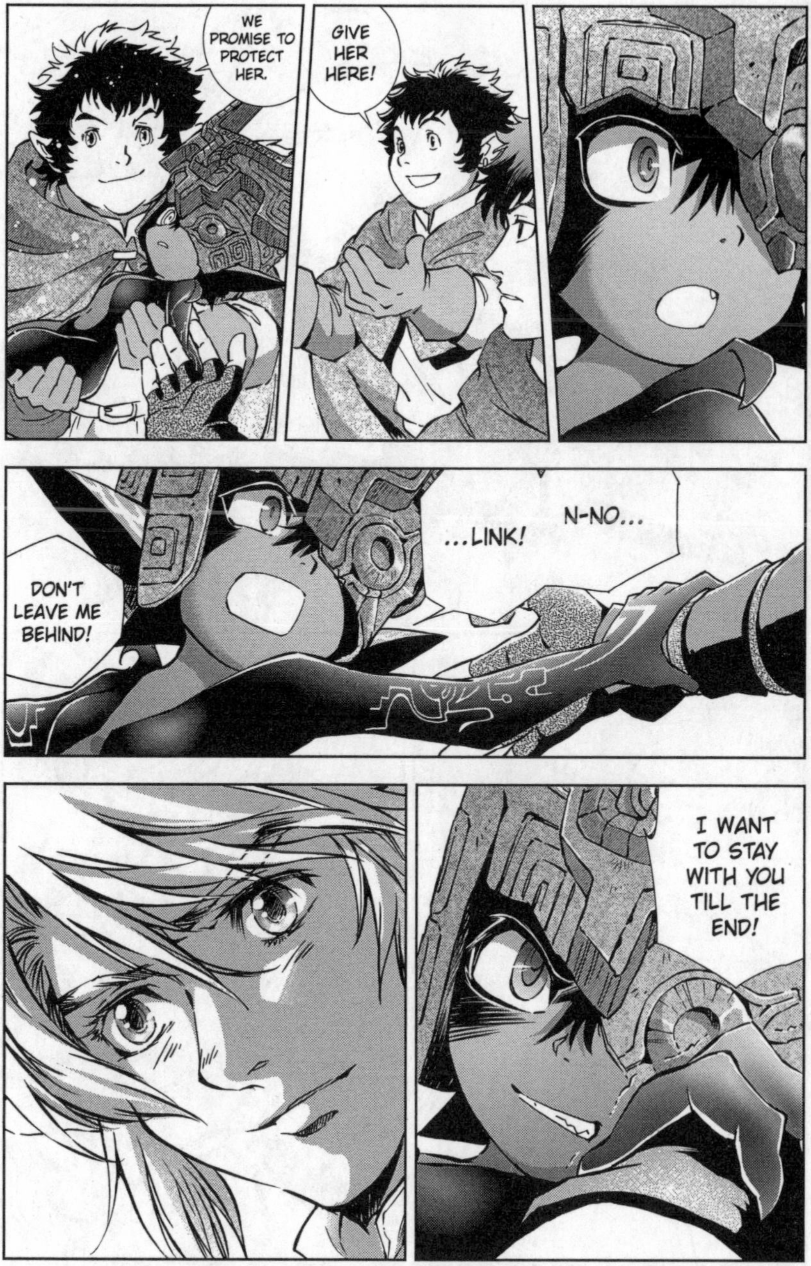
GIVE HER HERE!
WE PROMISE TO PROTECT HER.
N-NO...
...LINK!
DON'T LEAVE ME BEHIND!
I WANT TO STAY WITH YOU TILL THE END!

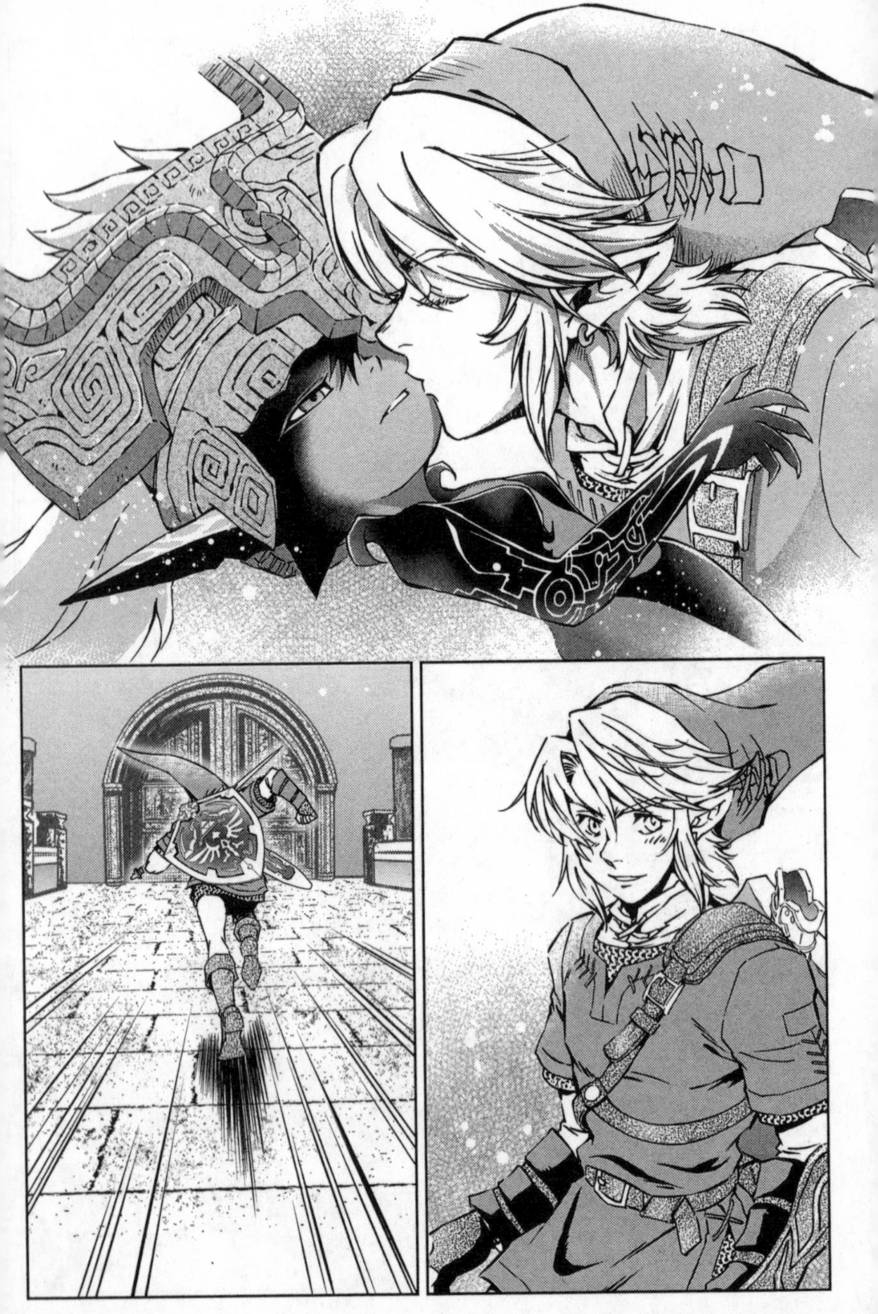

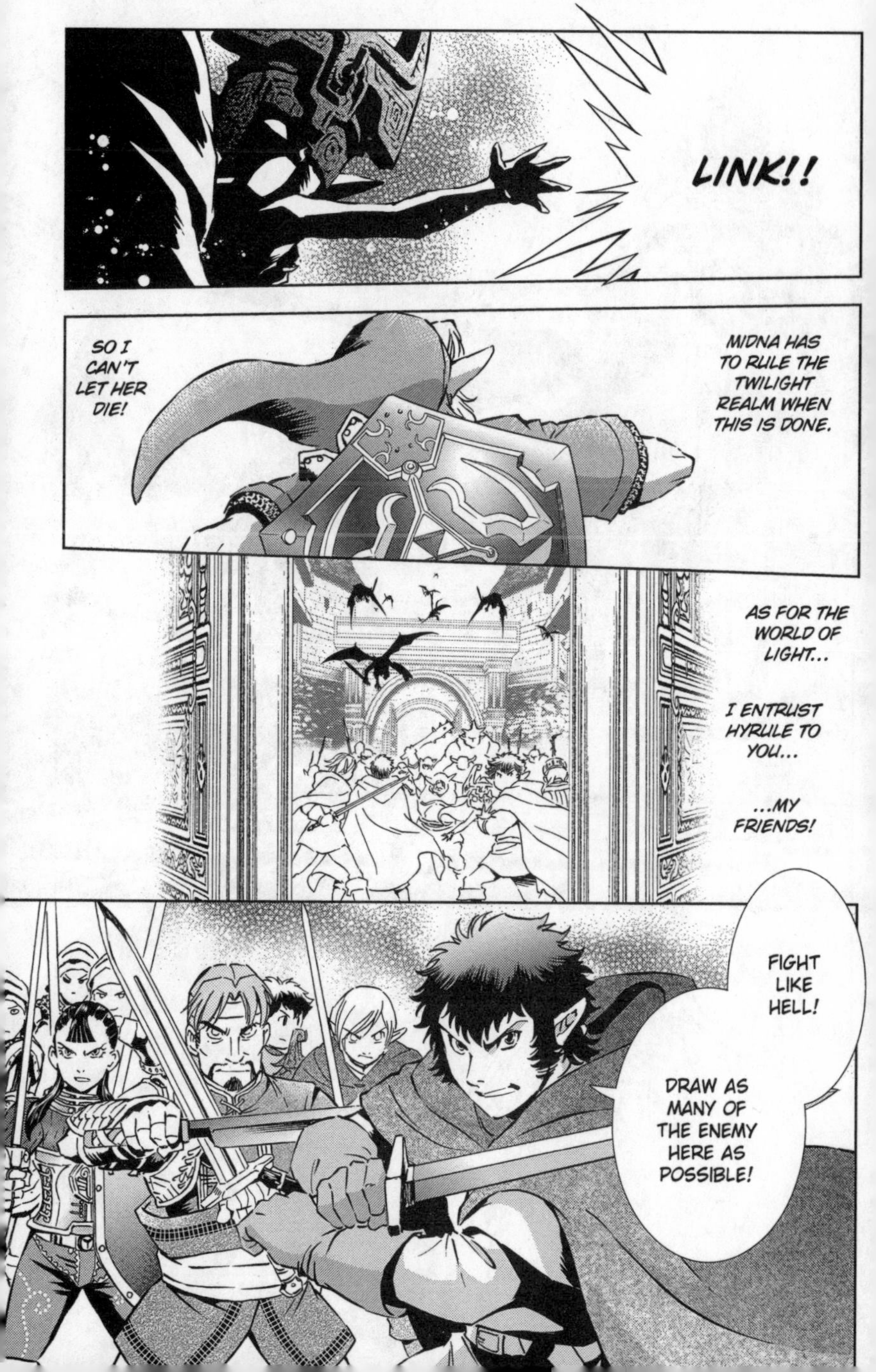
LINK!!
MIDNA HAS TO RULE THE TWILIGHT REALM WHEN THIS IS DONE.
SO I CAN'T LET HER DIE!
AS FOR THE WORLD OF LIGHT...
I ENTRUST HYRULE TO YOU...
...MY FRIENDS!
FIGHT LIKE HELL!
DRAW AS MANY OF THE ENEMY HERE AS POSSIBLE!

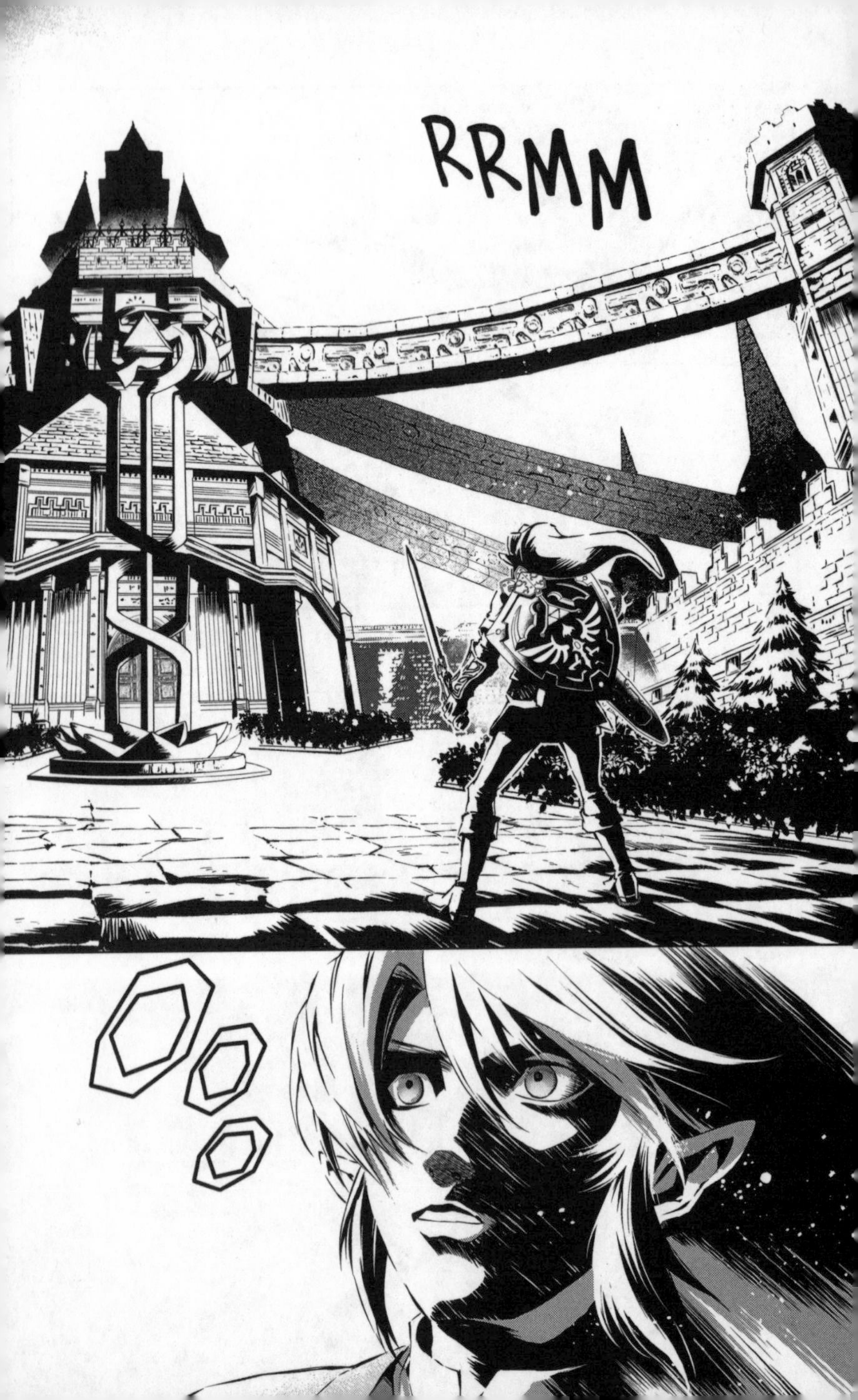
RRMM

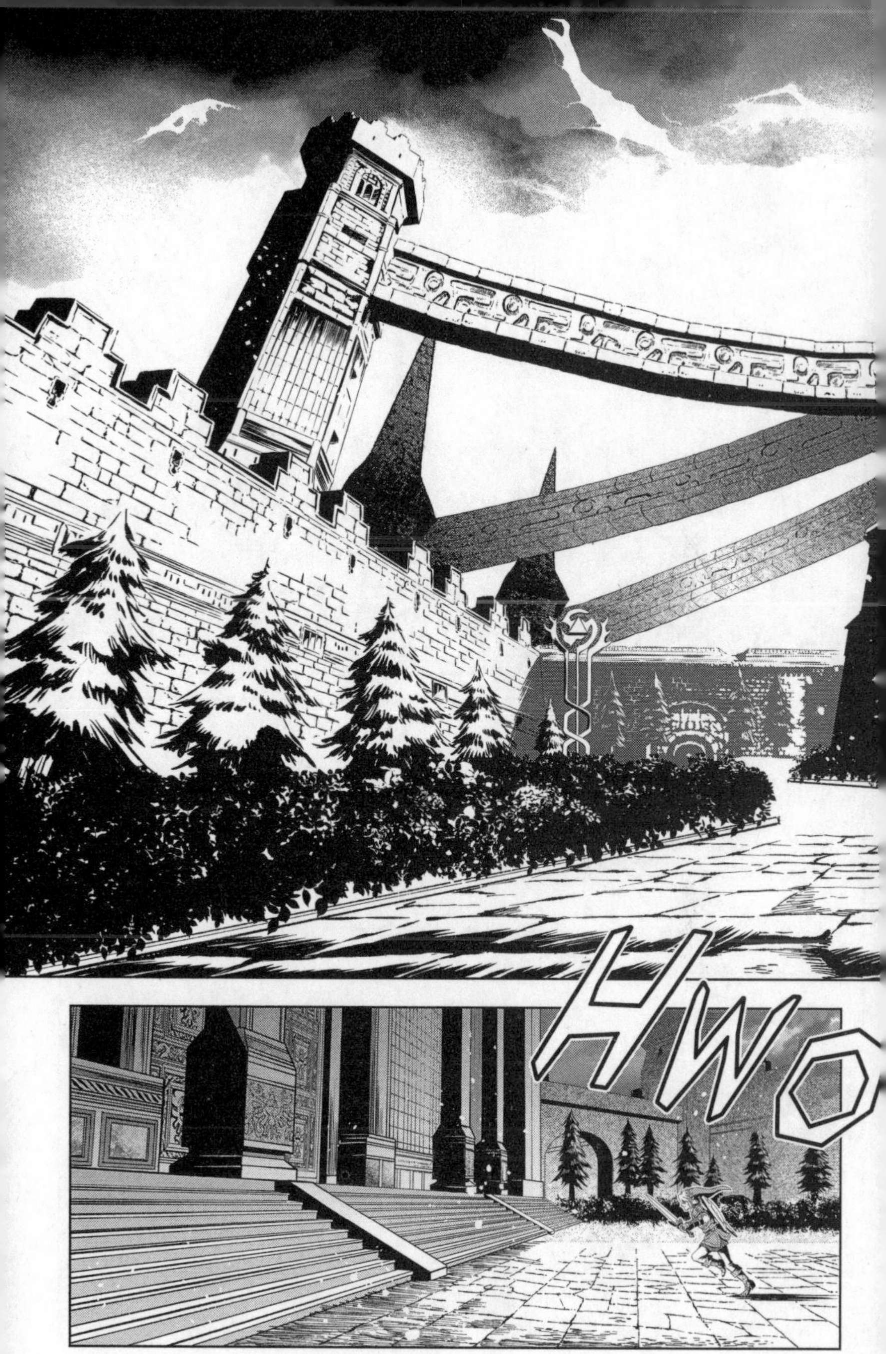
HWO

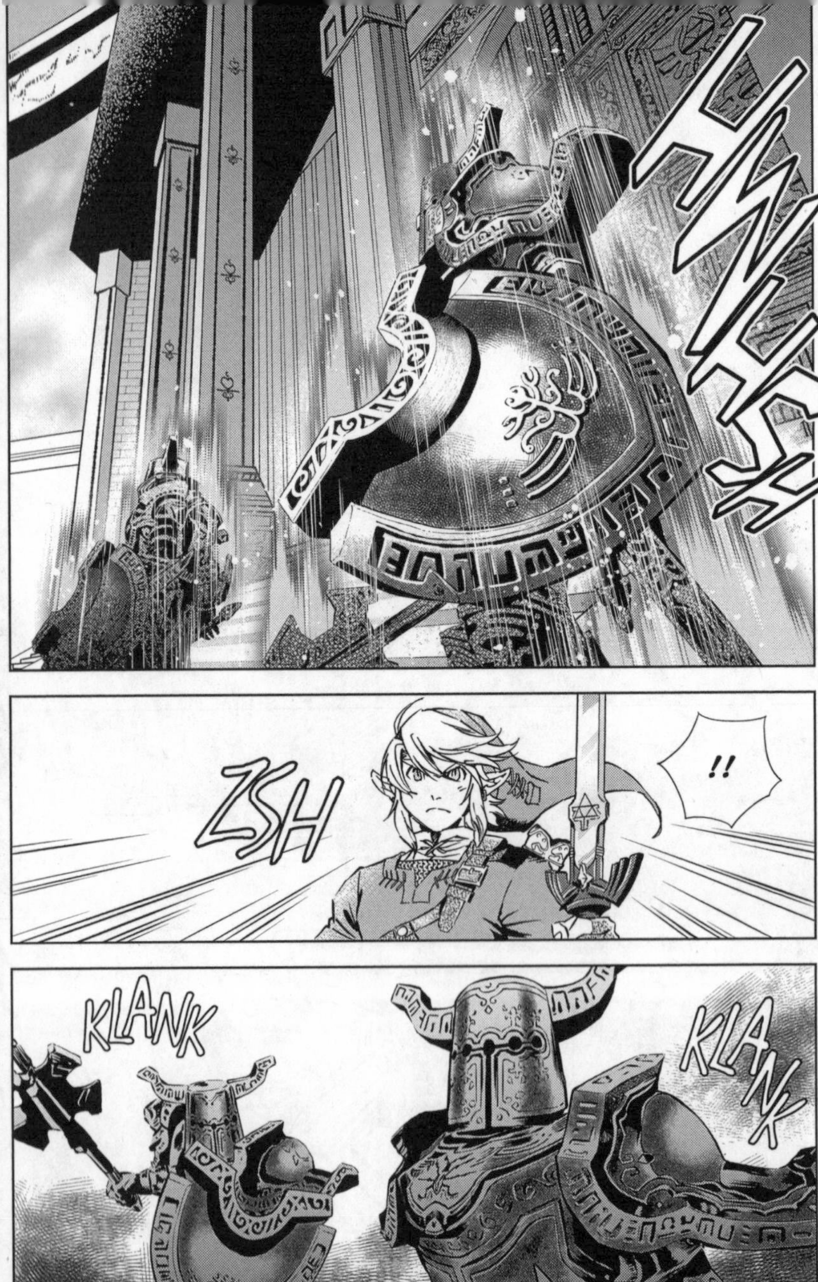
HWHSH
!!
ZSH
KLANK
KLANK

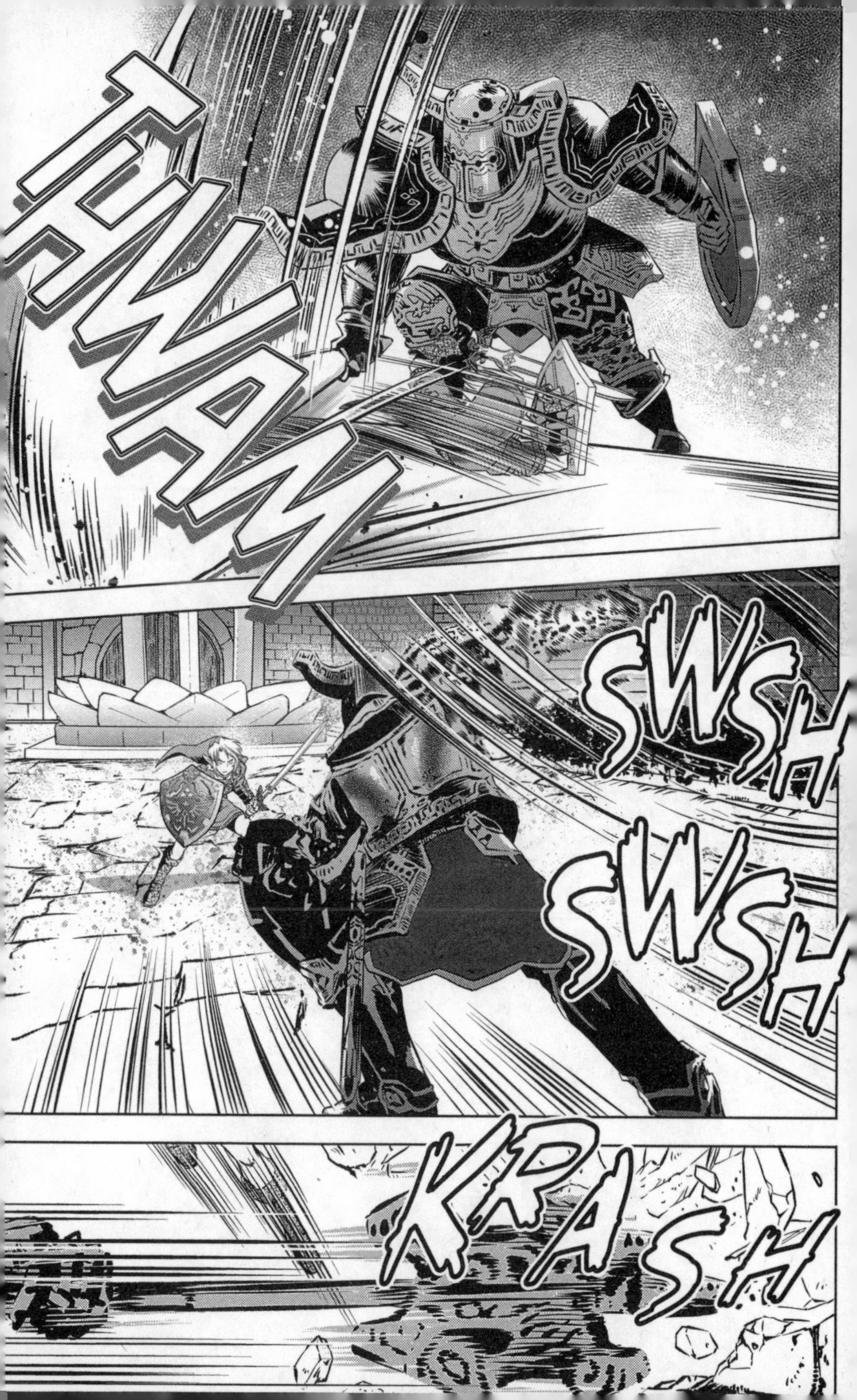
THWAM
SWSH
SWSH
KRASH

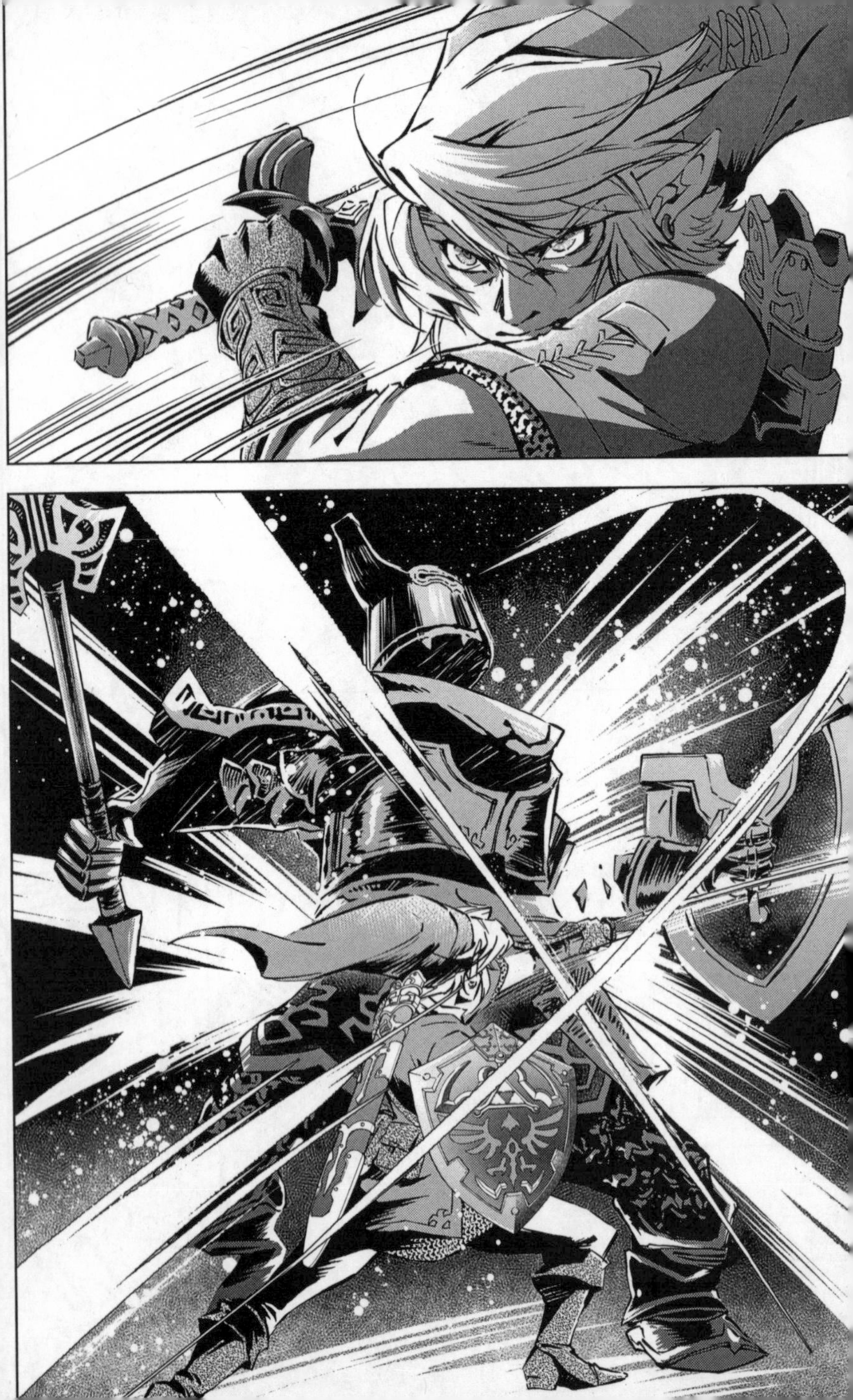

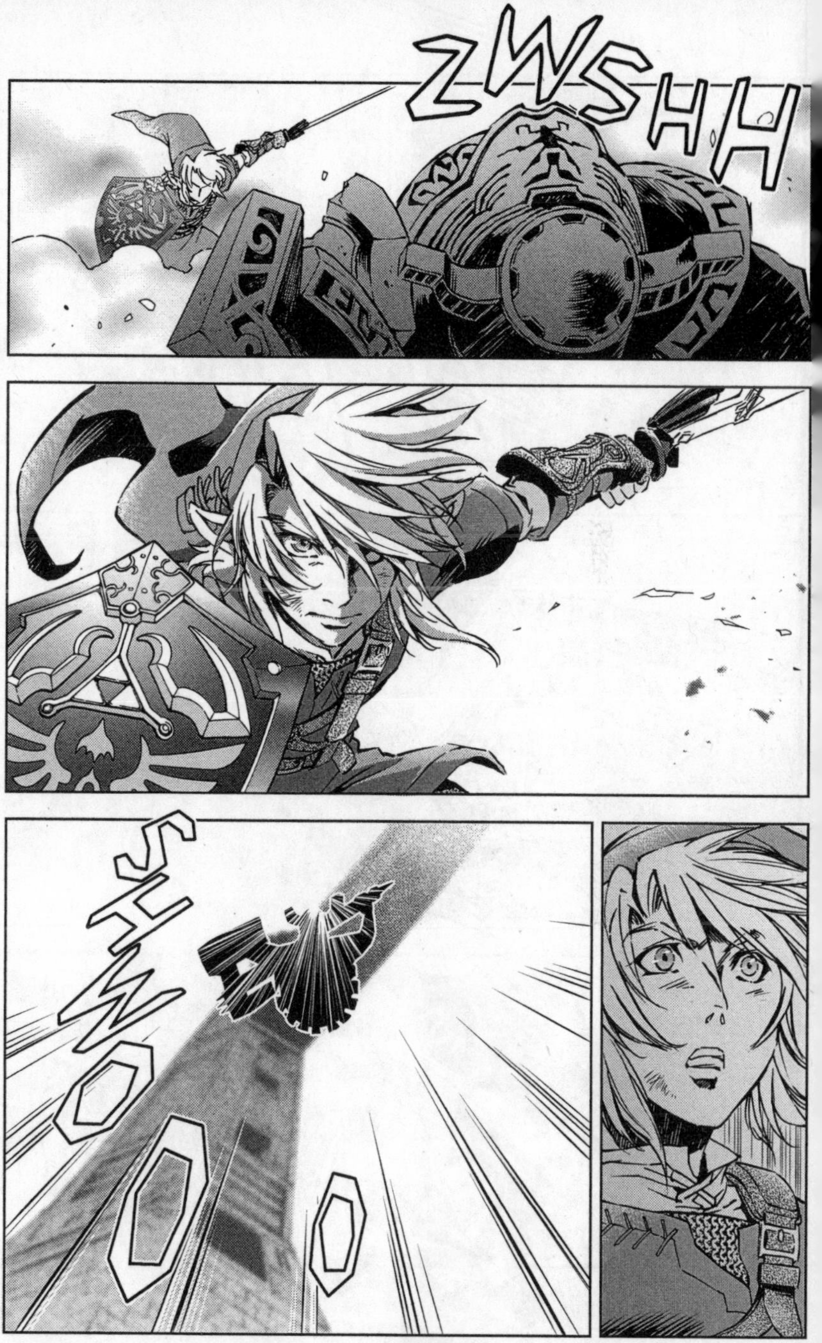
ZWSHH
SHWOOO

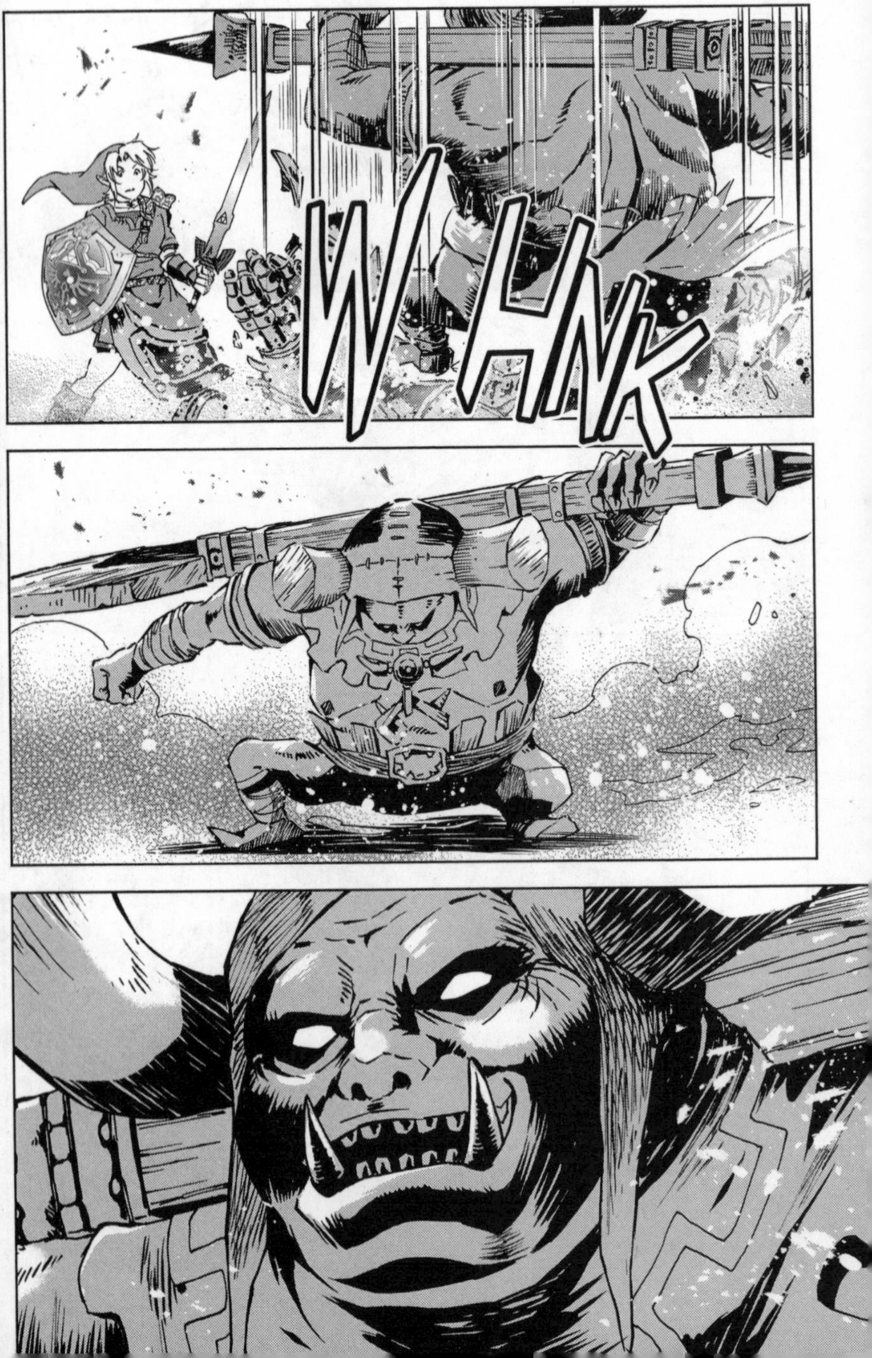
WHNK

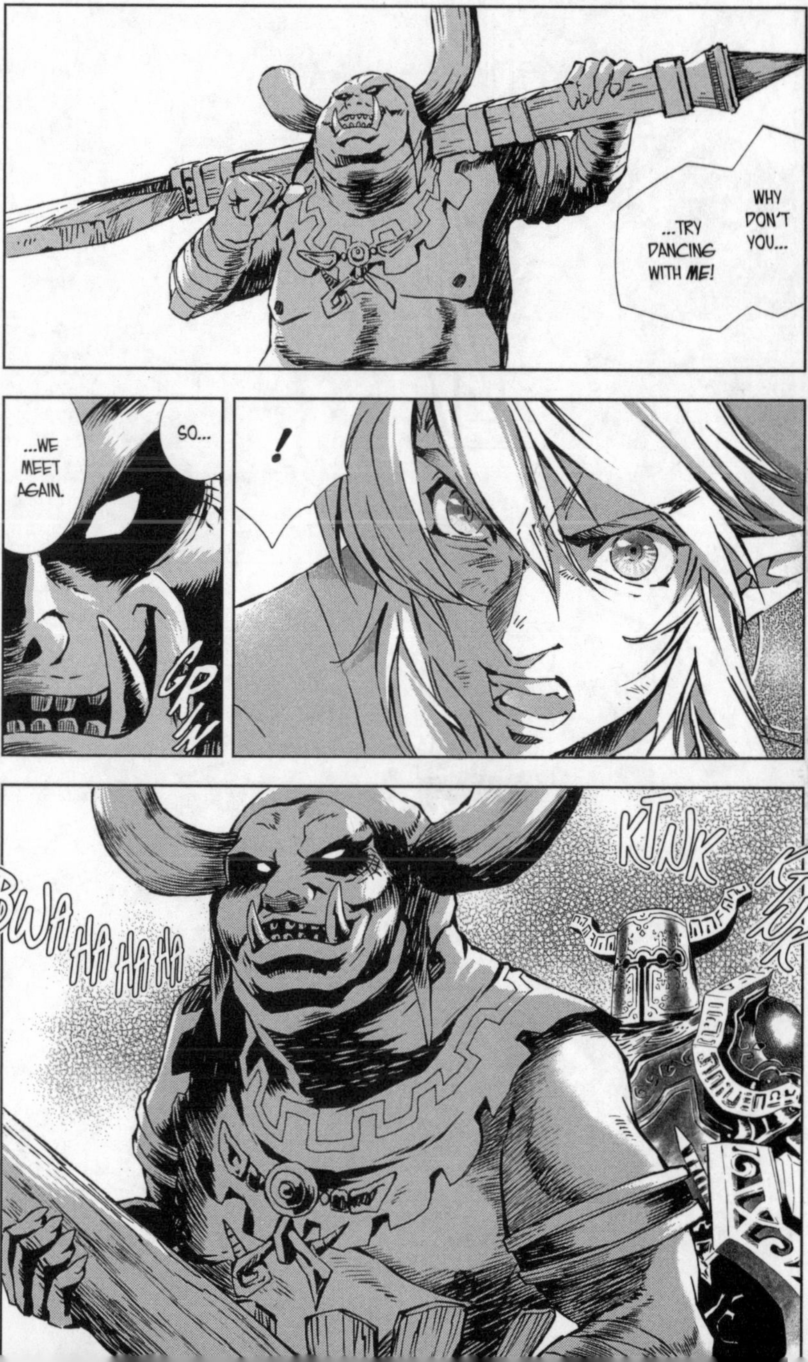
WHY DON'T YOU...
...TRY DANCING WITH ME!
!
SO...
...WE MEET AGAIN.
GRIN
KTNK
KTNK
BWA HA HA HA

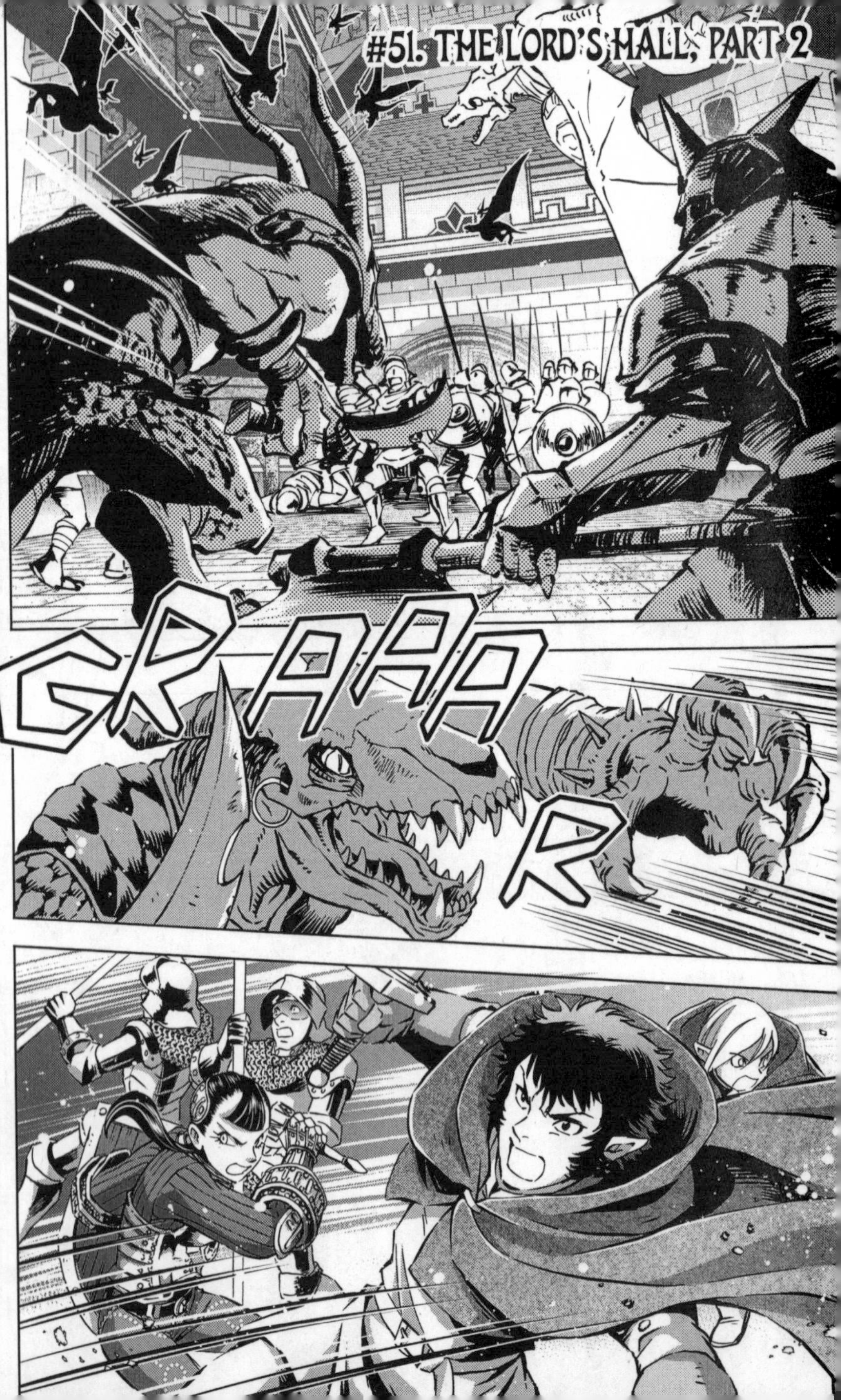
#51. THE LORD'S HALL, PART 2
GRAAAAR

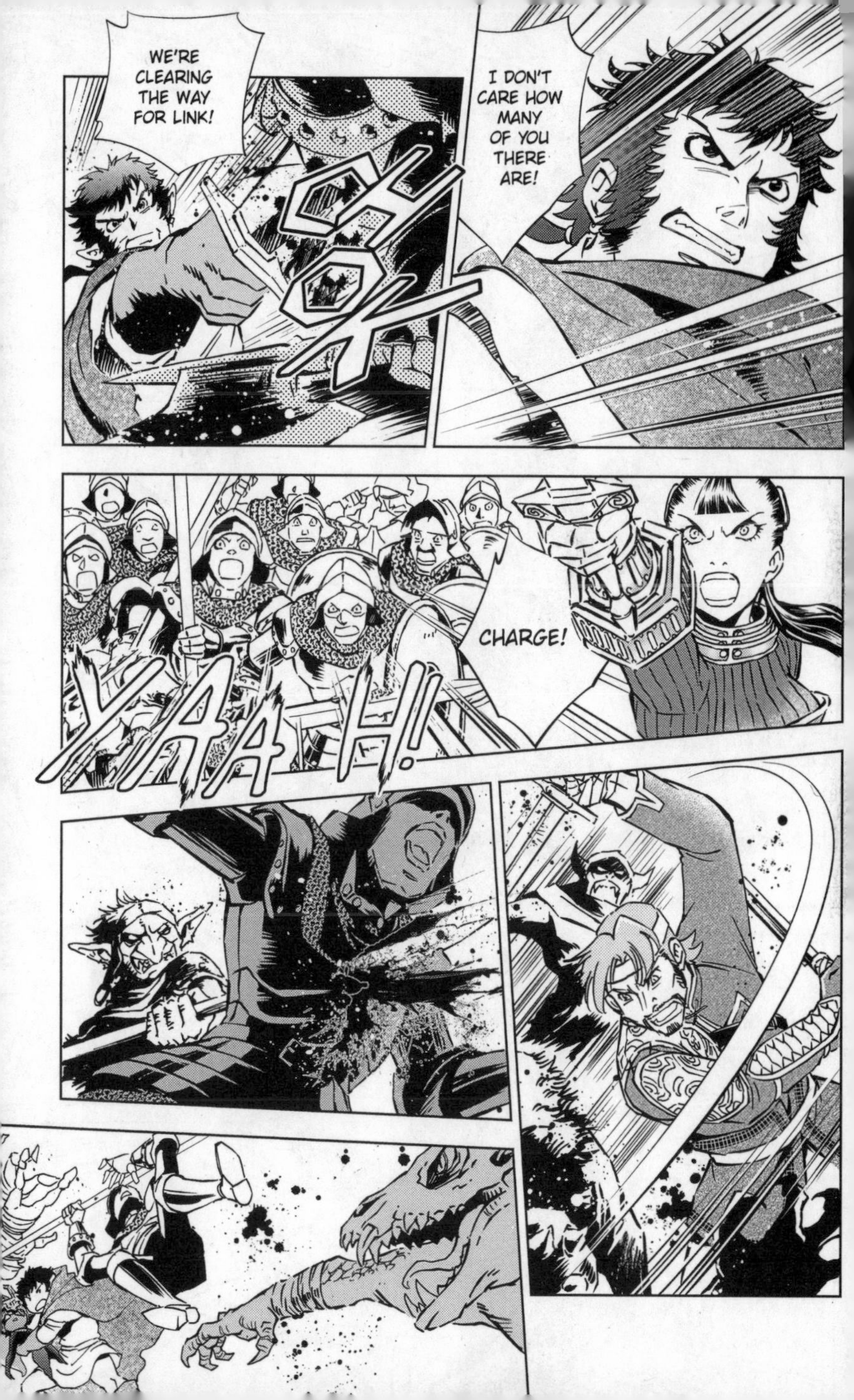
I DON'T CARE HOW MANY OF YOU THERE ARE!
WE'RE CLEARING THE WAY FOR LINK!
CHARGE!
YAAH!

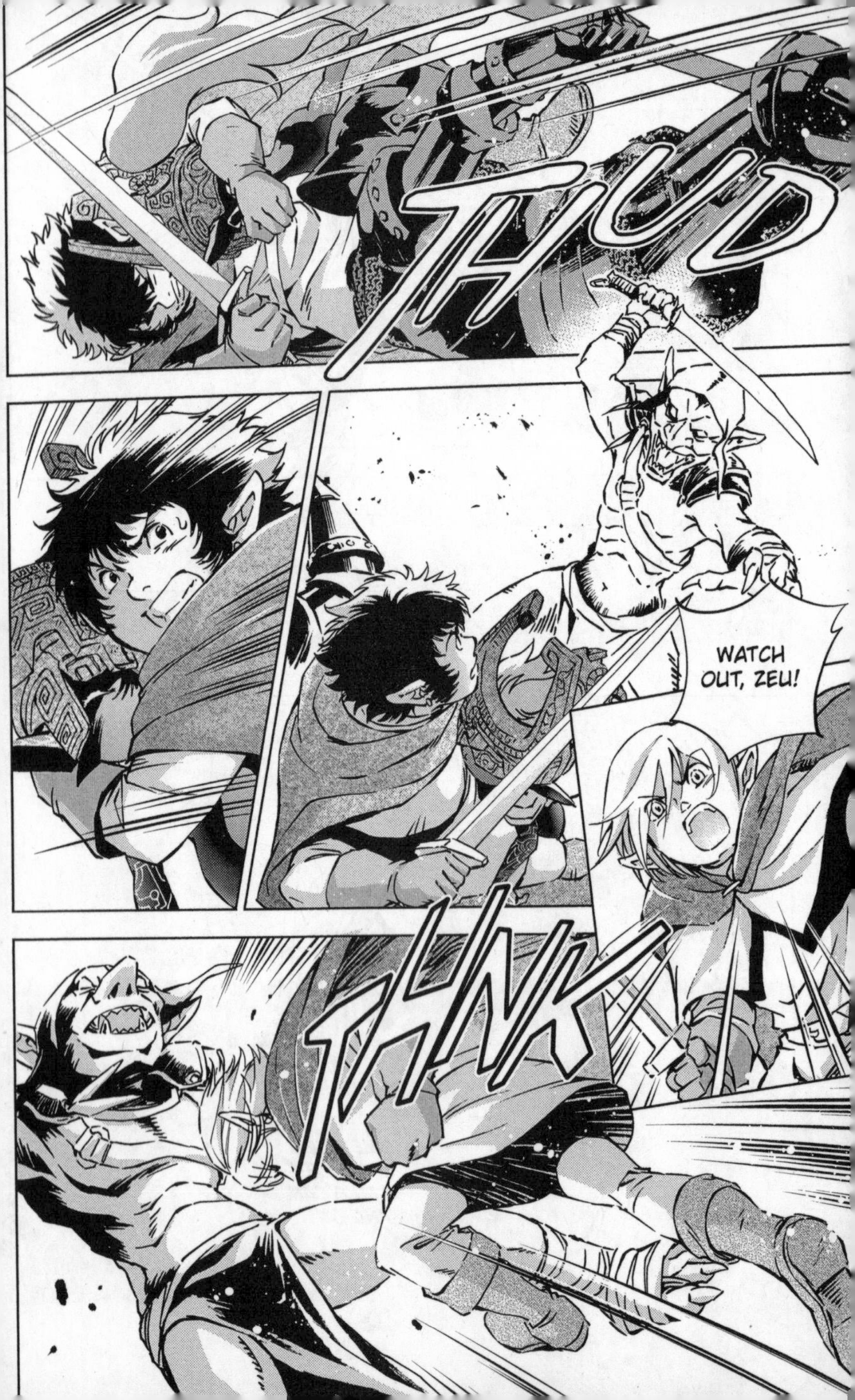
THUD
WATCH OUT, ZEU!
THNK

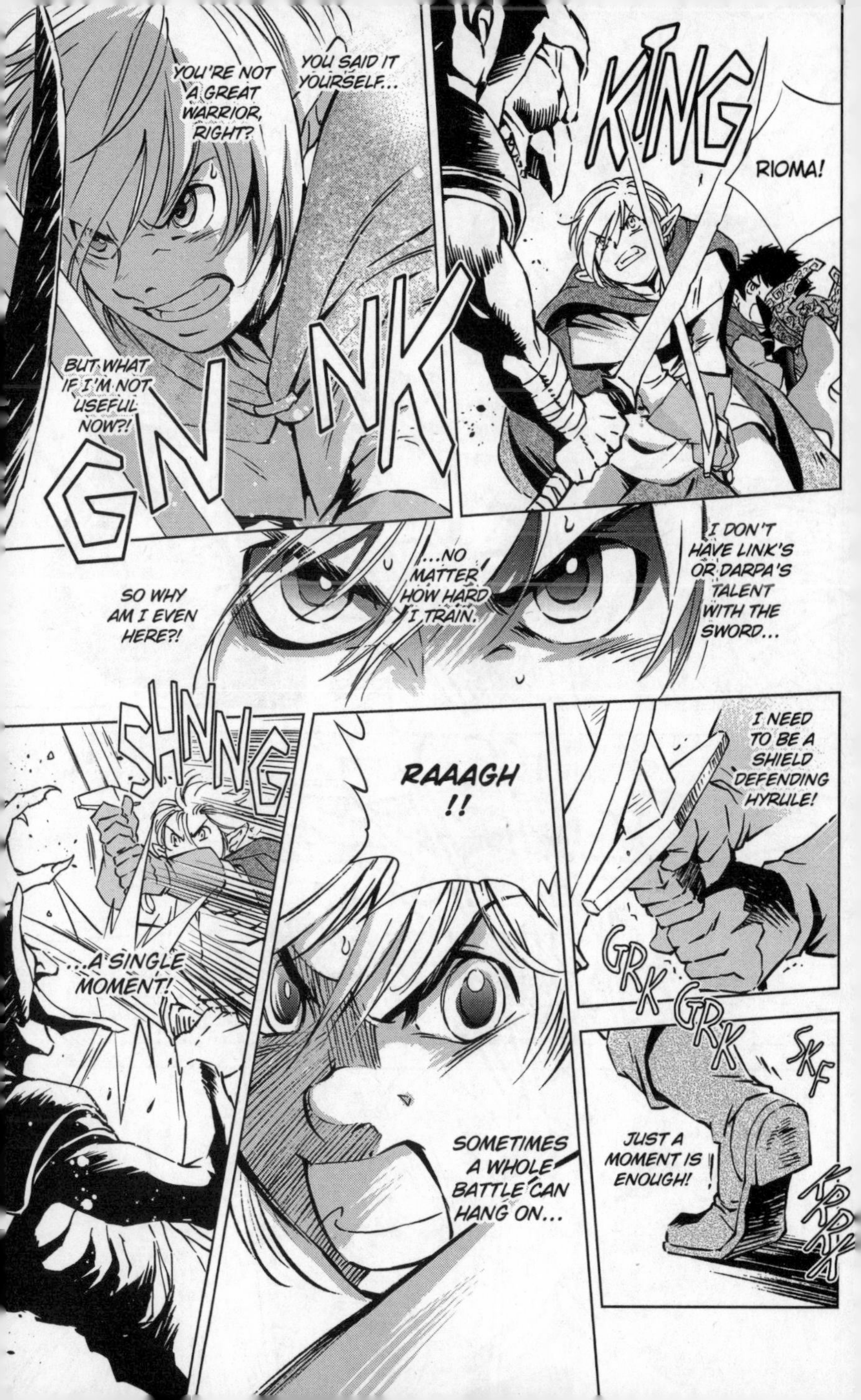
KING
RIOMA!
YOU SAID IT YOURSELF...
YOU'RE NOT A GREAT WARRIOR, RIGHT?
BUT WHAT IF I'M NOT USEFUL NOW?!
GNNK
I DON'T HAVE LINK'S OR DARPA'S TALENT WITH THE SWORD...
...NO MATTER HOW HARD I TRAIN.
SO WHY AM I EVEN HERE?!
I NEED TO BE A SHIELD DEFENDING HYRULE!
GRK GRK
SKF
JUST A MOMENT IS ENOUGH!
KRRAK
RAAAGH!!
SOMETIMES A WHOLE BATTLE CAN HANG ON...
SHNNG
...A SINGLE MOMENT!

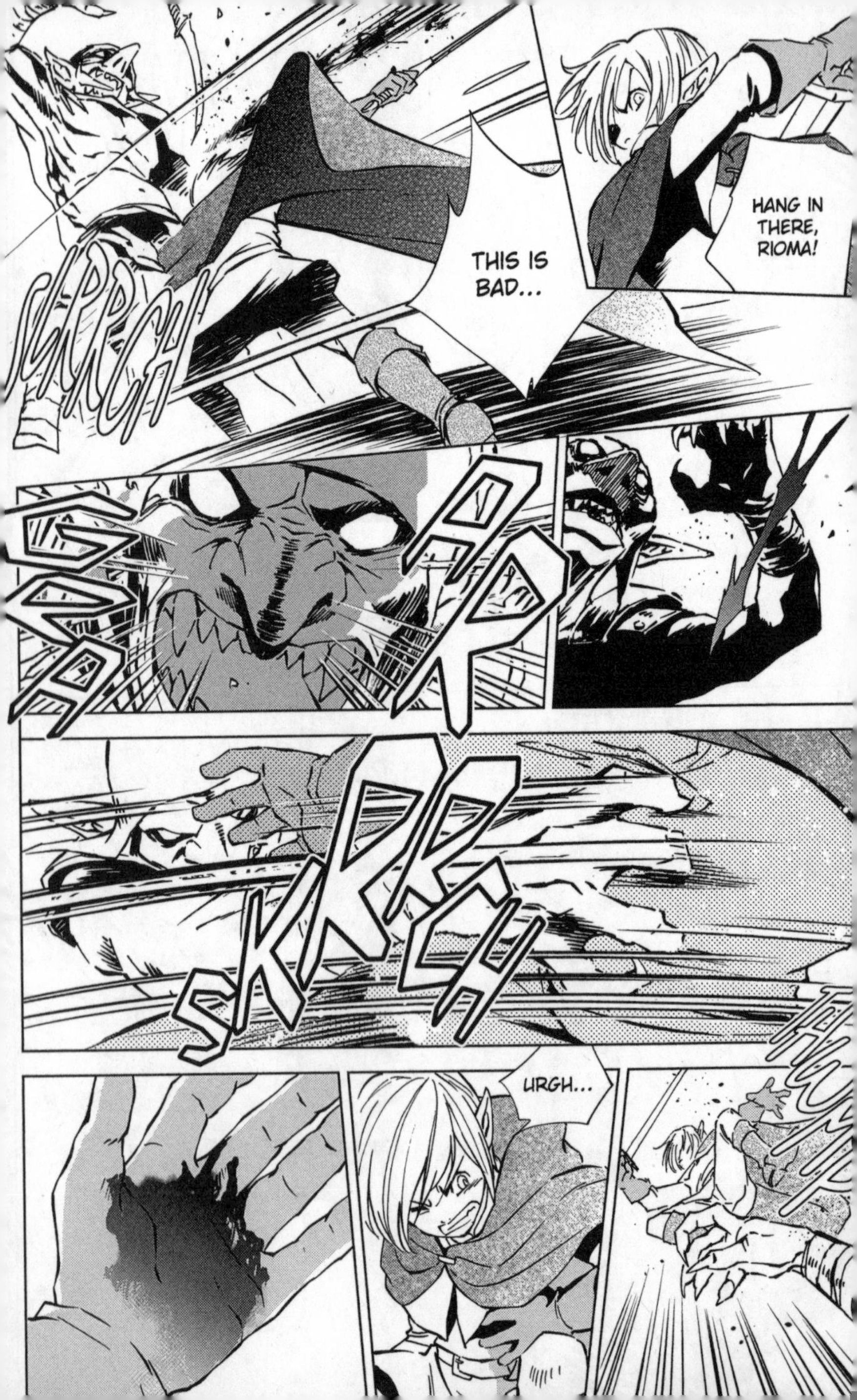
HANG IN THERE, RIOMA!
THIS IS BAD...
SCRRCH
SKRRCH
THUMP
URGH...

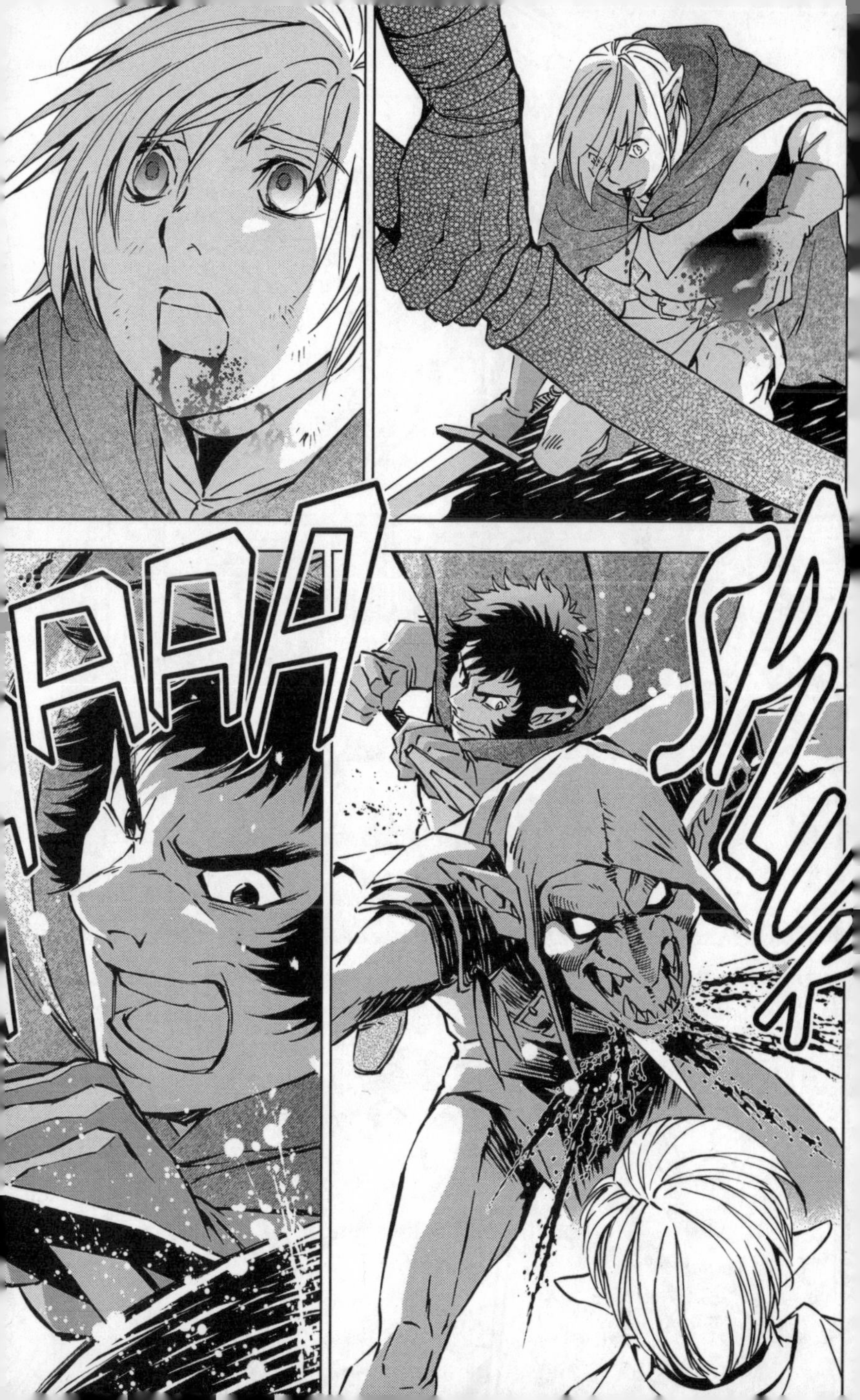
SPLUK
AAAA

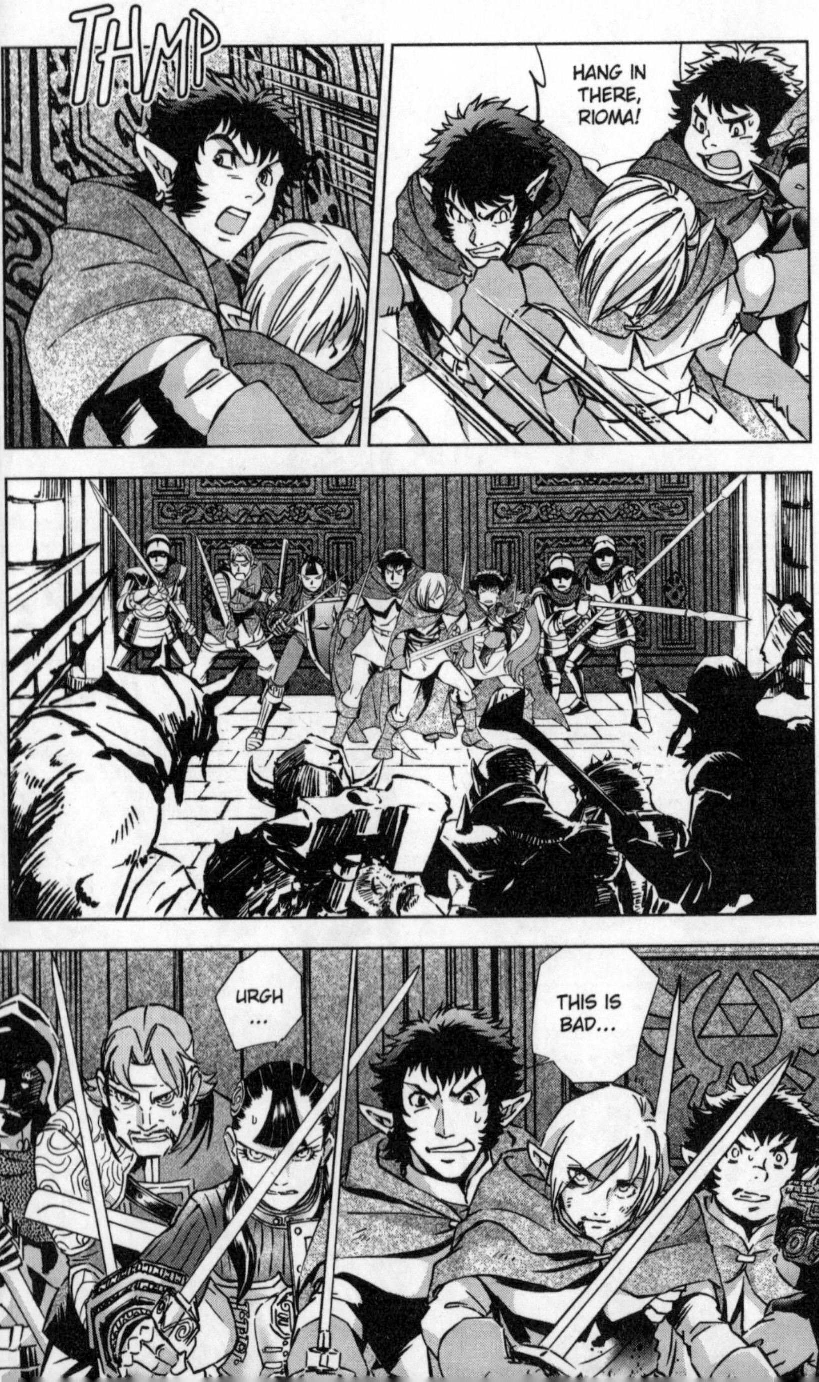
HANG IN THERE, RIOMA!
THMP
THIS IS BAD...
URGH ...

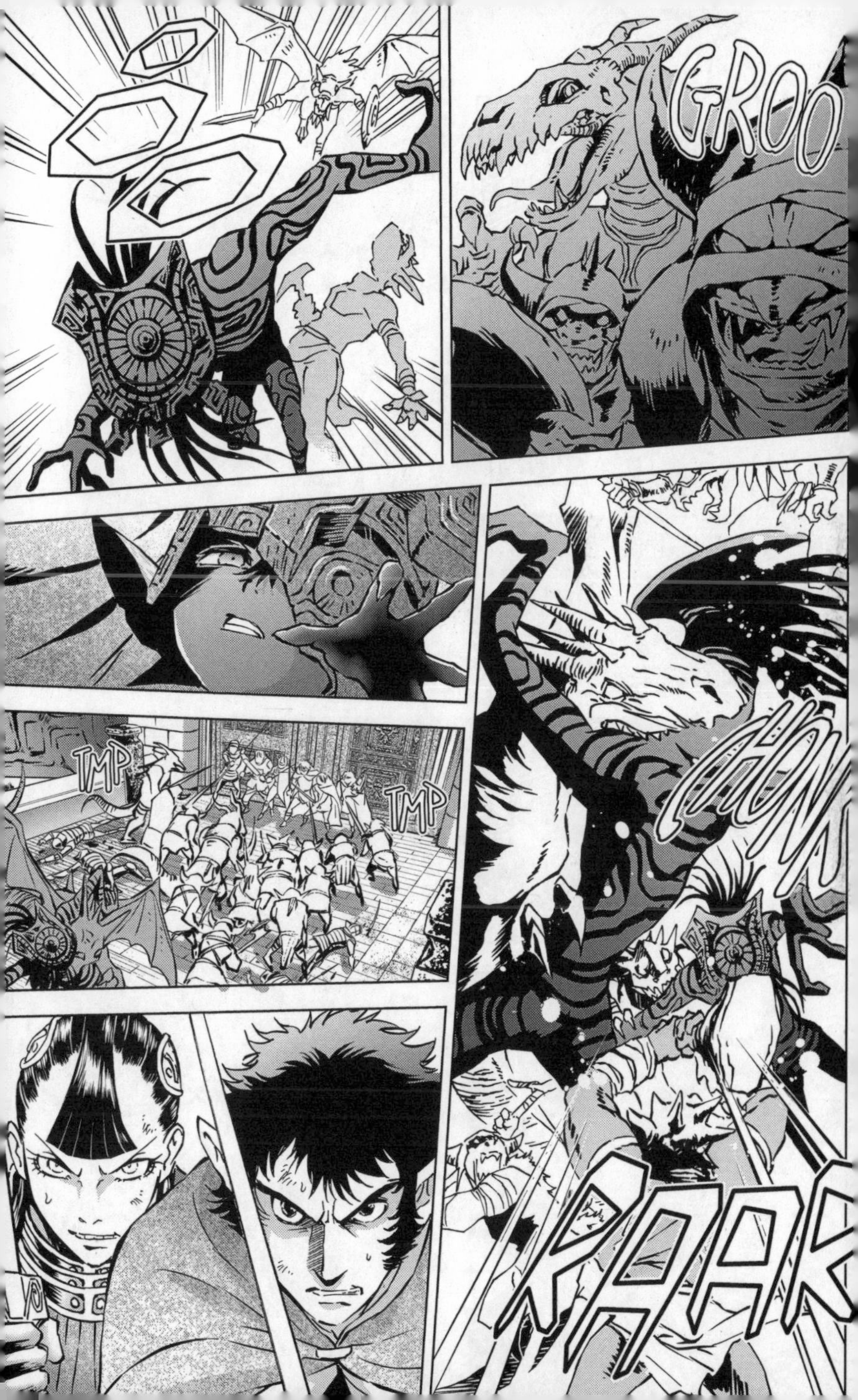
GROO
RAAR
TMP
TMP

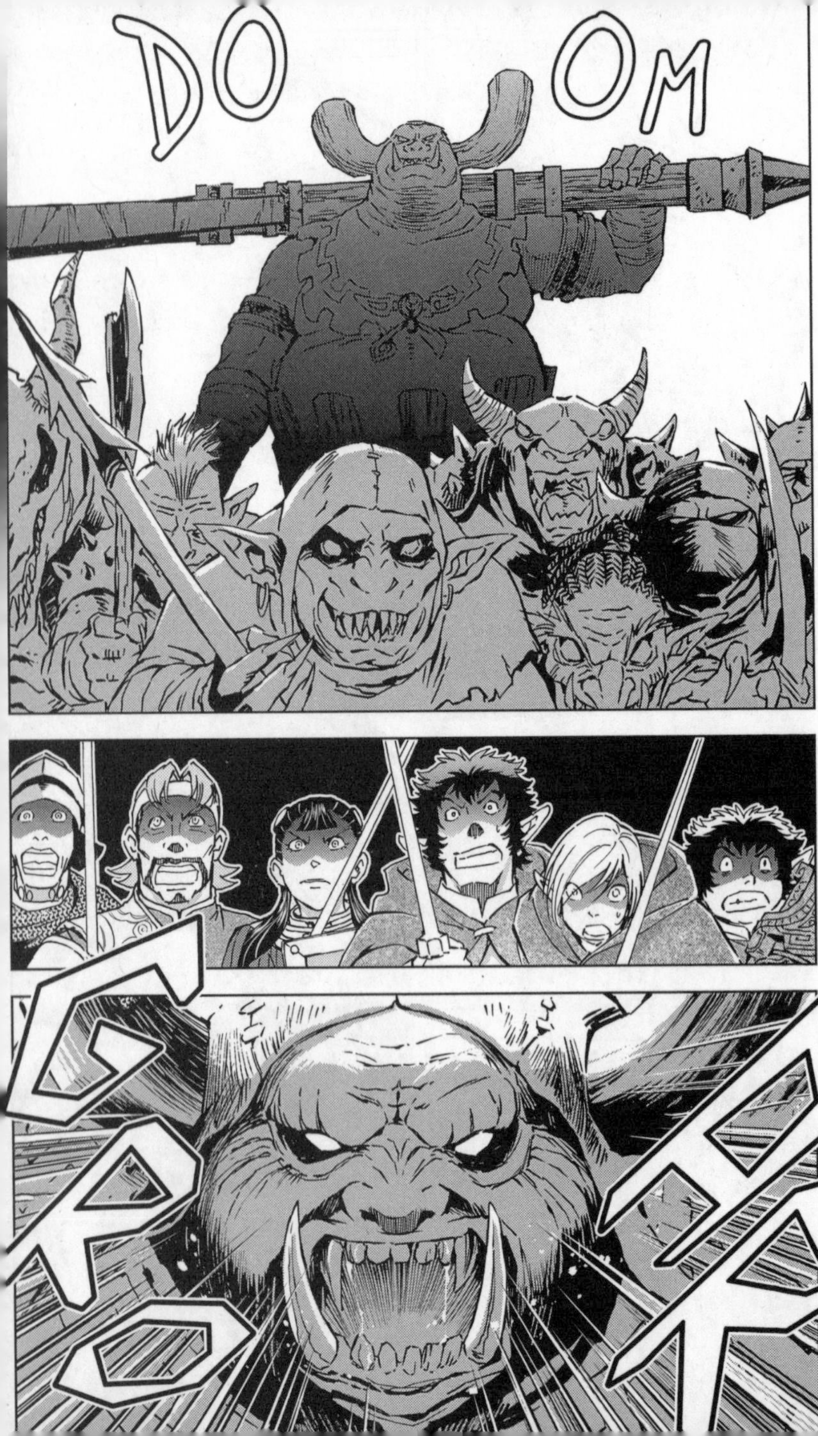
DOOM

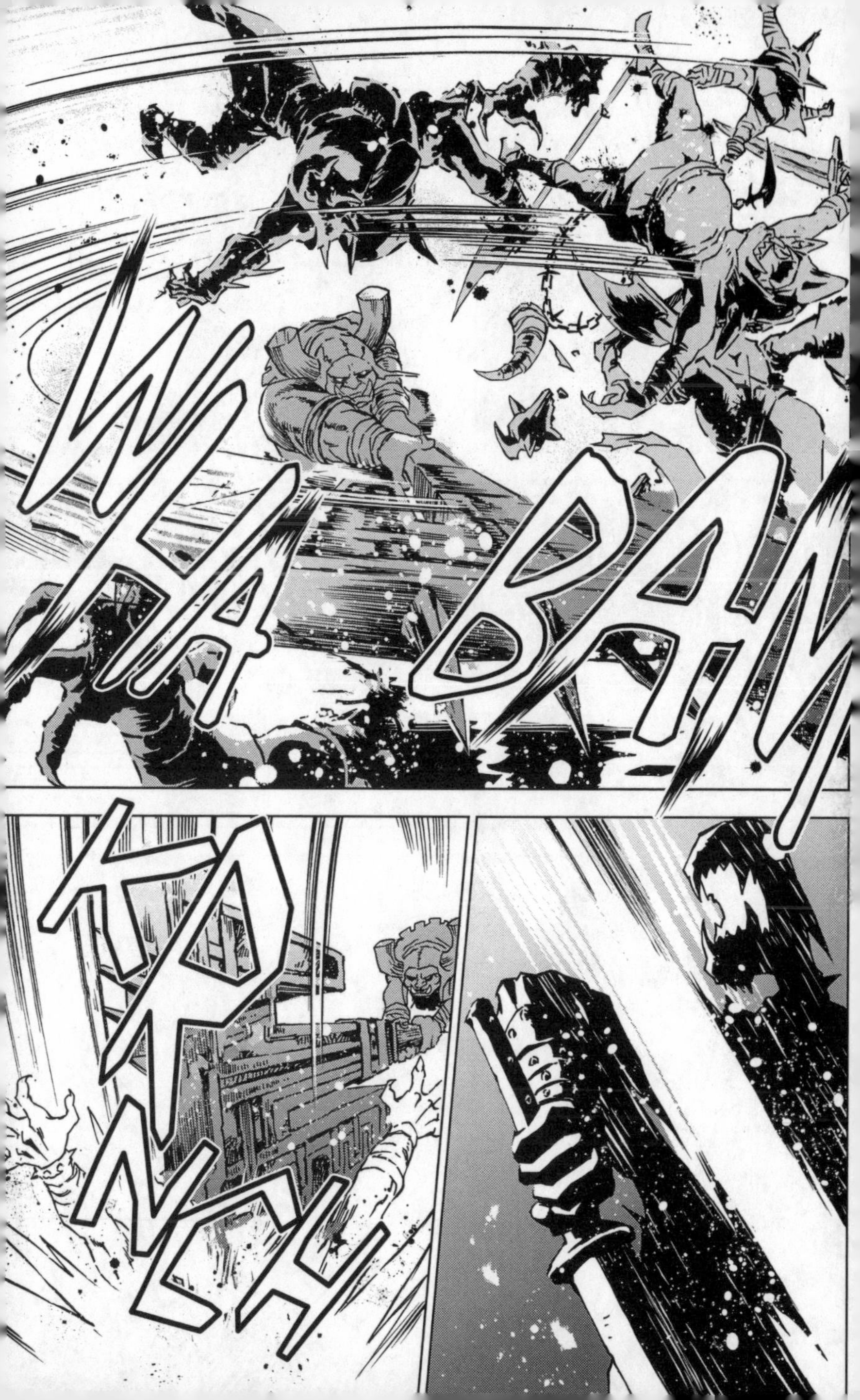
WHABAM
KRANCH

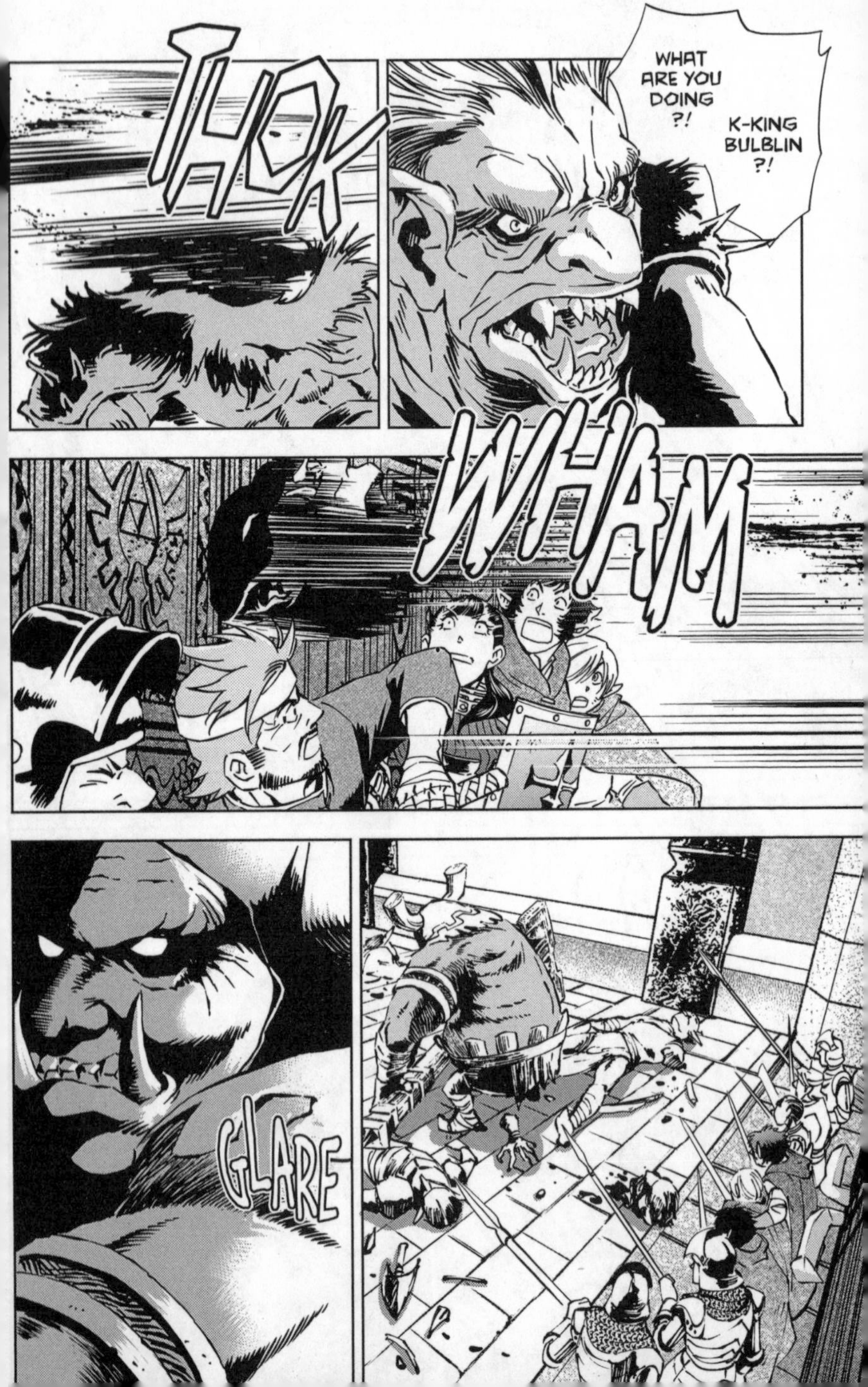
WHAT ARE YOU DOING ?!
K-KING BULBLIN ?!
THOK
WHAM
GLARE

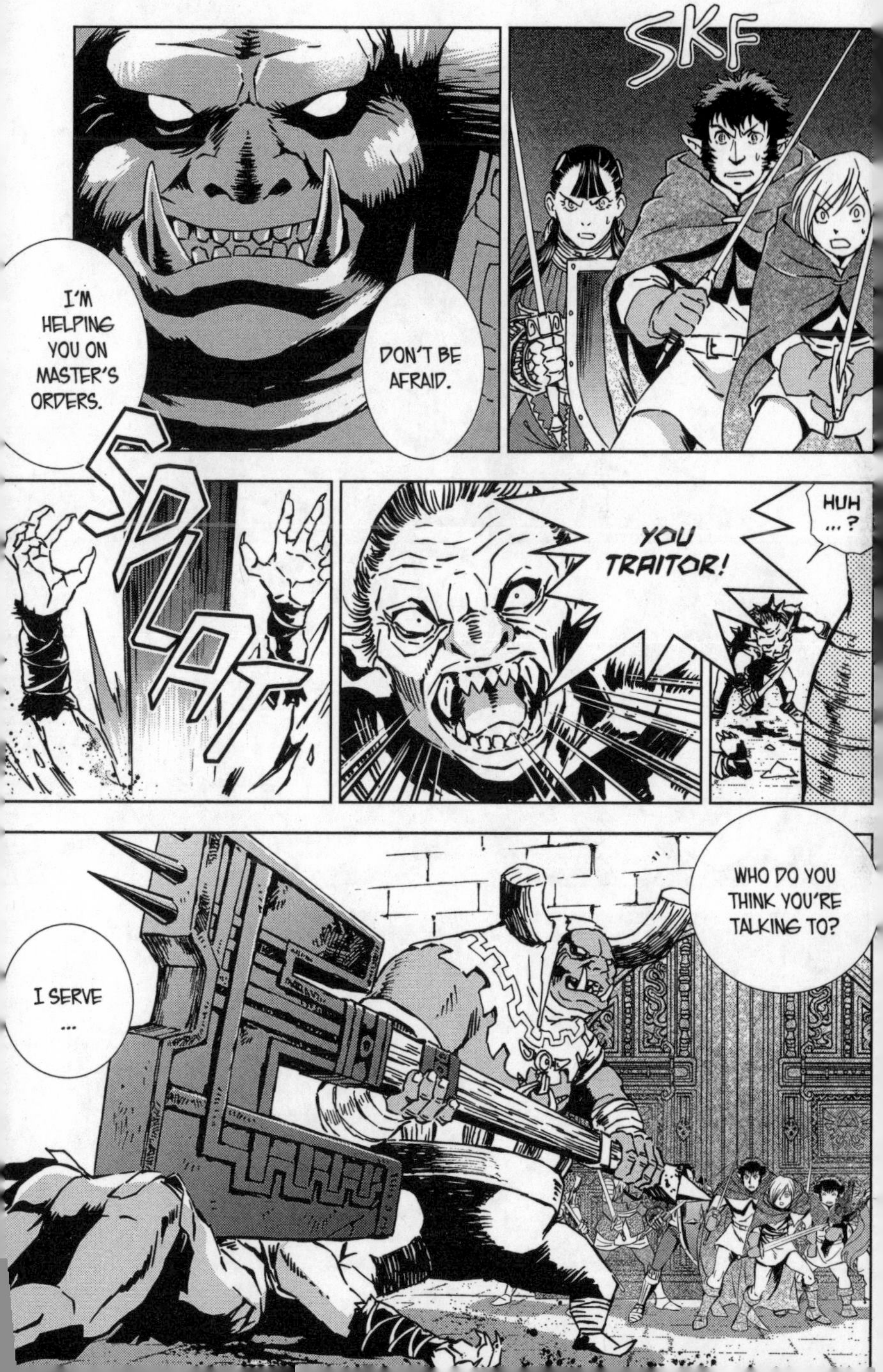
SKF
DON'T BE AFRAID.
I'M HELPING YOU ON MASTER'S ORDERS.
HUH ...?
YOU TRAITOR!
SPLAT
WHO DO YOU THINK YOU'RE TALKING TO?
I SERVE ...

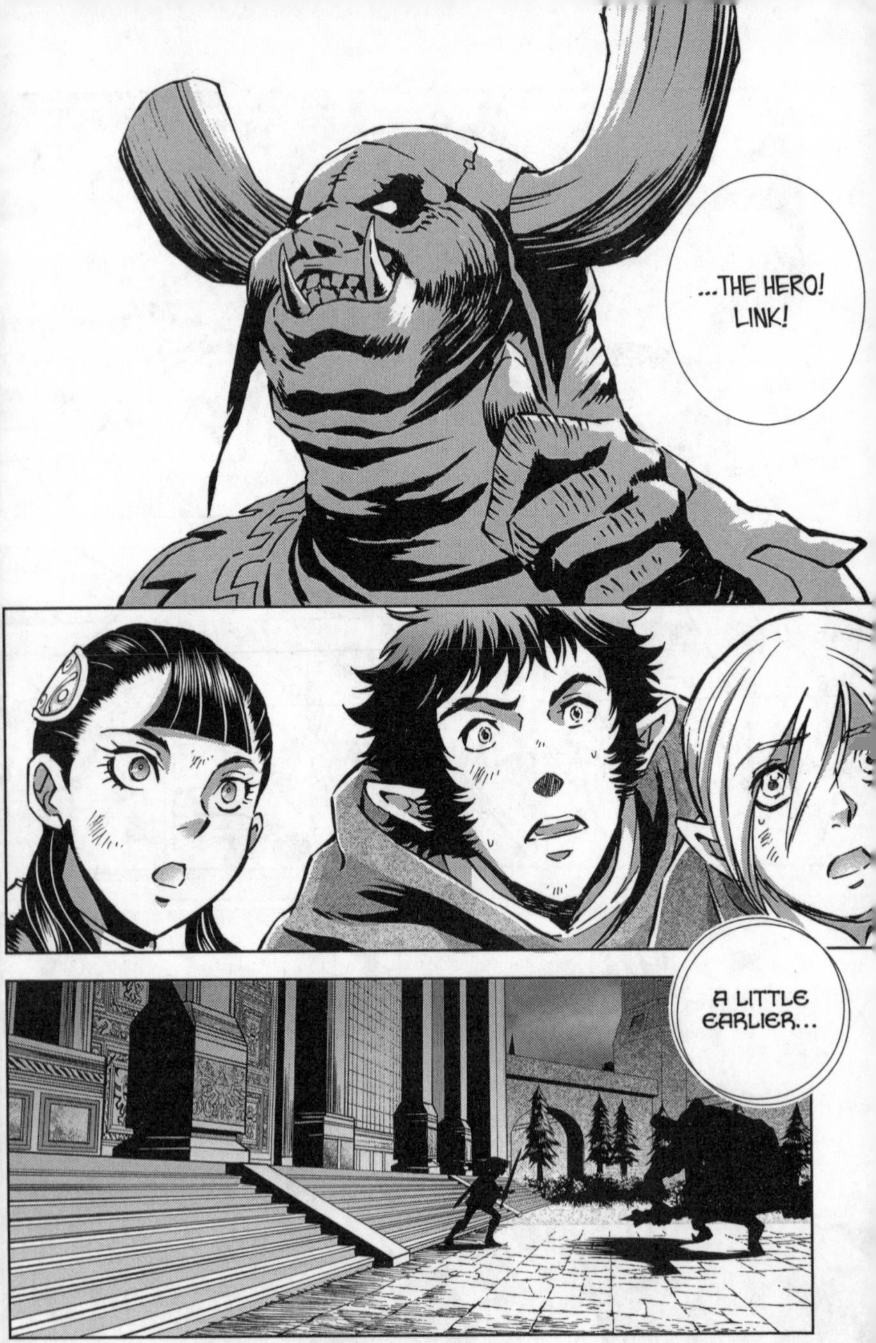
...THE HERO! LINK!
A LITTLE EARLIER...

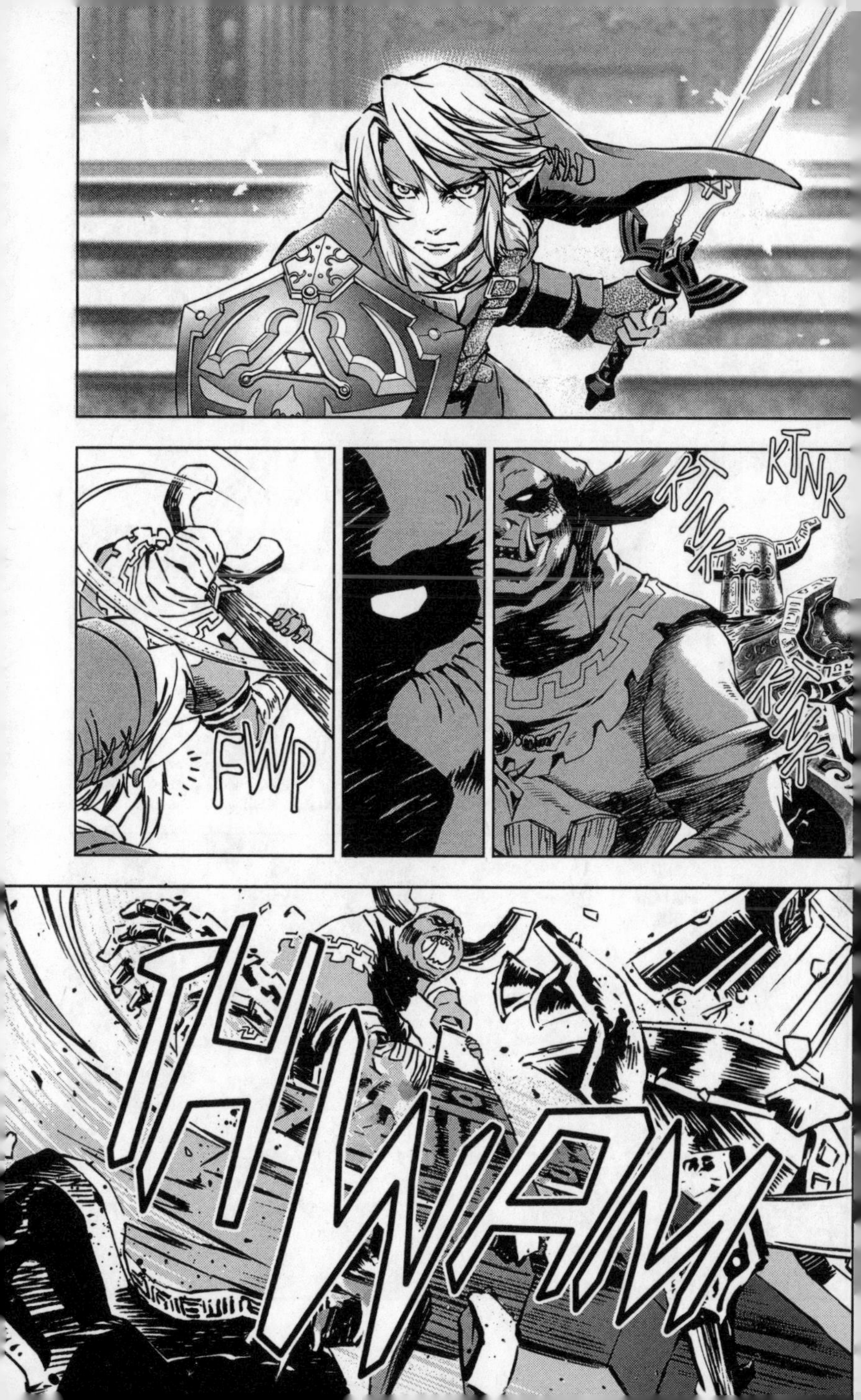
KTNK
KTNK
KTNK
FWP
THWAM

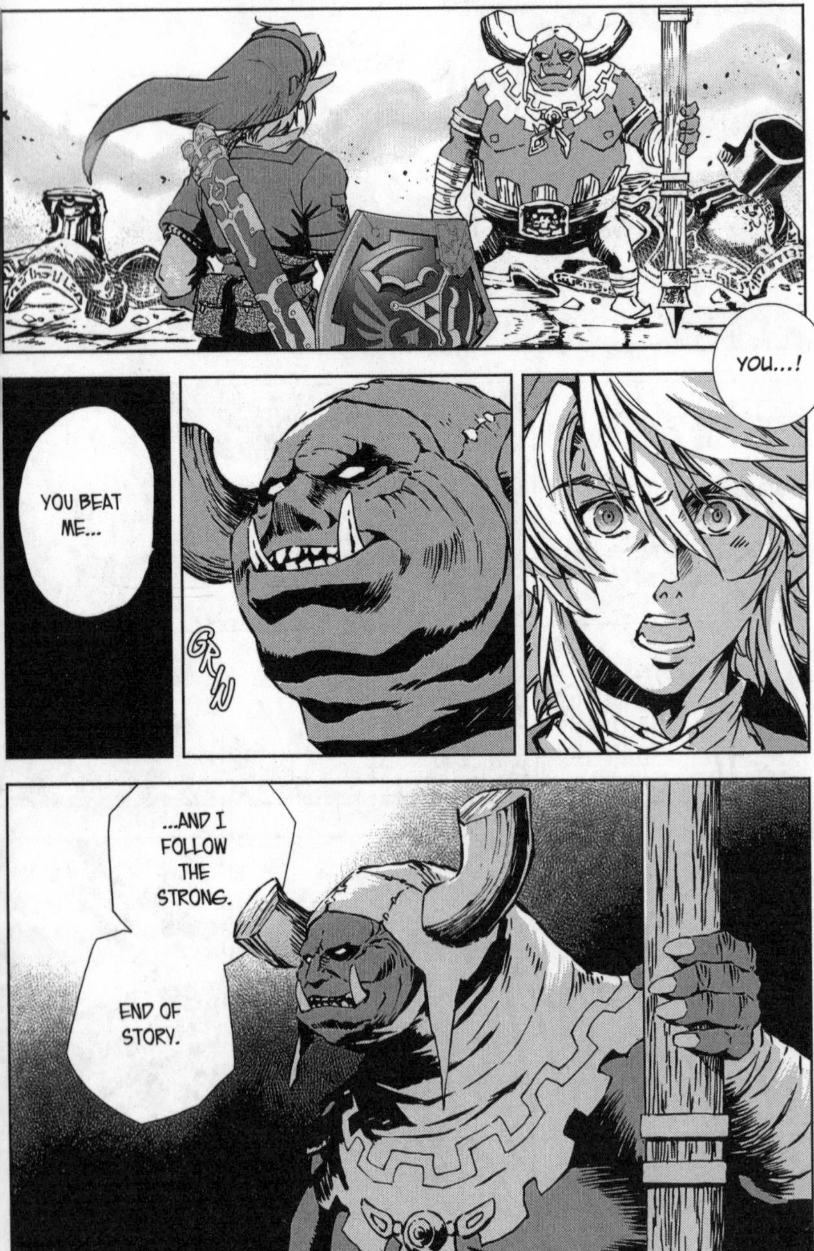
YOU...!
GRIN
YOU BEAT ME...
...AND I FOLLOW THE STRONG.
END OF STORY.

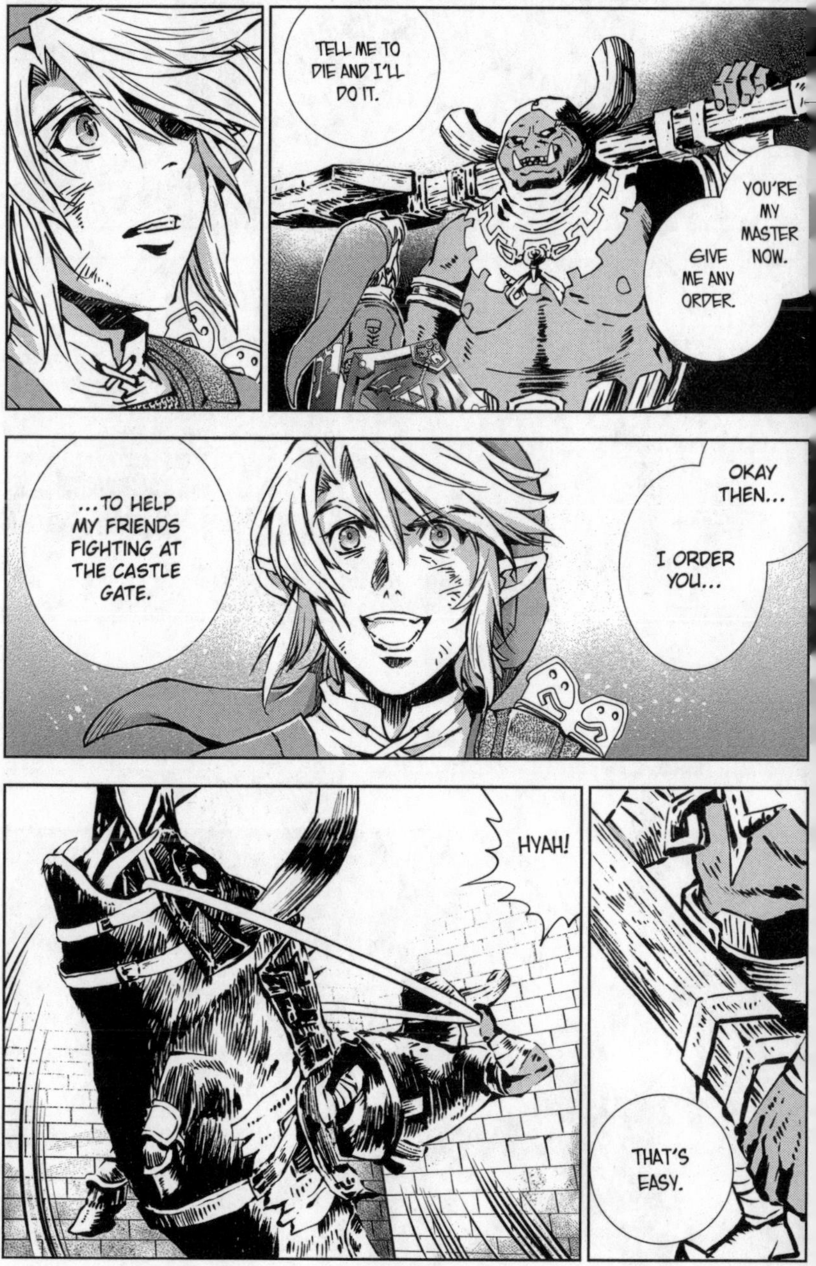
YOU'RE MY MASTER NOW.
GIVE ME ANY ORDER.
TELL ME TO DIE AND I'LL DO IT.
OKAY THEN...
I ORDER YOU...
...TO HELP MY FRIENDS FIGHTING AT THE CASTLE GATE.
THAT'S EASY.
HYAH!

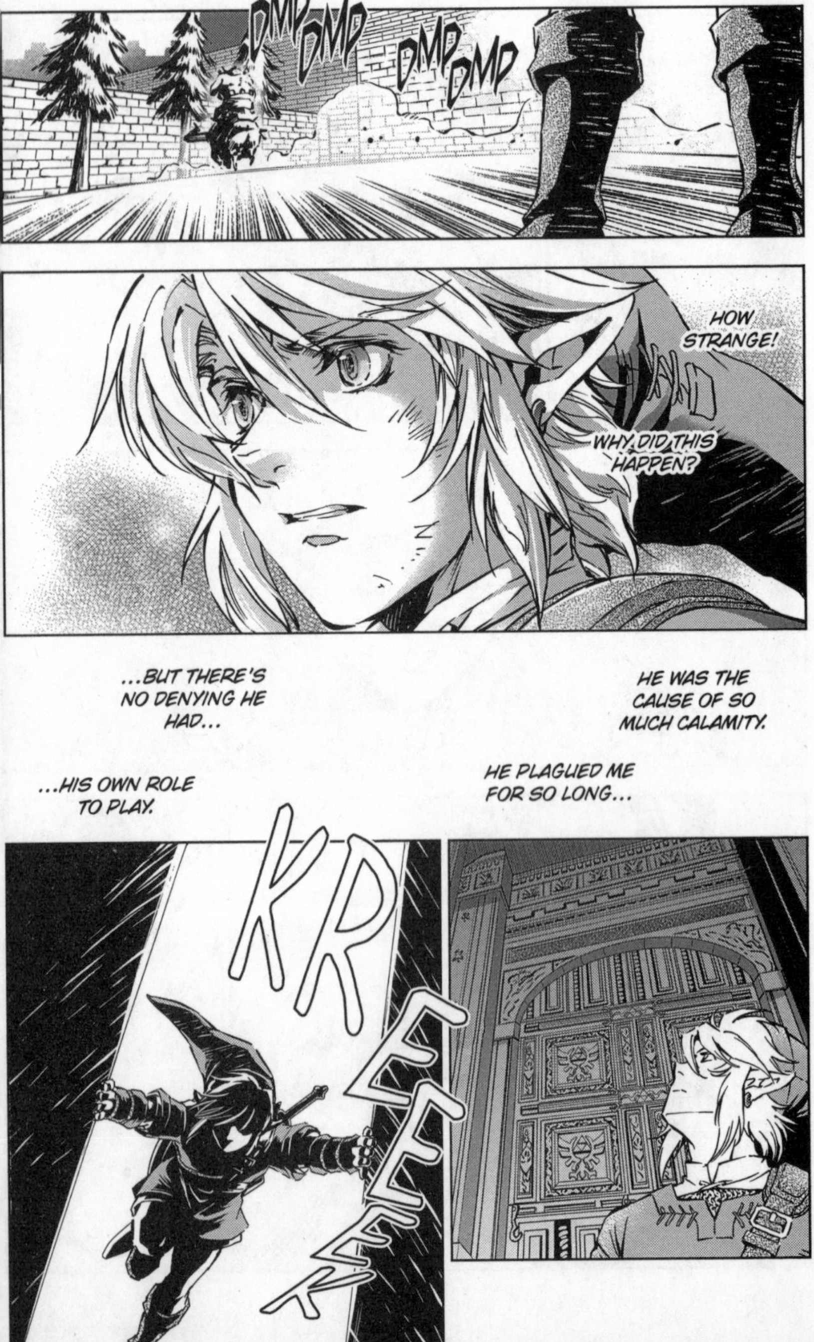
DMP DMP
DMP DMP
HOW STRANGE!
WHY DID THIS HAPPEN?
HE WAS THE CAUSE OF SO MUCH CALAMITY.
HE PLAGUED ME FOR SO LONG...
...BUT THERE'S NO DENYING HE HAD...
...HIS OWN ROLE TO PLAY.
KREEEEEK

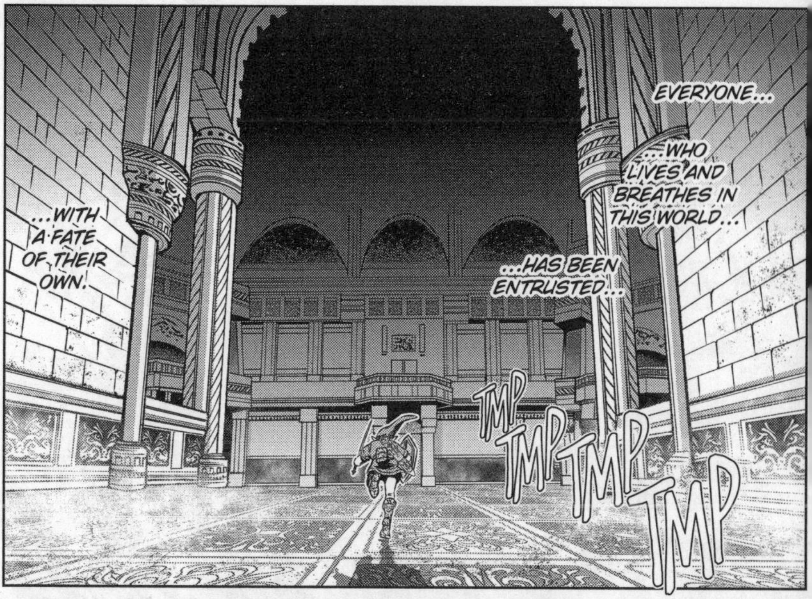
EVERYONE...
...WHO LIVES AND BREATHES IN THIS WORLD...
...HAS BEEN ENTRUSTED...
...WITH A FATE OF THEIR OWN.
TMP TMP TMP TMP

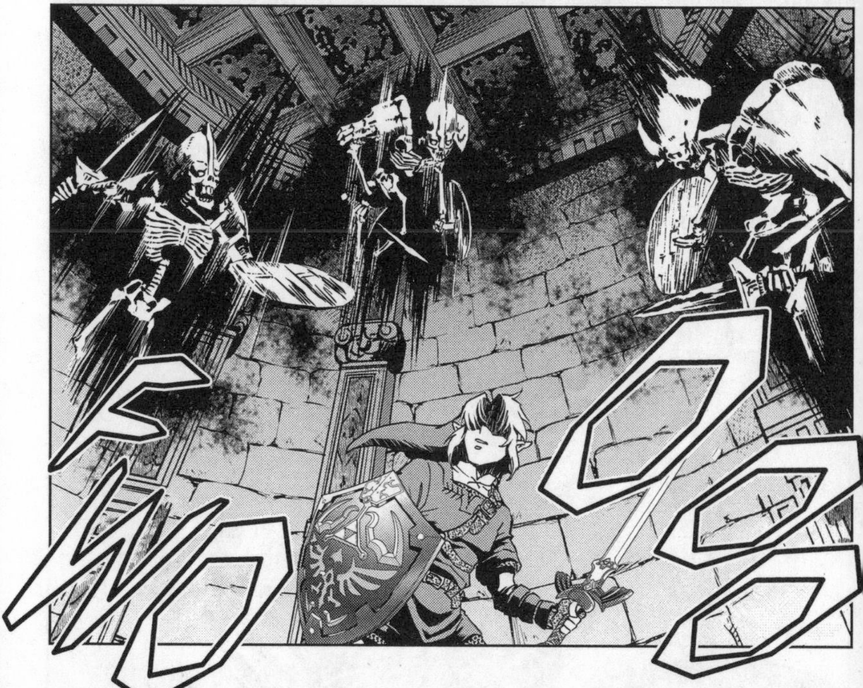

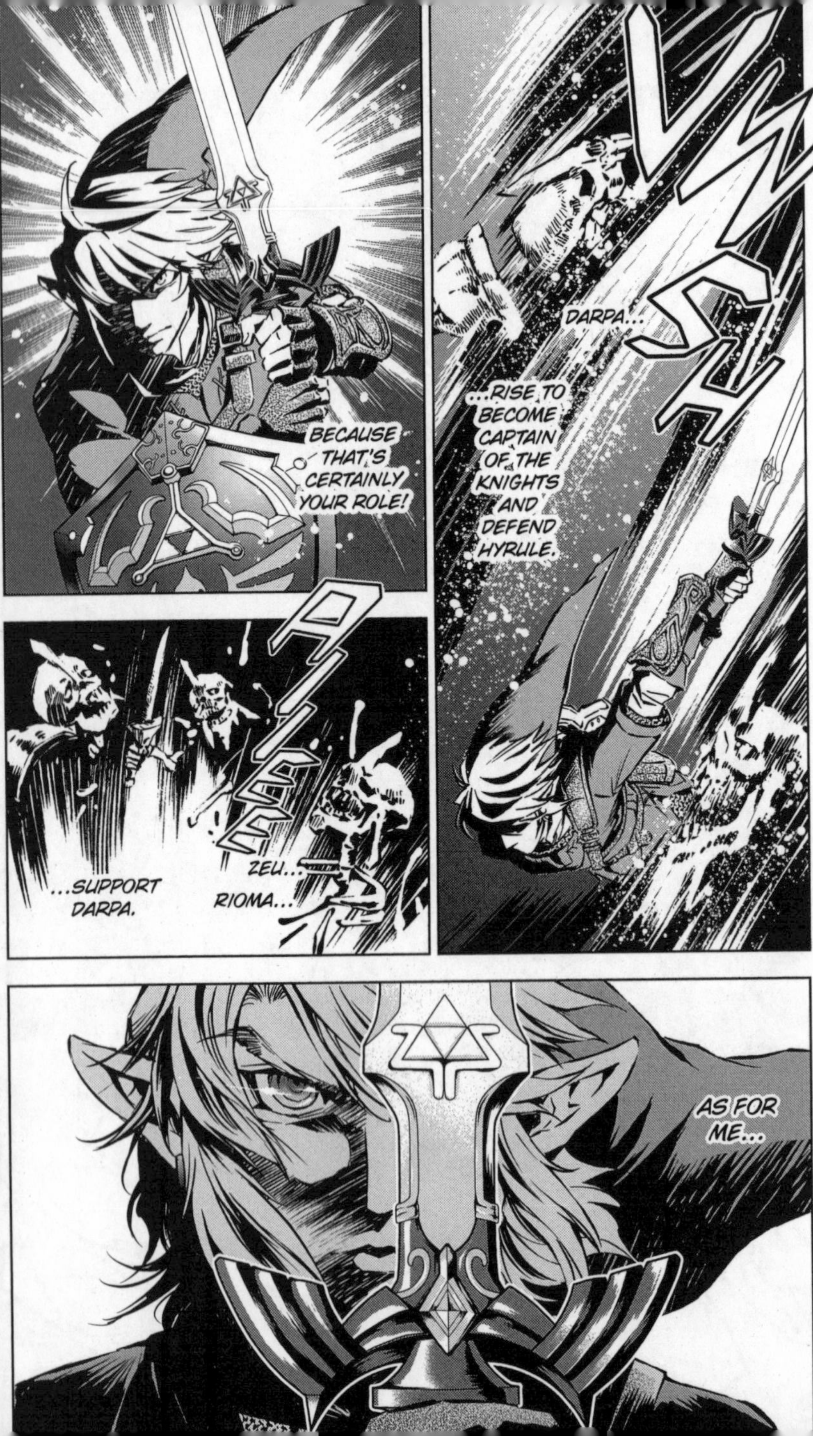
VWSH
DARPA...
...RISE TO BECOME CAPTAIN OF THE KNIGHTS AND DEFEND HYRULE.
BECAUSE THAT'S CERTAINLY YOUR ROLE!
ZEU...
RIOMA...
...SUPPORT DARPA.
AS FOR ME...

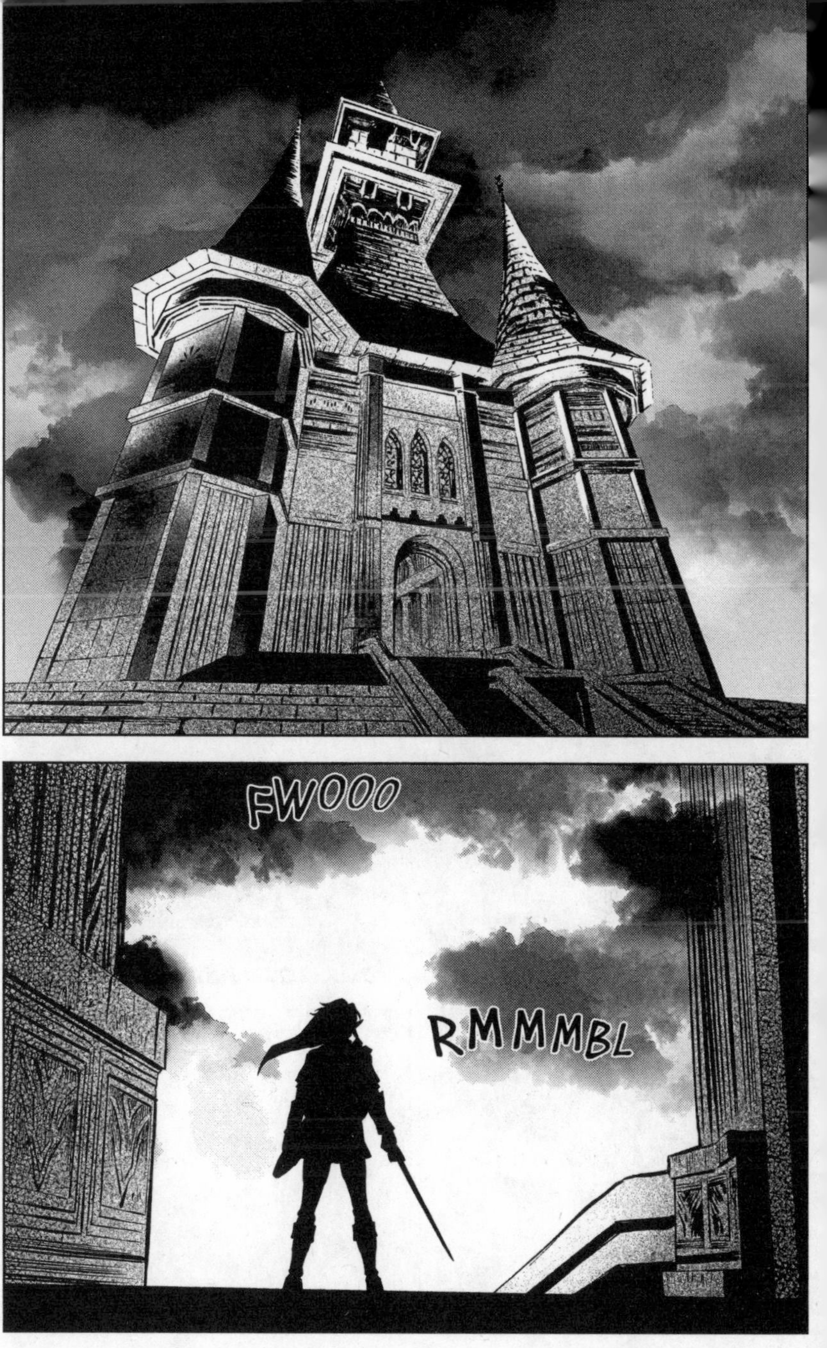
FWOOO
RMMMBL

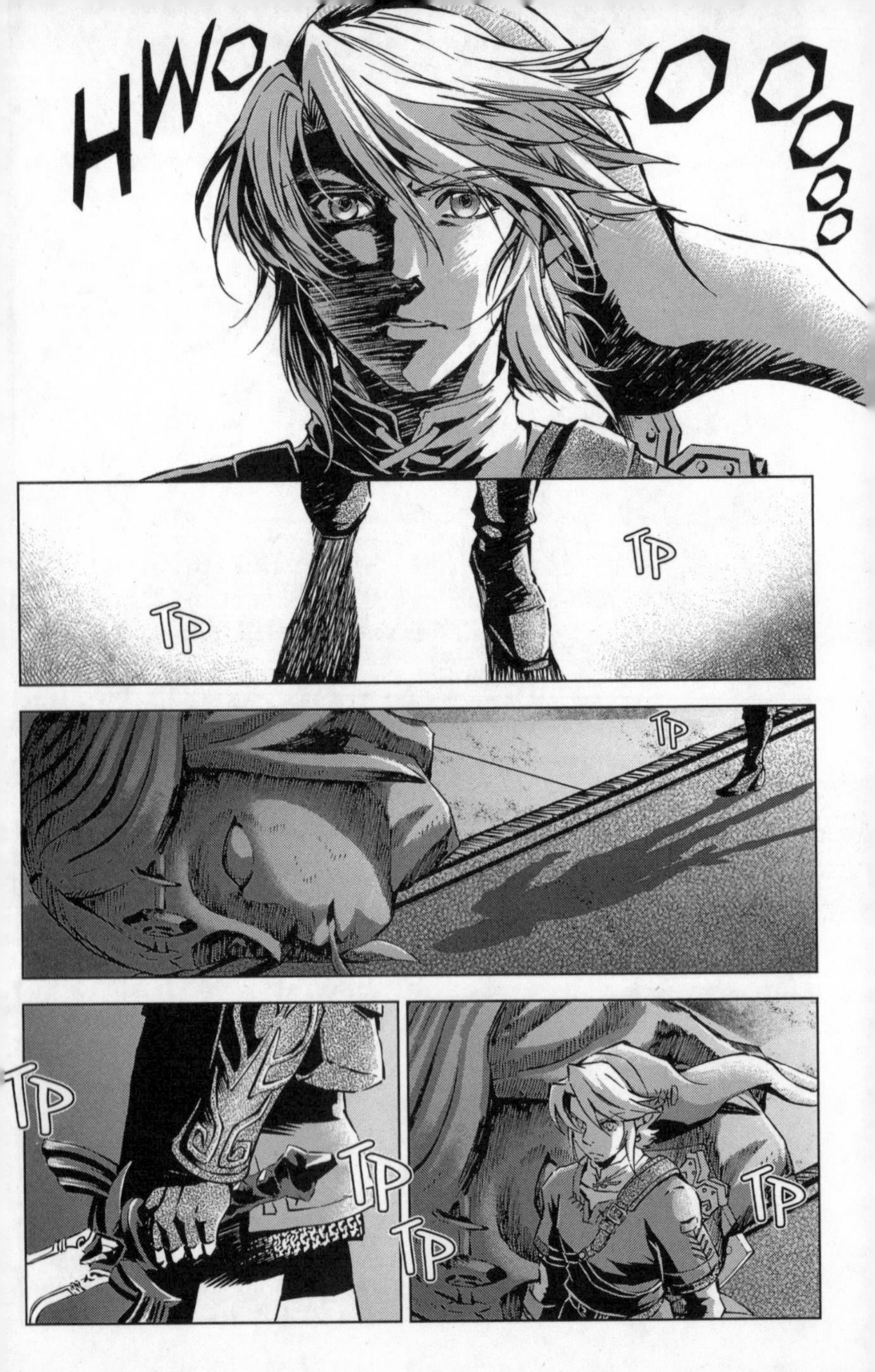

HWOOOOOO
TP
TP
TP
TP
TP
TP
TP

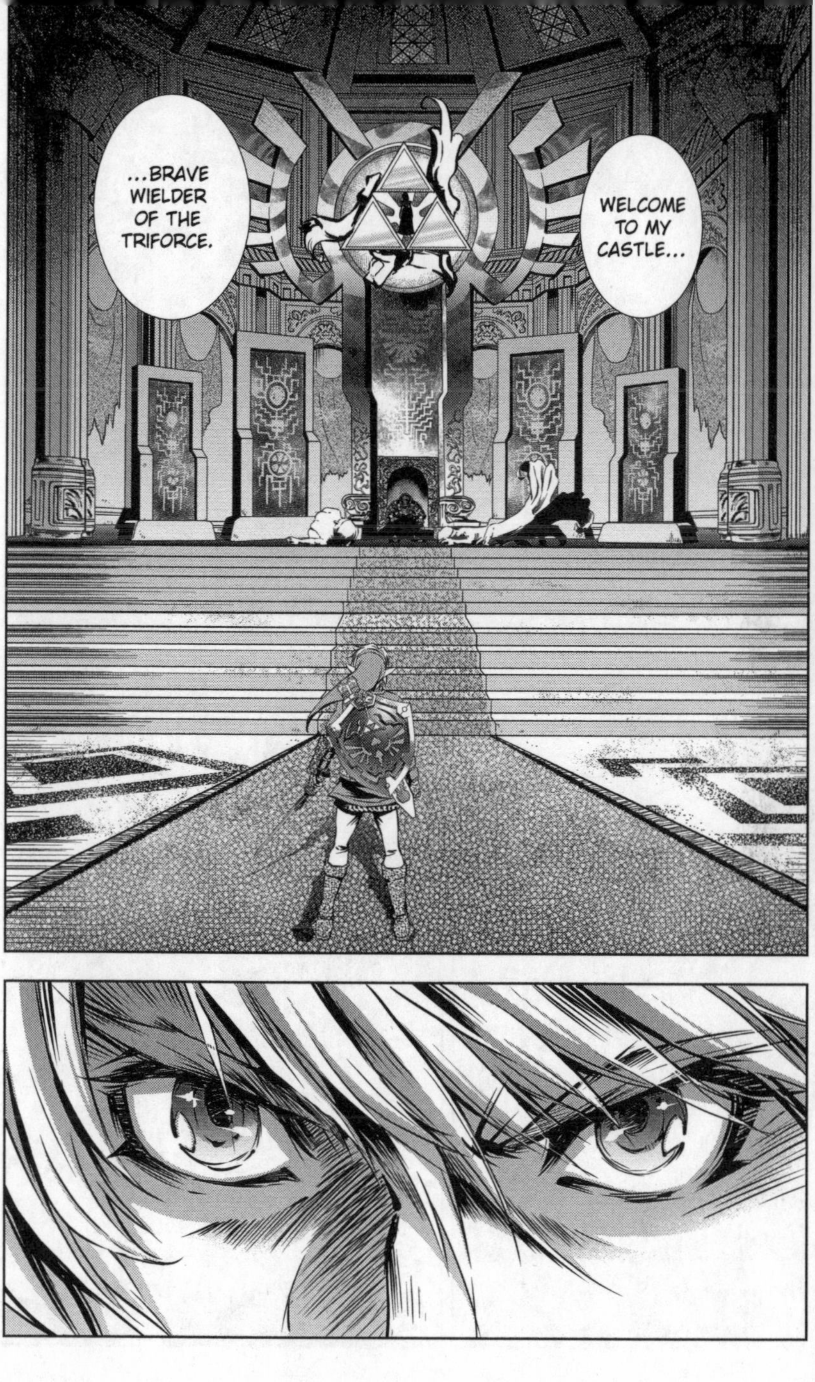
WELCOME TO MY CASTLE...
...BRAVE WIELDER OF THE TRIFORCE.

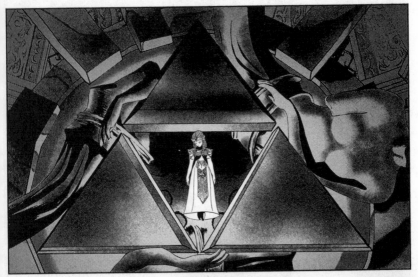

PRINCESS ZELDA!

!!

AT LONG LAST, THE PLAYERS ARE ALL ONSTAGE.

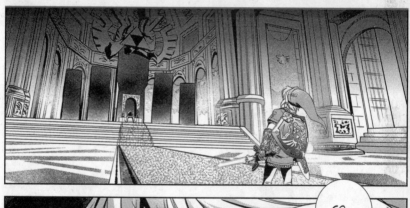

SO...

...YOU'RE GANONDORF, EH?

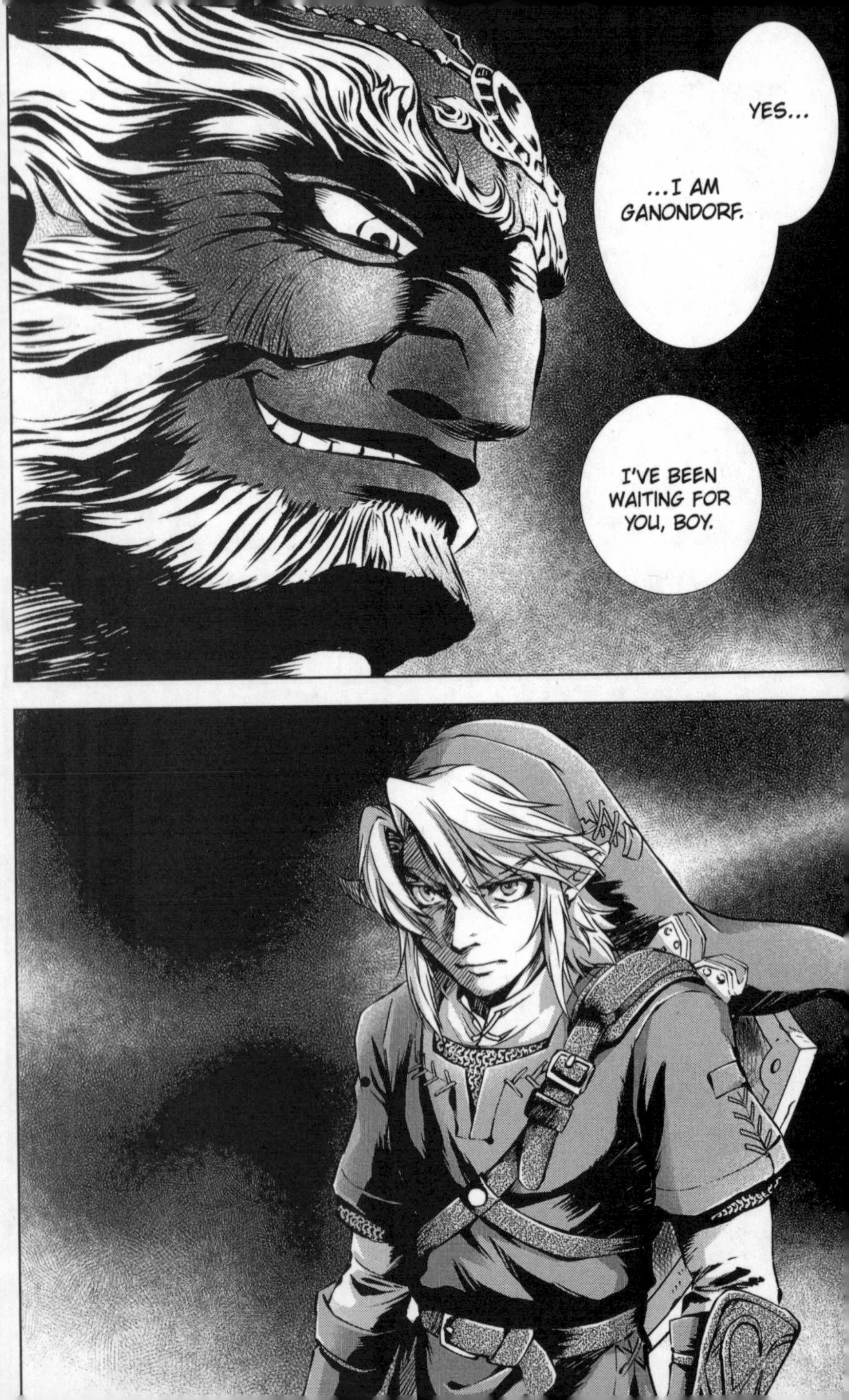
YES...
...I AM GANONDORF.
I'VE BEEN WAITING FOR YOU, BOY.

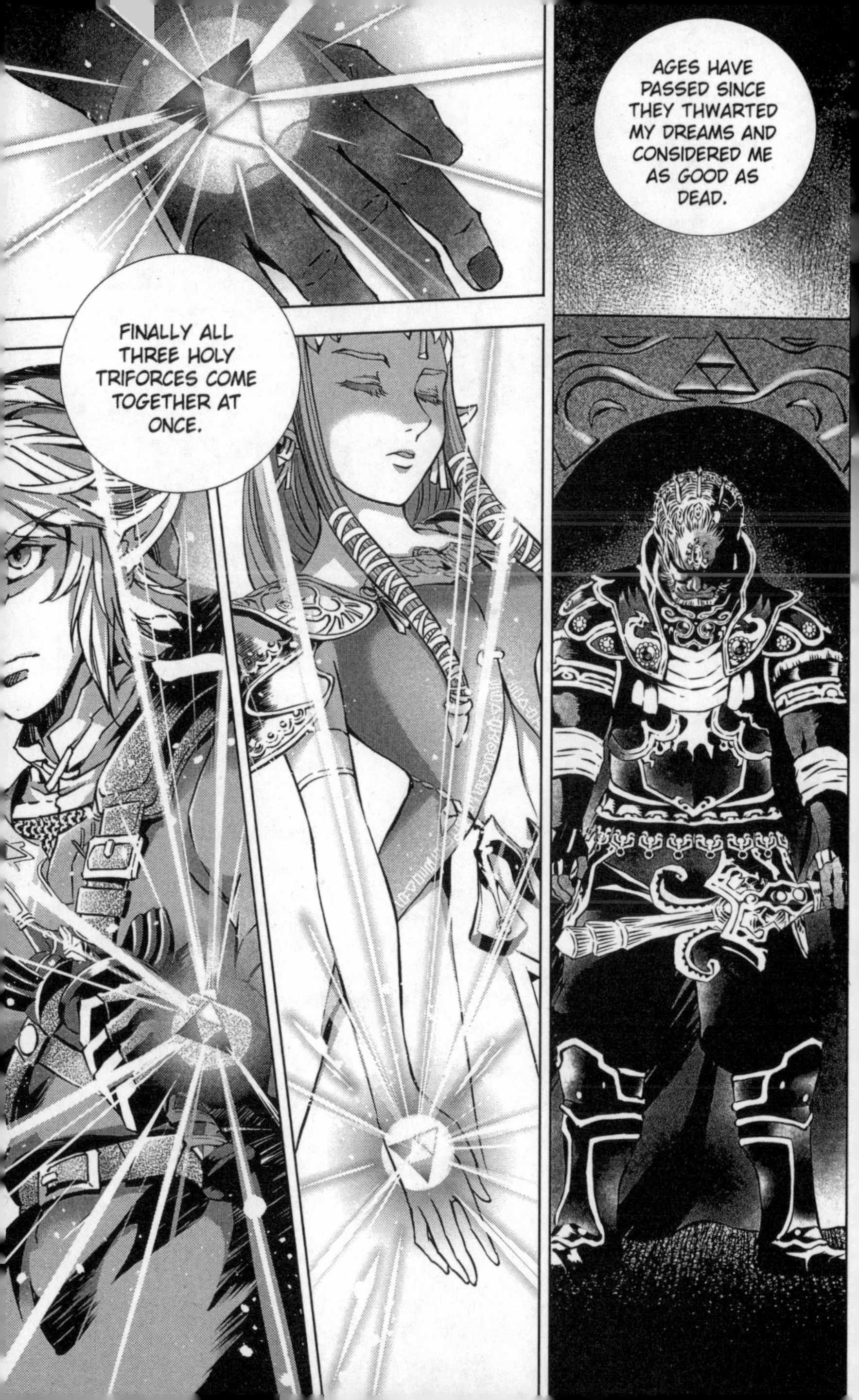
AGES HAVE PASSED SINCE THEY THWARTED MY DREAMS AND CONSIDERED ME AS GOOD AS DEAD.
FINALLY ALL THREE HOLY TRIFORCES COME TOGETHER AT ONCE.

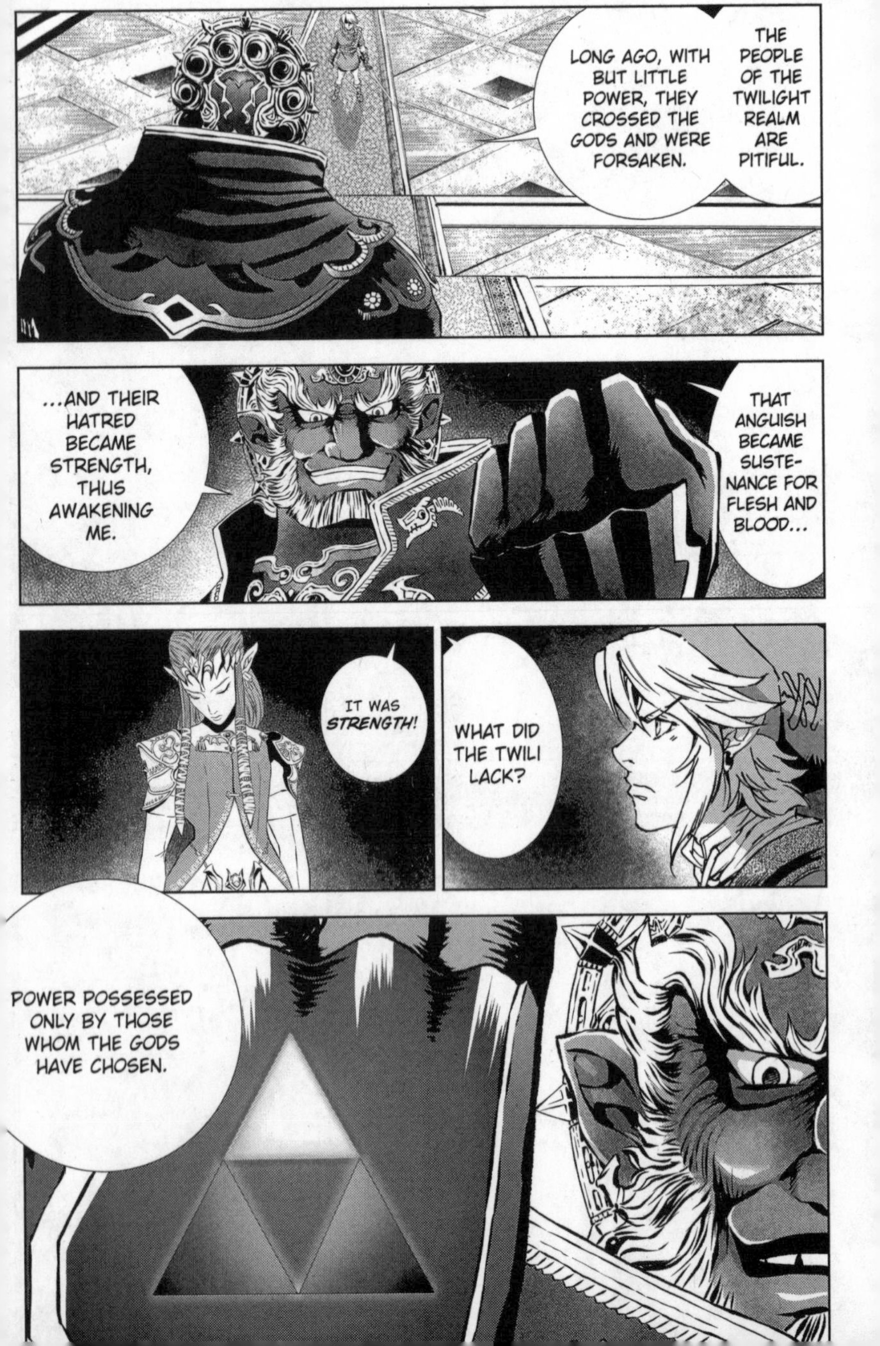
THE PEOPLE OF THE TWILIGHT REALM ARE PITIFUL.
LONG AGO, WITH BUT LITTLE POWER, THEY CROSSED THE GODS AND WERE FORSAKEN.
THAT ANGUISH BECAME SUSTE-NANCE FOR FLESH AND BLOOD...
...AND THEIR HATRED BECAME STRENGTH, THUS AWAKENING ME.
WHAT DID THE TWILI LACK?
IT WAS *STRENGTH*!
POWER POSSESSED ONLY BY THOSE WHOM THE GODS HAVE CHOSEN.

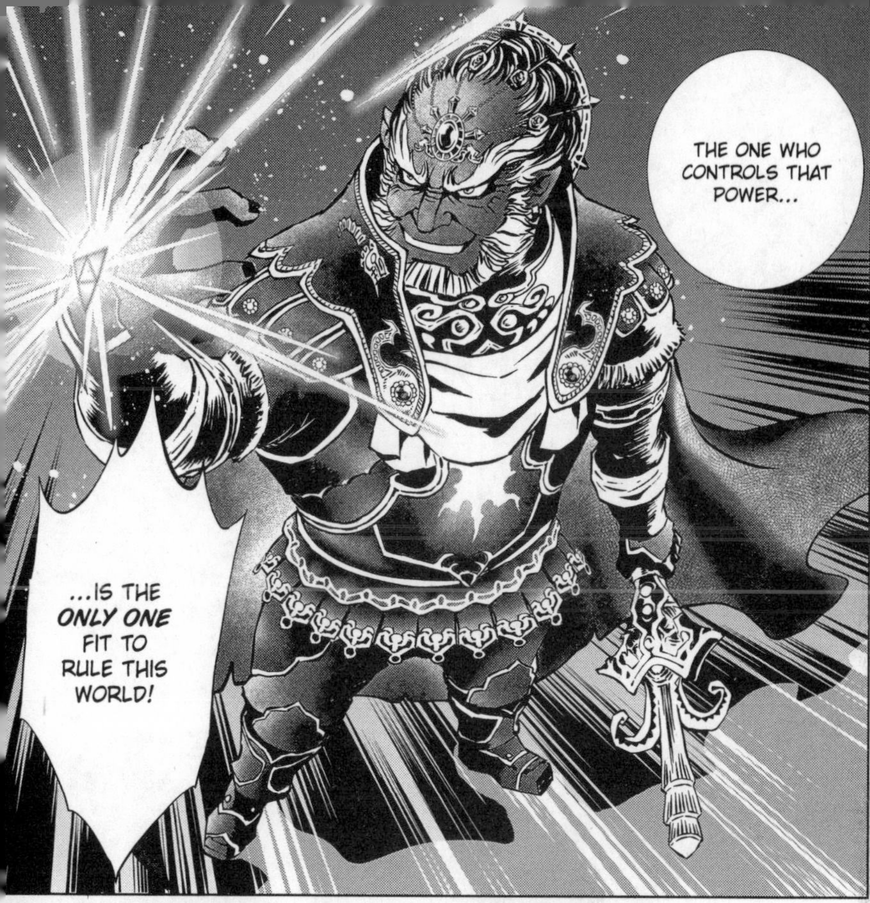
THE ONE WHO CONTROLS THAT POWER...
...IS THE ***ONLY ONE*** FIT TO RULE THIS WORLD!

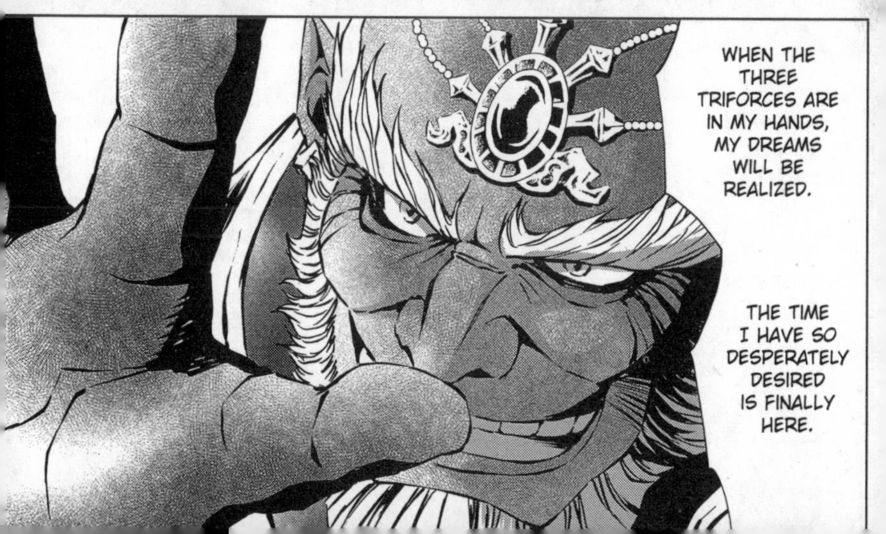
WHEN THE THREE TRIFORCES ARE IN MY HANDS, MY DREAMS WILL BE REALIZED.
THE TIME I HAVE SO DESPERATELY DESIRED IS FINALLY HERE.

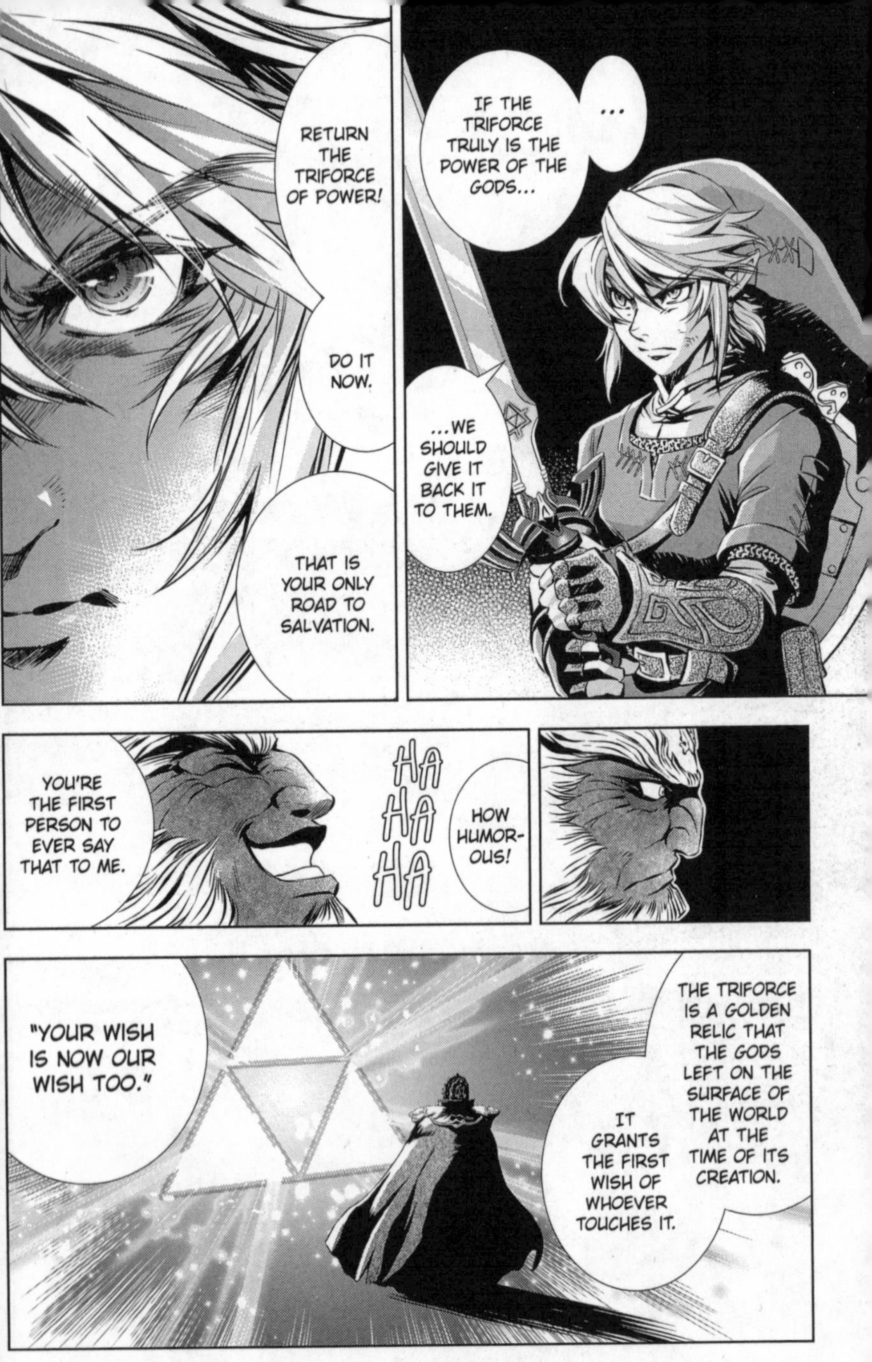
...
IF THE TRIFORCE TRULY IS THE POWER OF THE GODS...
...WE SHOULD GIVE IT BACK IT TO THEM.
RETURN THE TRIFORCE OF POWER!
DO IT NOW.
THAT IS YOUR ONLY ROAD TO SALVATION.
HA HA HA
HOW HUMOR-OUS!
YOU'RE THE FIRST PERSON TO EVER SAY THAT TO ME.
THE TRIFORCE IS A GOLDEN RELIC THAT THE GODS LEFT ON THE SURFACE OF THE WORLD AT THE TIME OF ITS CREATION.
IT GRANTS THE FIRST WISH OF WHOEVER TOUCHES IT.
"YOUR WISH IS NOW OUR WISH TOO."

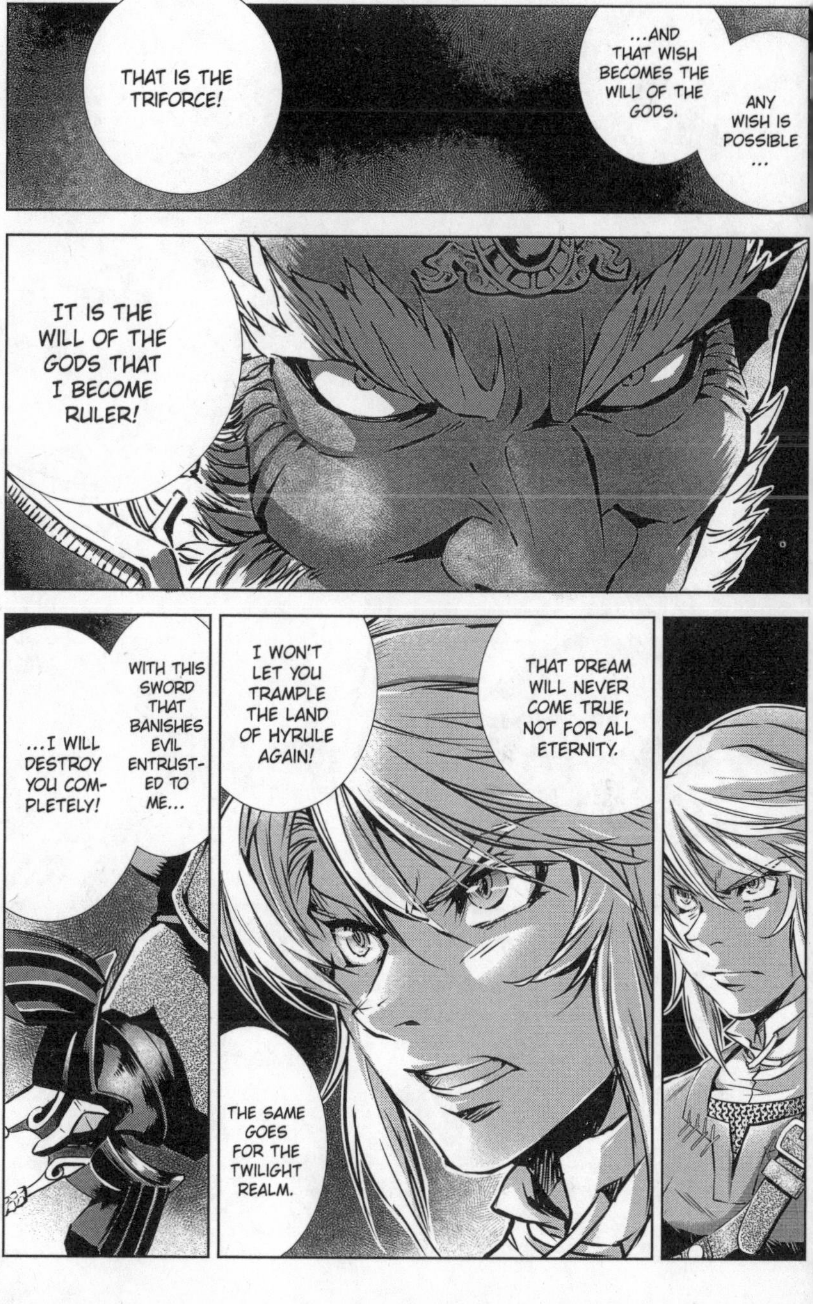
ANY WISH IS POSSIBLE ...
...AND THAT WISH BECOMES THE WILL OF THE GODS.
THAT IS THE TRIFORCE!
IT IS THE WILL OF THE GODS THAT I BECOME RULER!
THAT DREAM WILL NEVER COME TRUE, NOT FOR ALL ETERNITY.
I WON'T LET YOU TRAMPLE THE LAND OF HYRULE AGAIN!
THE SAME GOES FOR THE TWILIGHT REALM.
WITH THIS SWORD THAT BANISHES EVIL ENTRUST-ED TO ME...
...I WILL DESTROY YOU COM-PLETELY!

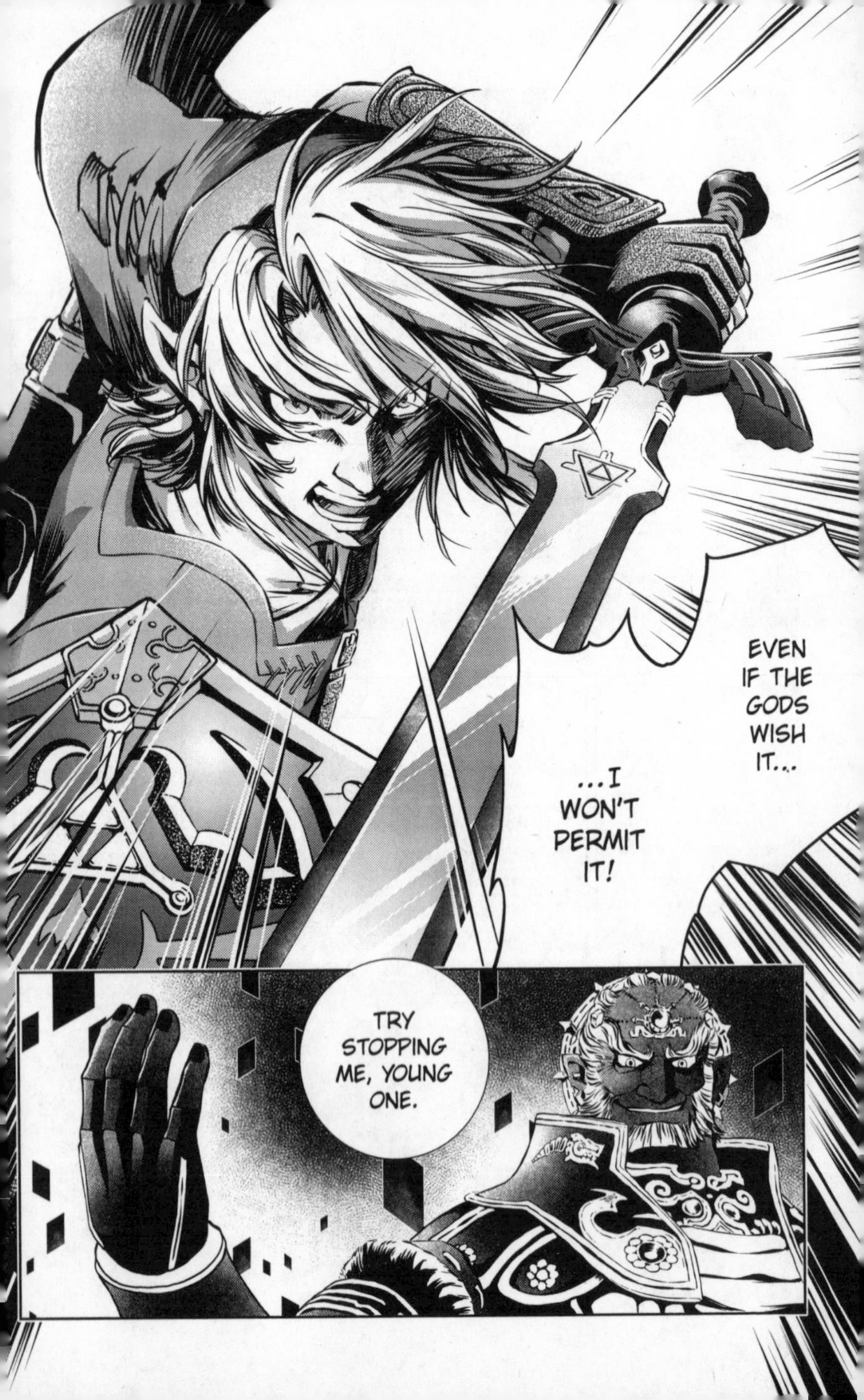
EVEN IF THE GODS WISH IT...
...I WON'T PERMIT IT!
TRY STOPPING ME, YOUNG ONE.

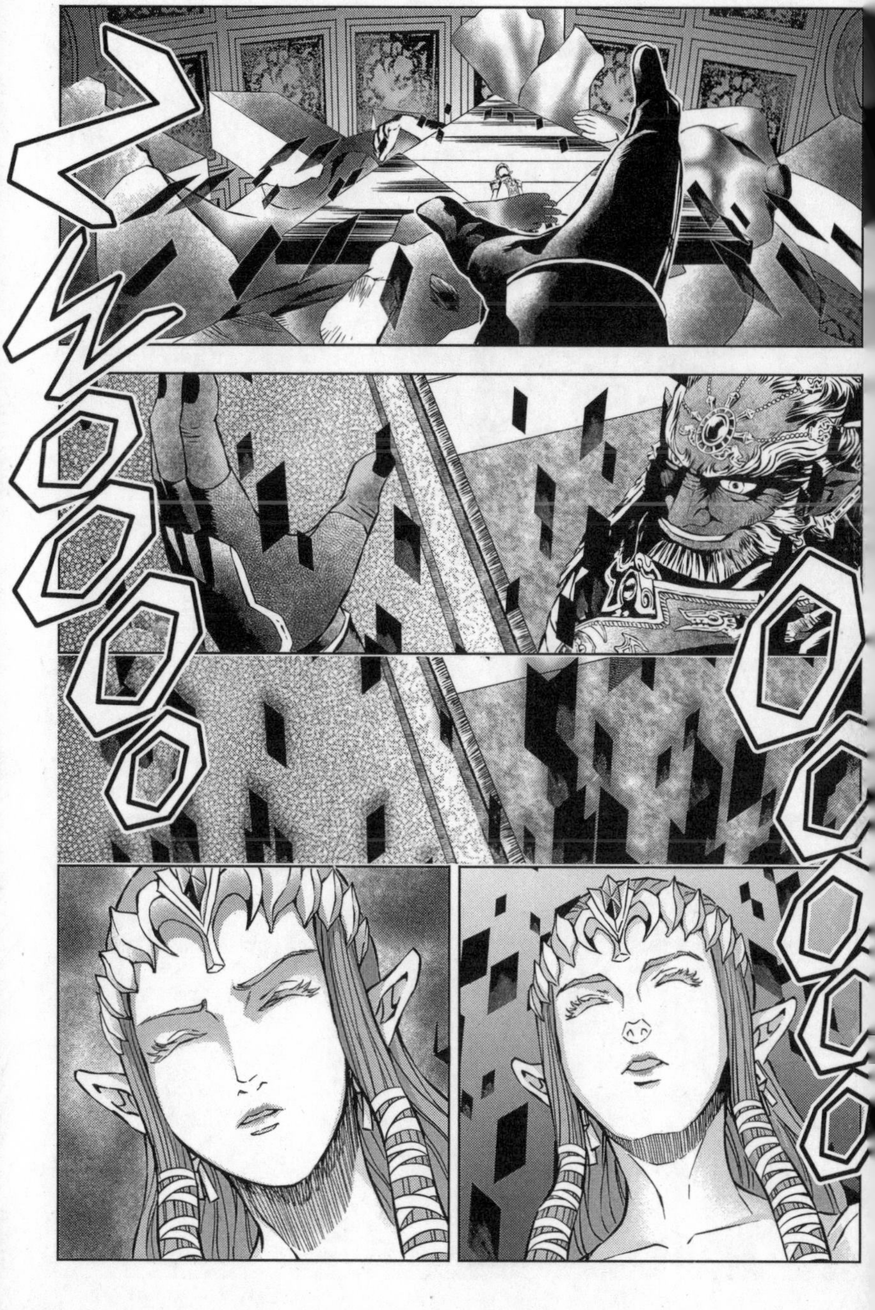
VWOOOO
OOOOOO

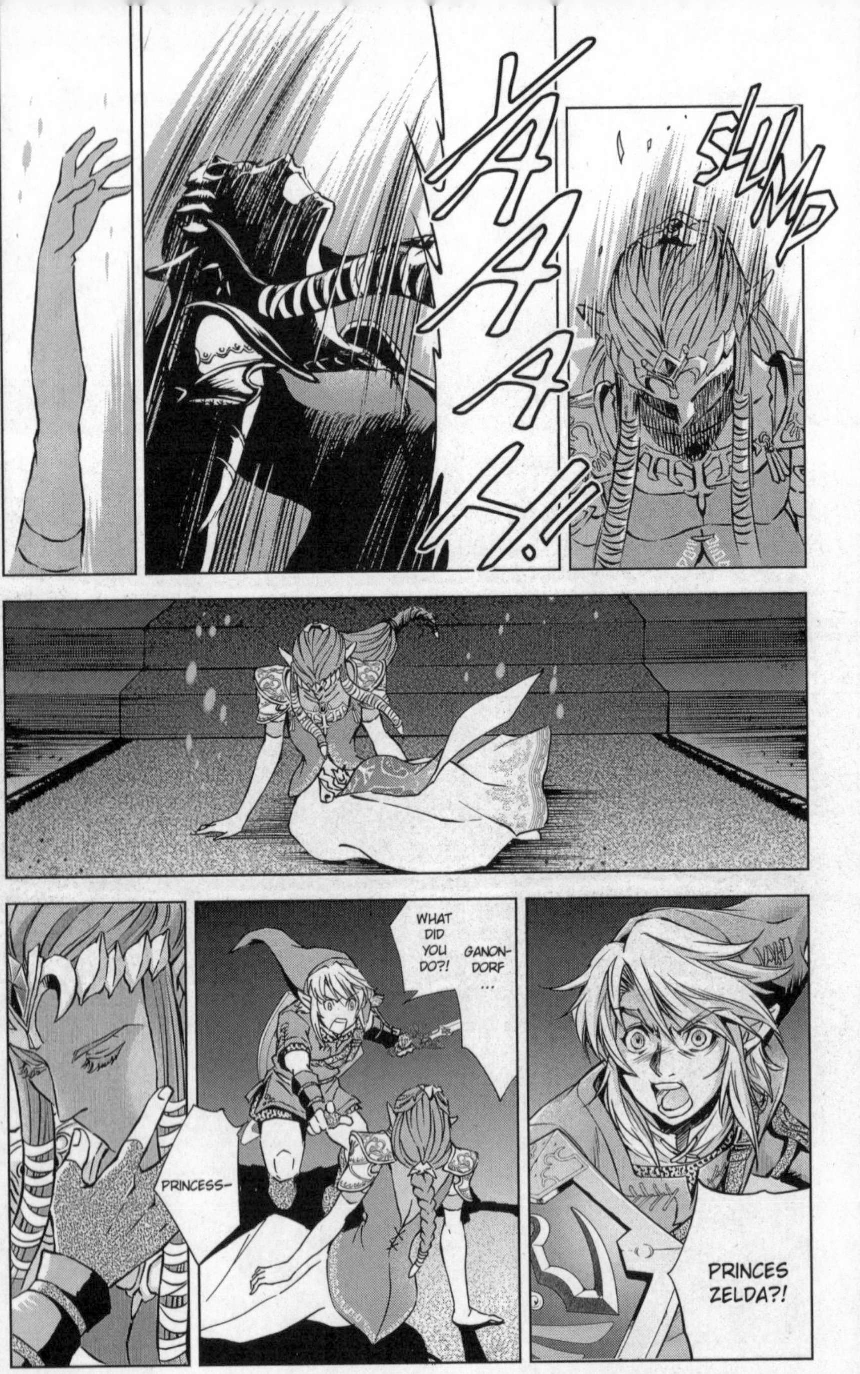
SLUMP
YAAAH!!
PRINCES ZELDA?!
GANON-DORF ...
WHAT DID YOU DO?!
PRINCESS-

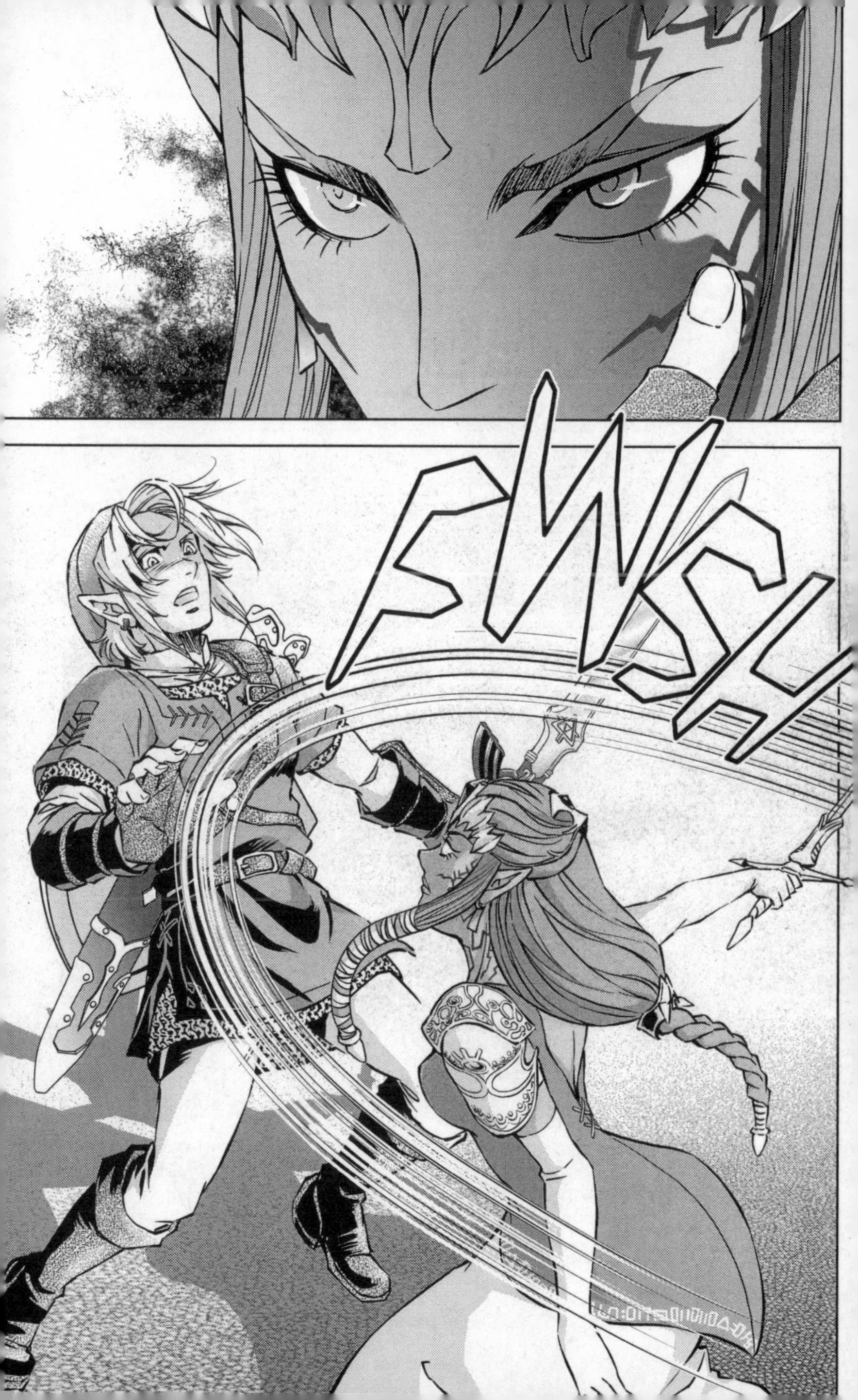
FWSH

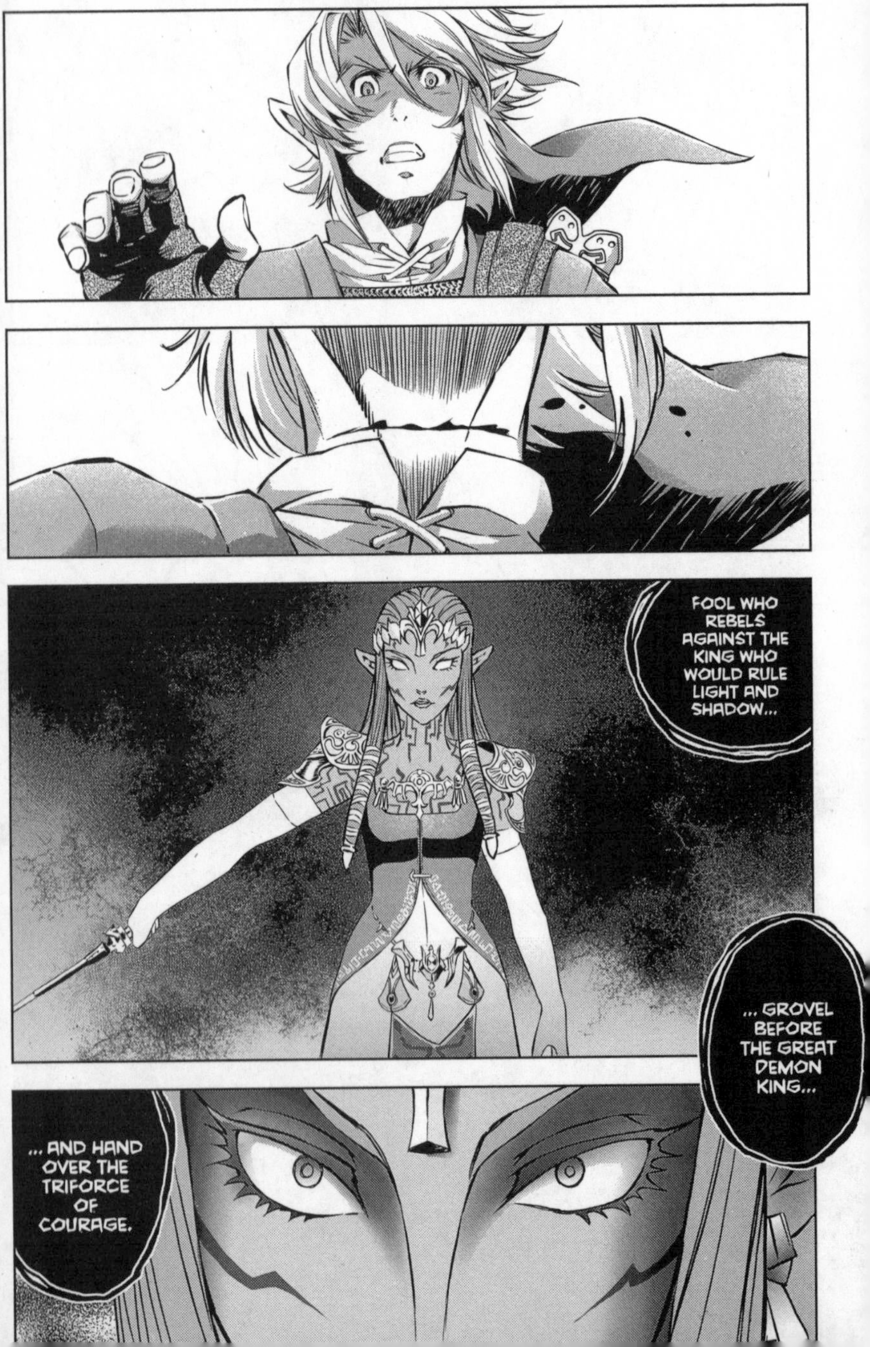

FOOL WHO REBELS AGAINST THE KING WHO WOULD RULE LIGHT AND SHADOW...
... GROVEL BEFORE THE GREAT DEMON KING...
... AND HAND OVER THE TRIFORCE OF COURAGE.

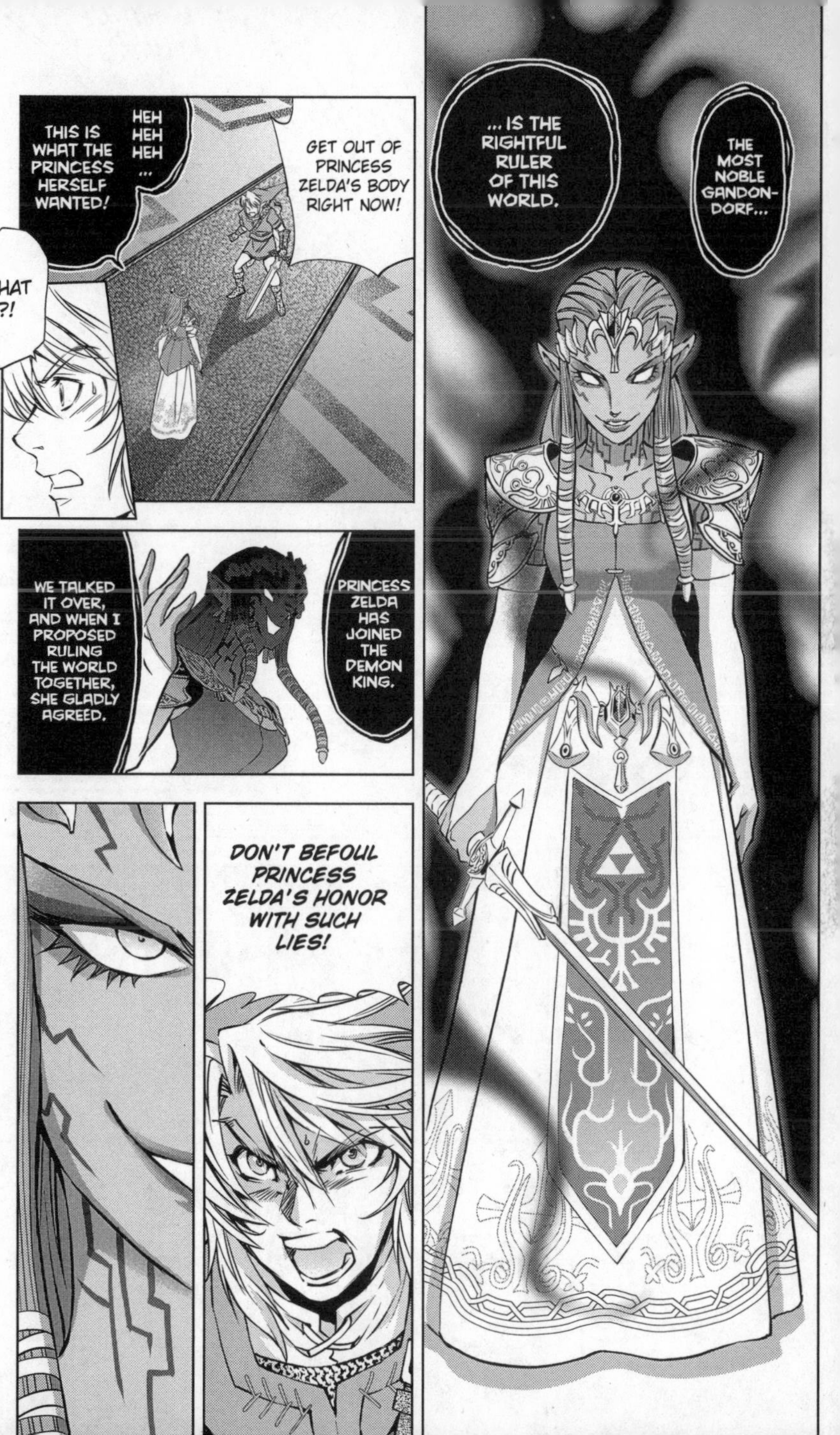
THE MOST NOBLE GANDON-DORF...
...IS THE RIGHTFUL RULER OF THIS WORLD.
GET OUT OF PRINCESS ZELDA'S BODY RIGHT NOW!
HEH HEH HEH ...
THIS IS WHAT THE PRINCESS HERSELF WANTED!
WHAT ?!
PRINCESS ZELDA HAS JOINED THE DEMON KING.
WE TALKED IT OVER, AND WHEN I PROPOSED RULING THE WORLD TOGETHER, SHE GLADLY AGREED.
DON'T BEFOUL PRINCESS ZELDA'S HONOR WITH SUCH LIES!

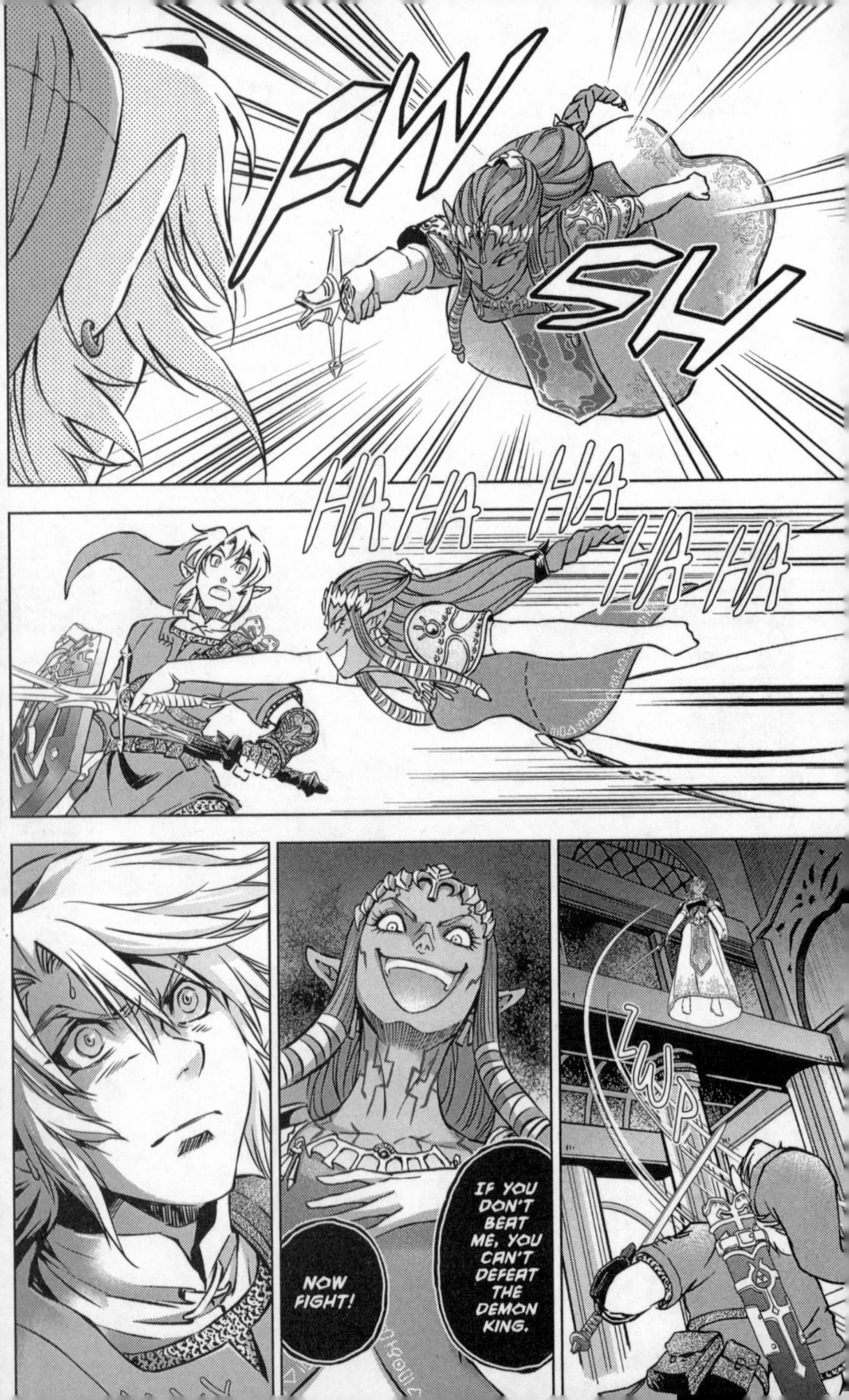
FW
SH
HA HA HA
HA HA
ZWP
IF YOU DON'T BEAT ME, YOU CAN'T DEFEAT THE DEMON KING.
NOW FIGHT!

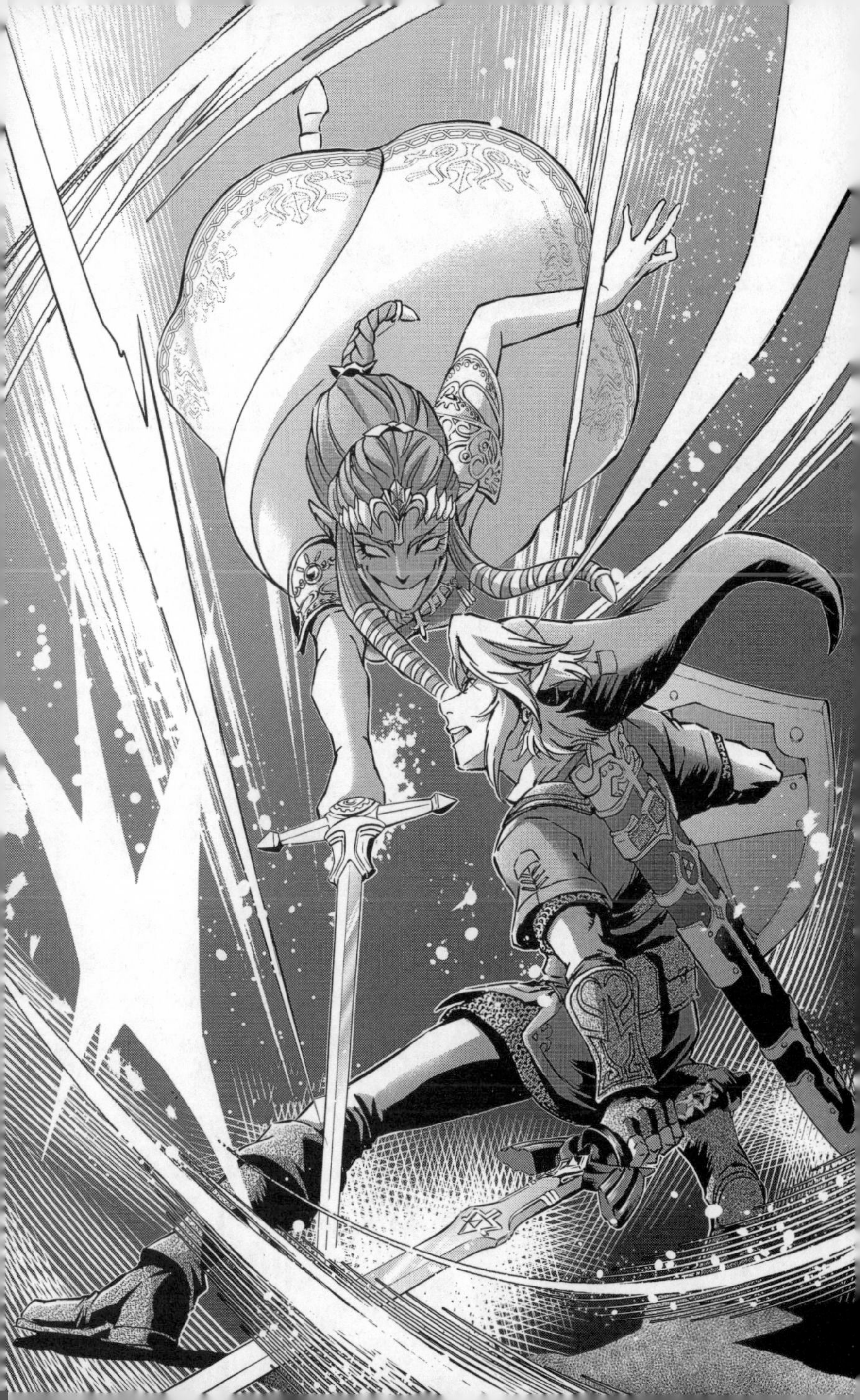

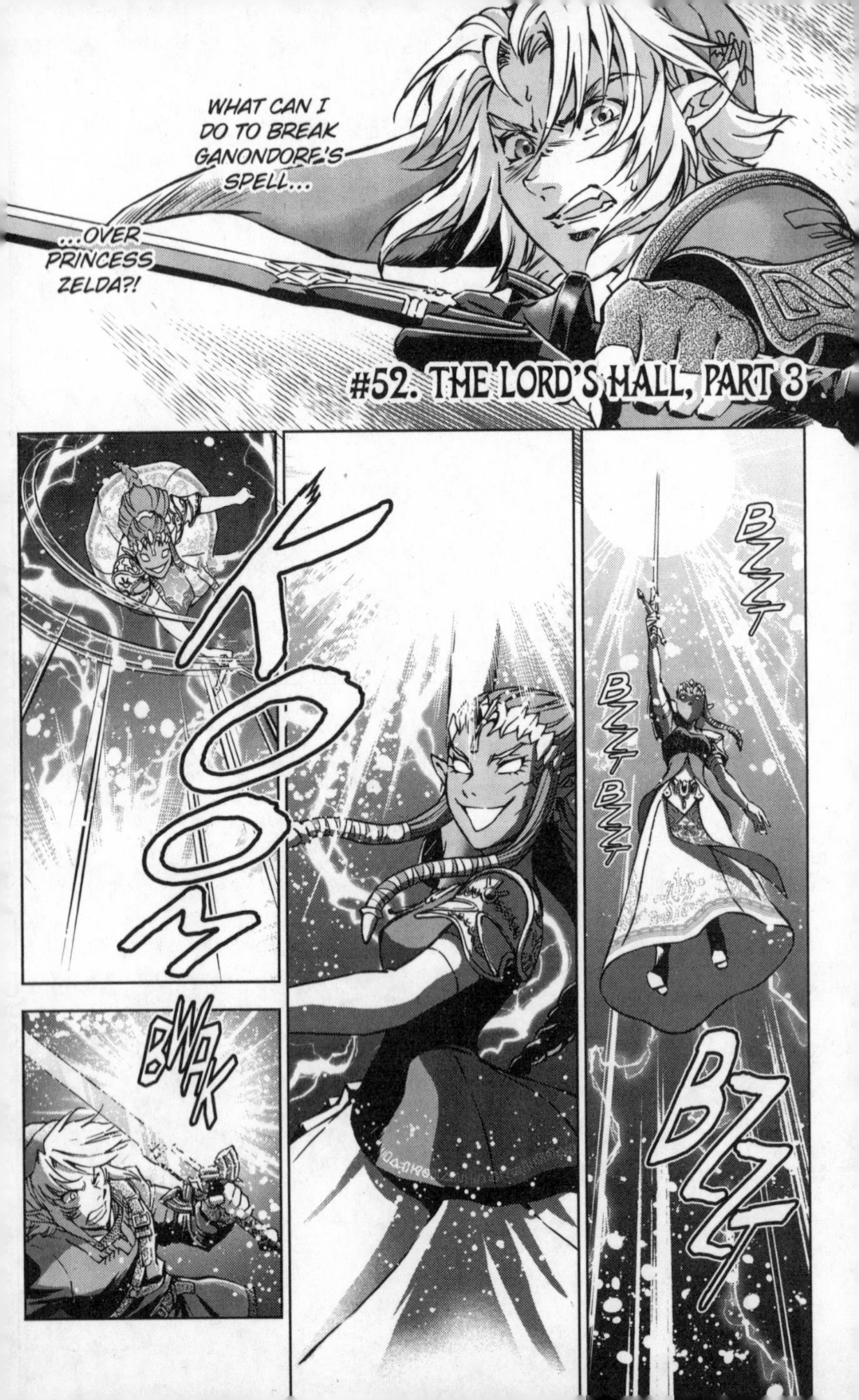
WHAT CAN I DO TO BREAK GANONDORF'S SPELL...
...OVER PRINCESS ZELDA?!
#52. THE LORD'S HALL, PART 3
BZZT
BZZT BZZT
BZZT
VOOM
BWAK

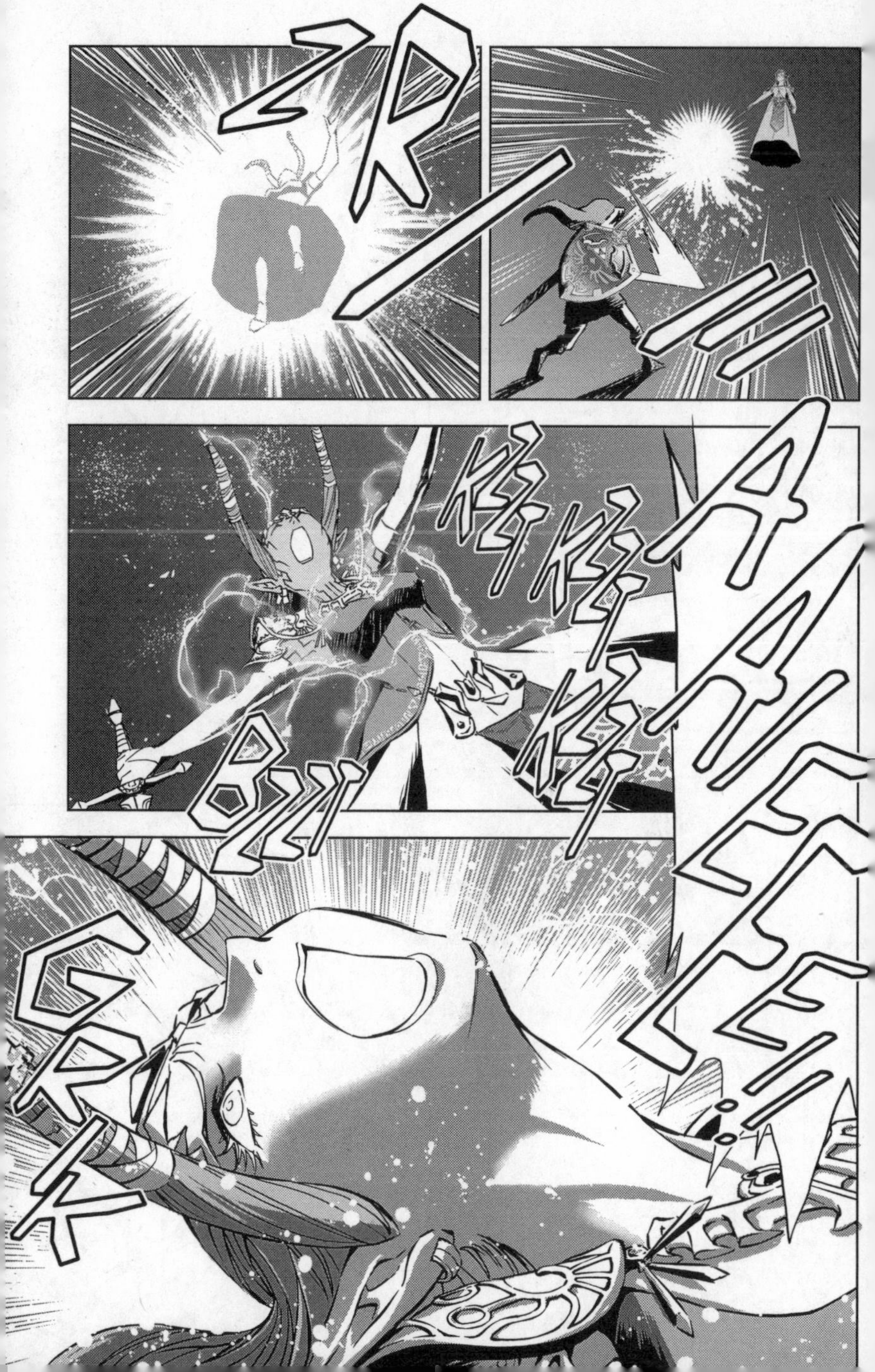
KZT KZT KZT KZT
BZZT

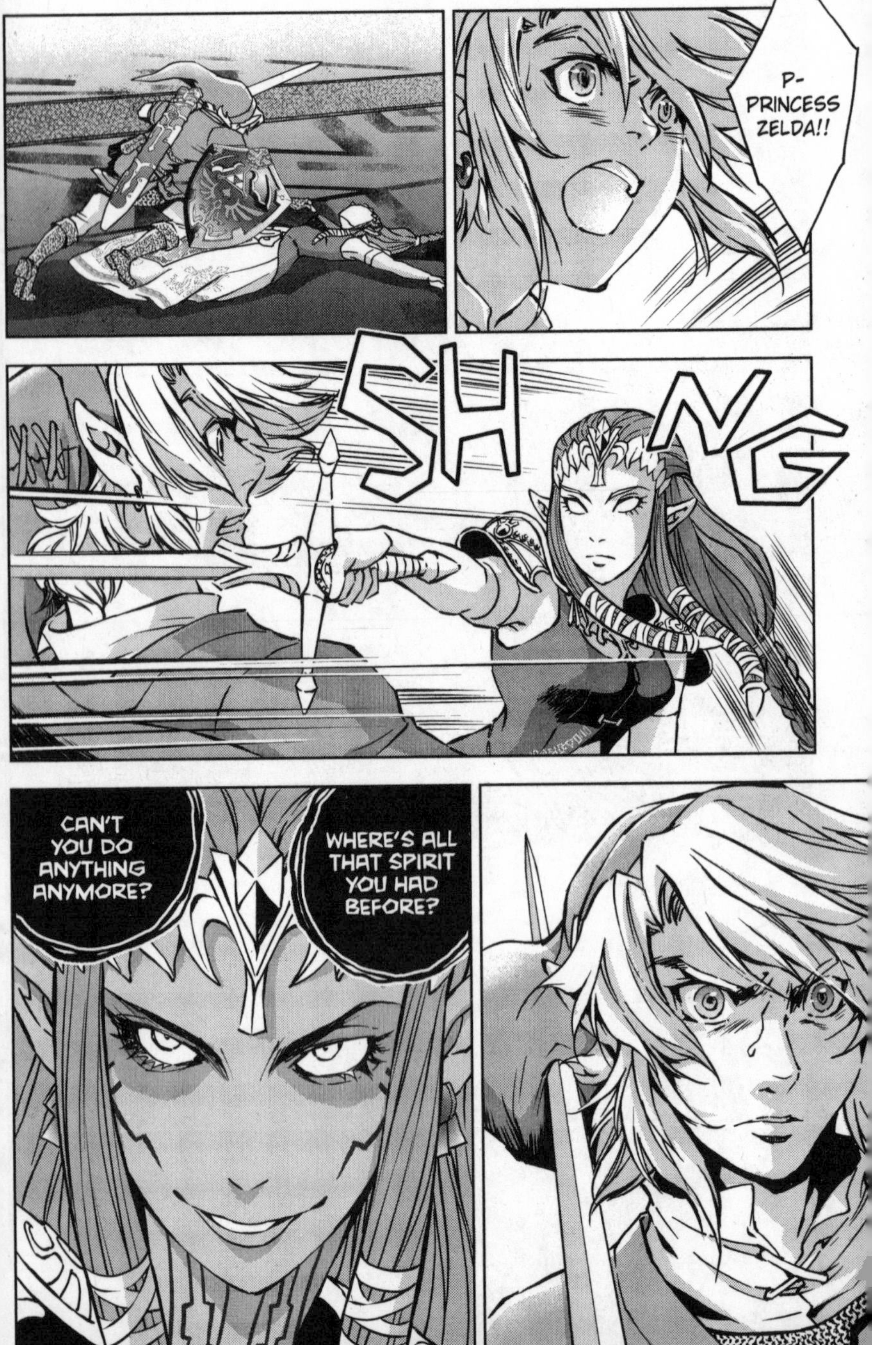
P- PRINCESS ZELDA!!
SH NG
WHERE'S ALL THAT SPIRIT YOU HAD BEFORE?
CAN'T YOU DO ANYTHING ANYMORE?

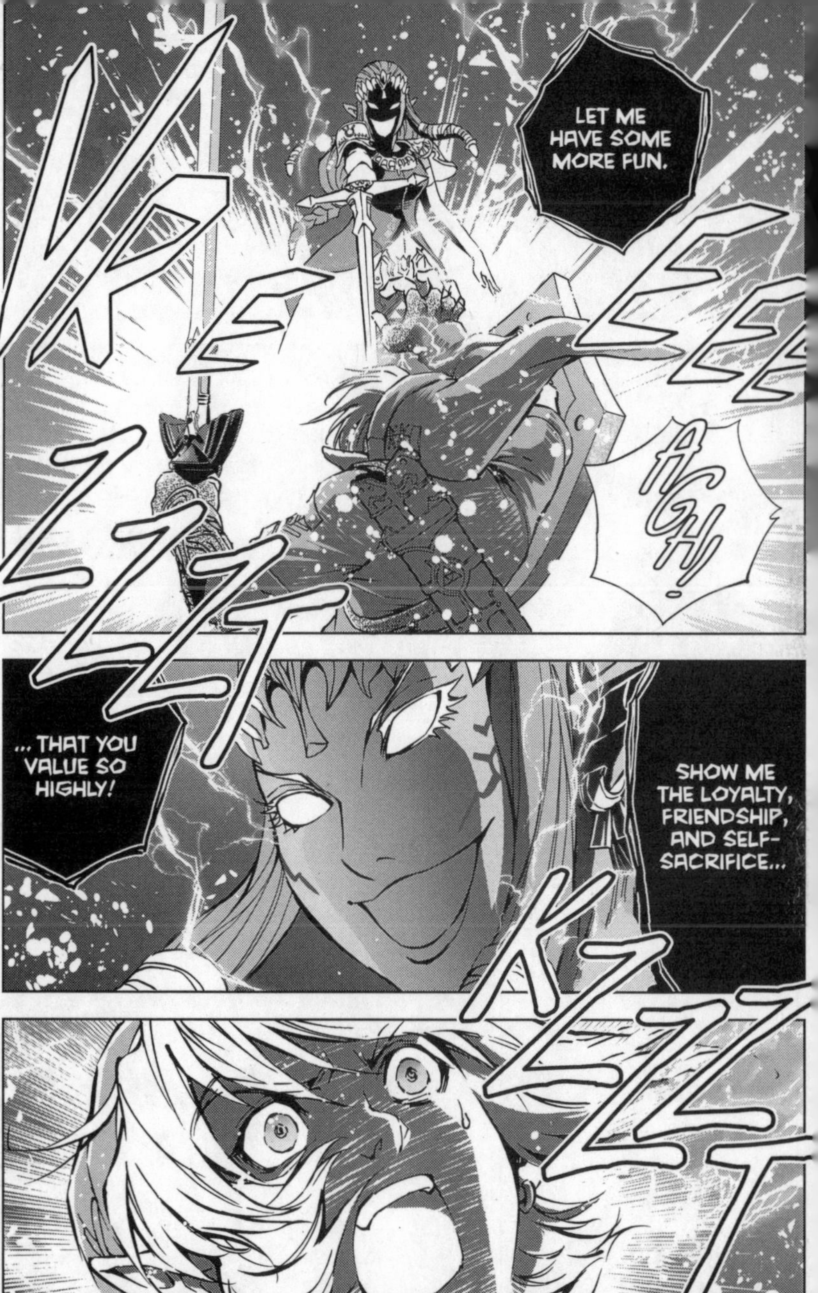
LET ME HAVE SOME MORE FUN.
AGH!
SHOW ME THE LOYALTY, FRIENDSHIP, AND SELF-SACRIFICE...
...THAT YOU VALUE SO HIGHLY!

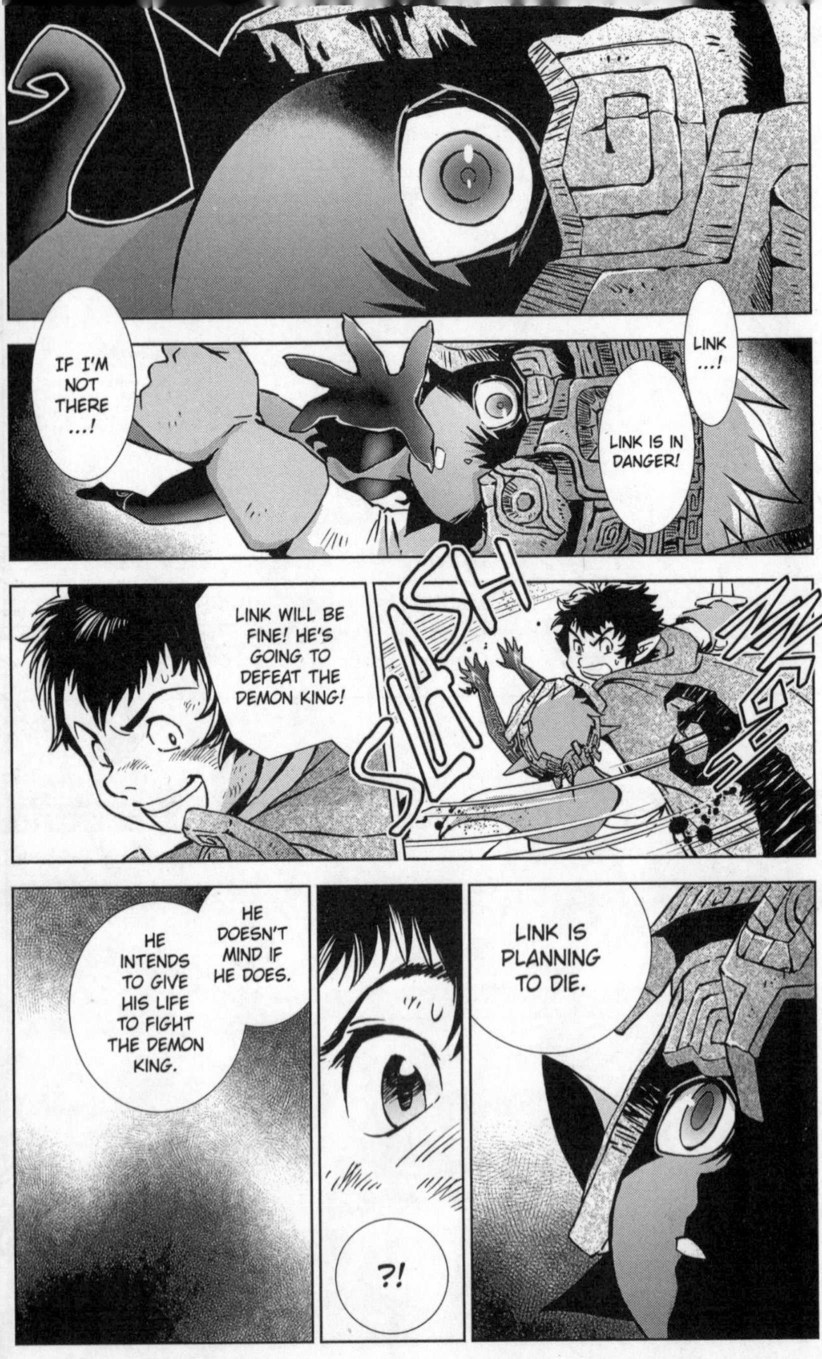
LINK ...!
LINK IS IN DANGER!
IF I'M NOT THERE ...!
SLASH
LINK WILL BE FINE! HE'S GOING TO DEFEAT THE DEMON KING!
LINK IS PLANNING TO DIE.
?!
HE DOESN'T MIND IF HE DOES.
HE INTENDS TO GIVE HIS LIFE TO FIGHT THE DEMON KING.

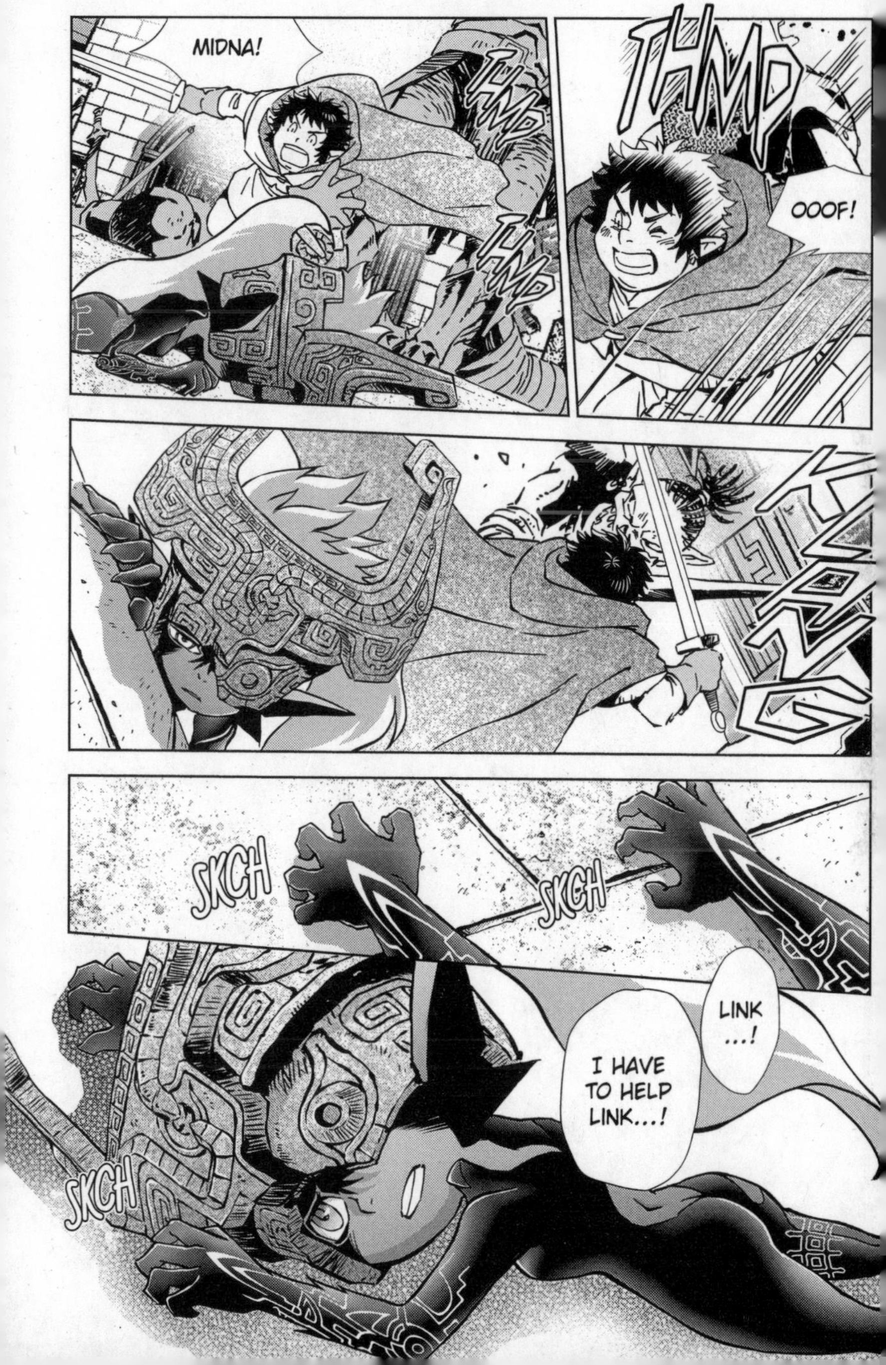
THMP
OOOF!
MIDNA!
THMP
THMP
KLANG
SKCH
SKCH
LINK...!
I HAVE TO HELP LINK...!
SKCH

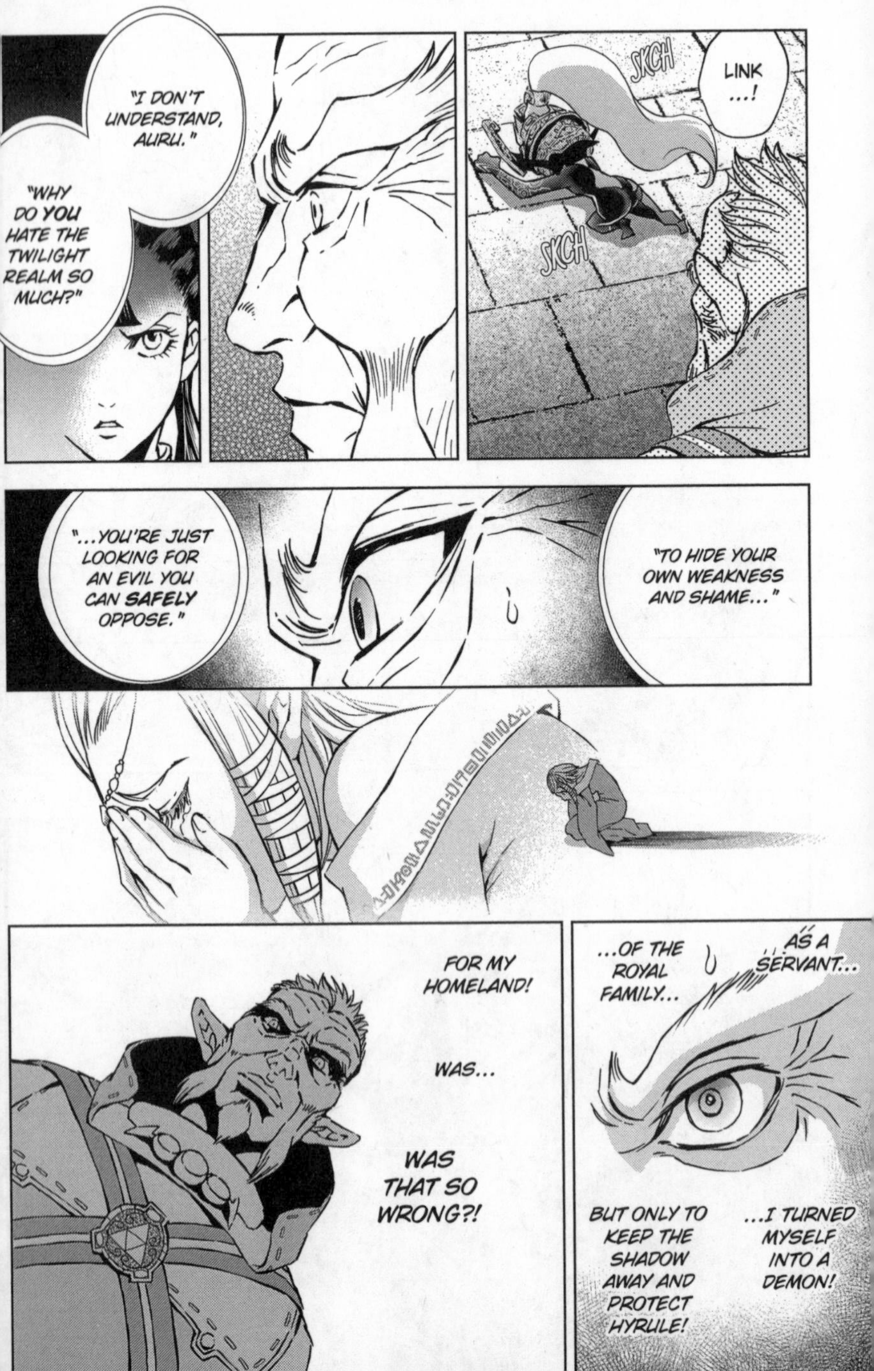
LINK ...!
SKCH
SKCH
"I DON'T UNDERSTAND, AURU."
"WHY DO YOU HATE THE TWILIGHT REALM SO MUCH?"
"TO HIDE YOUR OWN WEAKNESS AND SHAME..."
"...YOU'RE JUST LOOKING FOR AN EVIL YOU CAN SAFELY OPPOSE."
AS A SERVANT...
...OF THE ROYAL FAMILY...
...I TURNED MYSELF INTO A DEMON!
BUT ONLY TO KEEP THE SHADOW AWAY AND PROTECT HYRULE!
FOR MY HOMELAND!
WAS...
WAS THAT SO WRONG?!

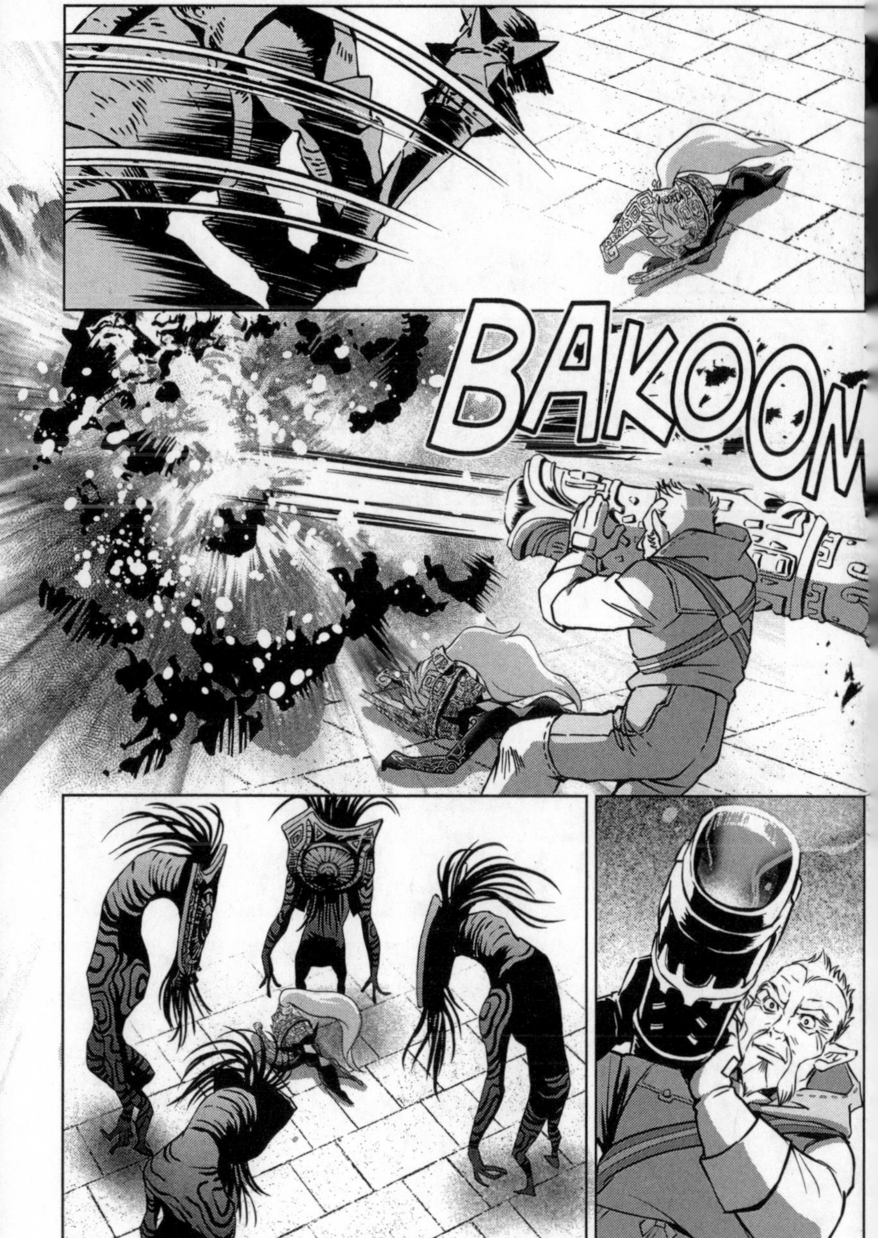
BAKOOM

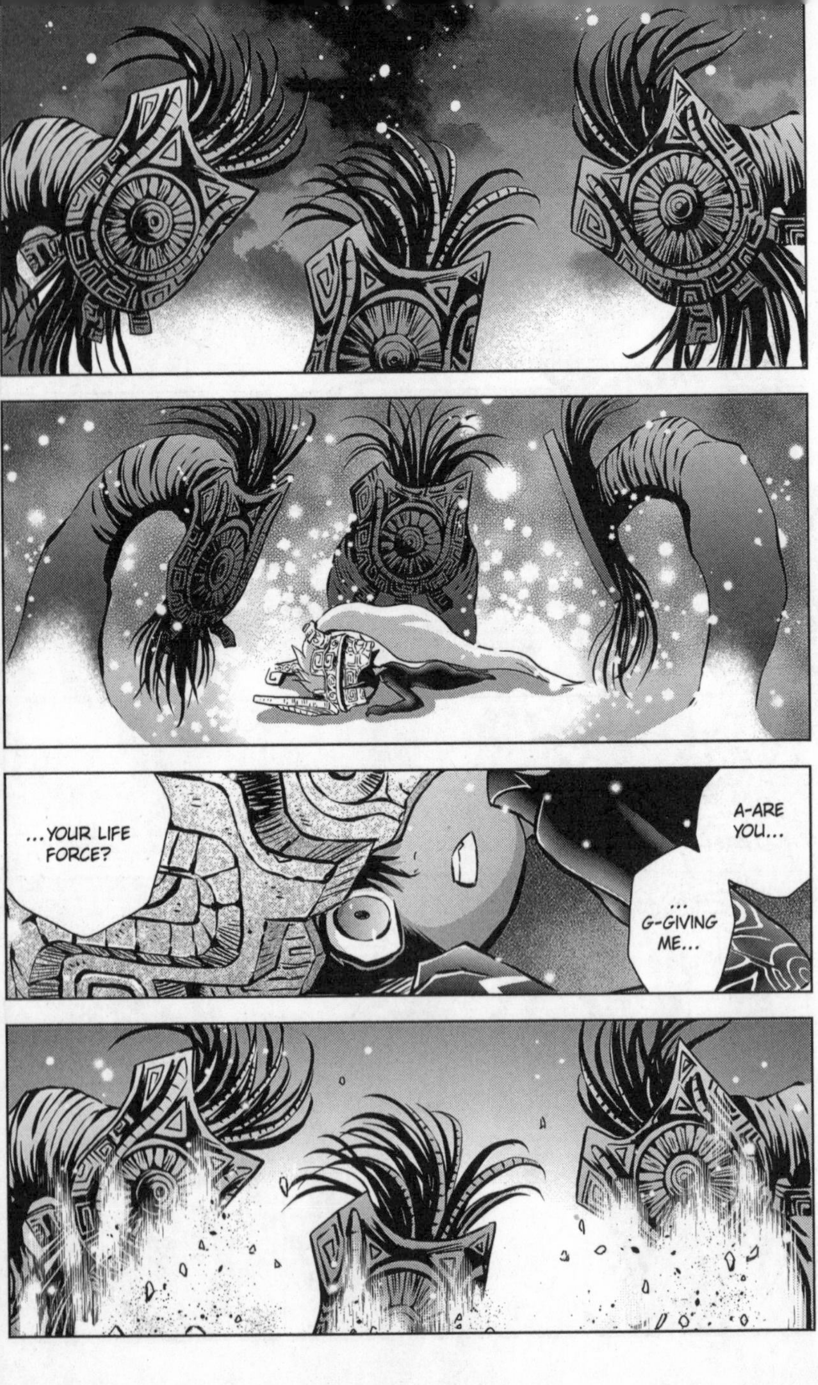
A-ARE YOU...
... G-GIVING ME...
...YOUR LIFE FORCE?

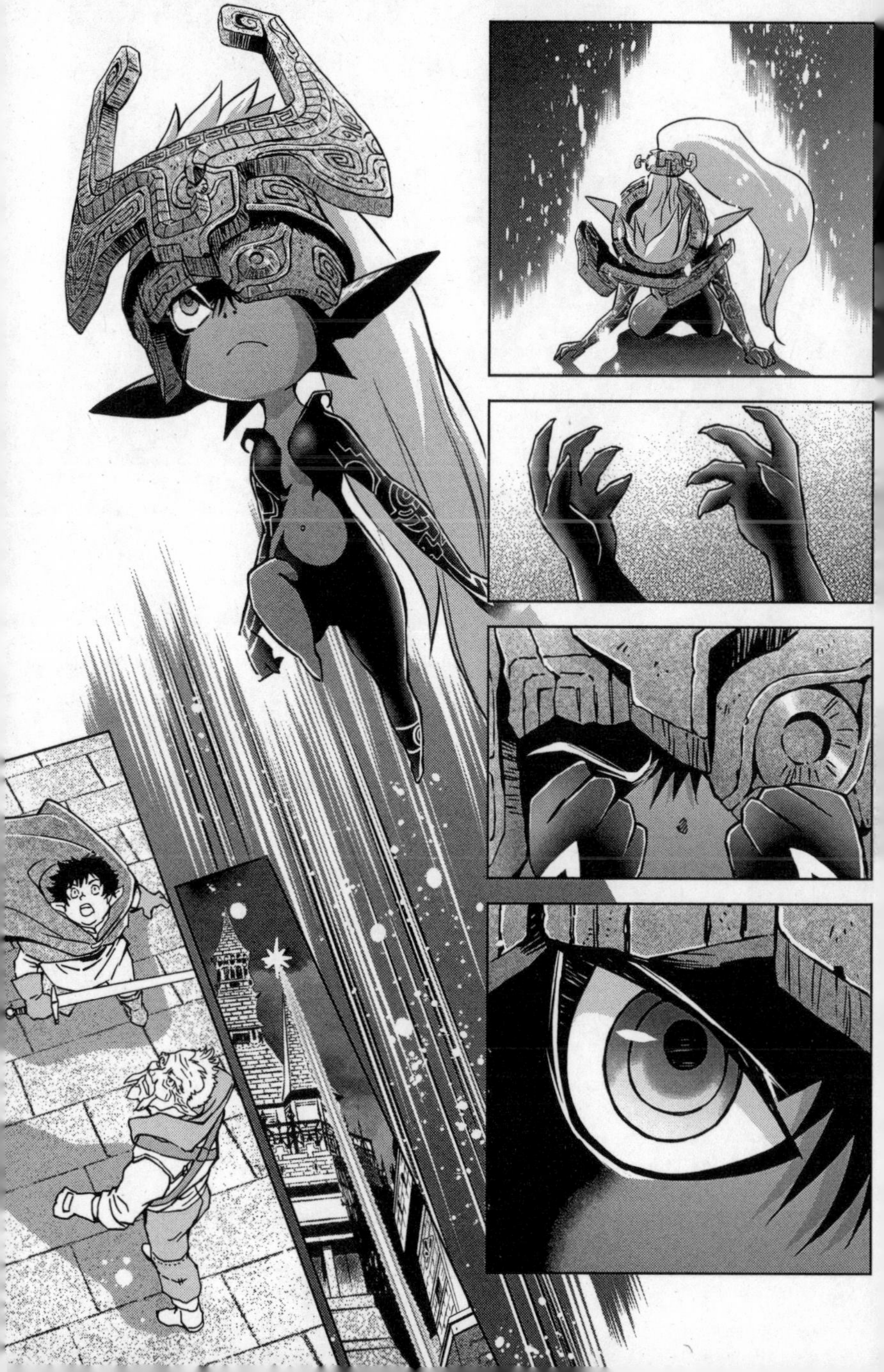

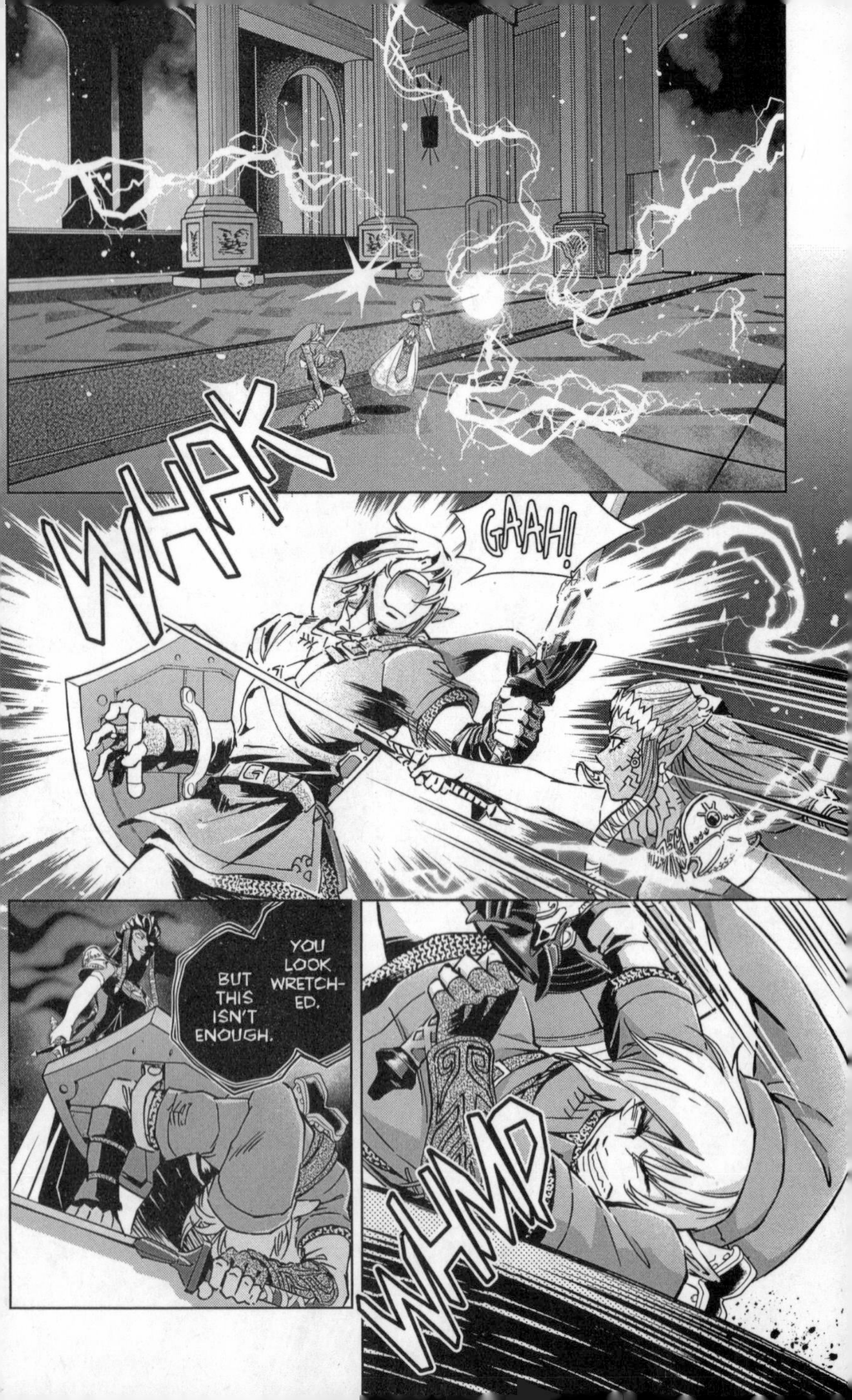
WHAK
GAAH!
WHMP
YOU LOOK WRETCHED. BUT THIS ISN'T ENOUGH.

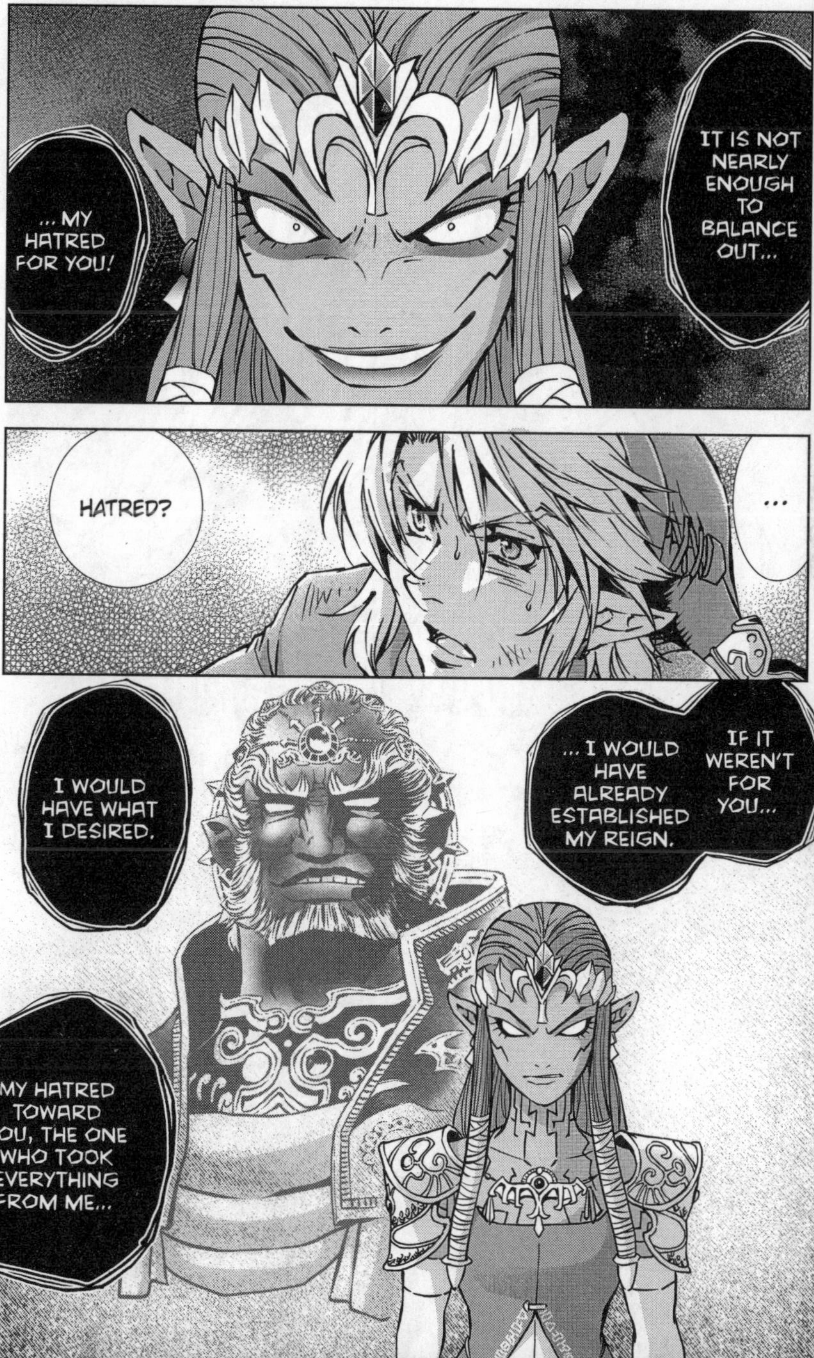
IT IS NOT NEARLY ENOUGH TO BALANCE OUT...
...MY HATRED FOR YOU!
...
HATRED?
IF IT WEREN'T FOR YOU...
...I WOULD HAVE ALREADY ESTABLISHED MY REIGN.
I WOULD HAVE WHAT I DESIRED.
MY HATRED TOWARD YOU, THE ONE WHO TOOK EVERYTHING FROM ME...

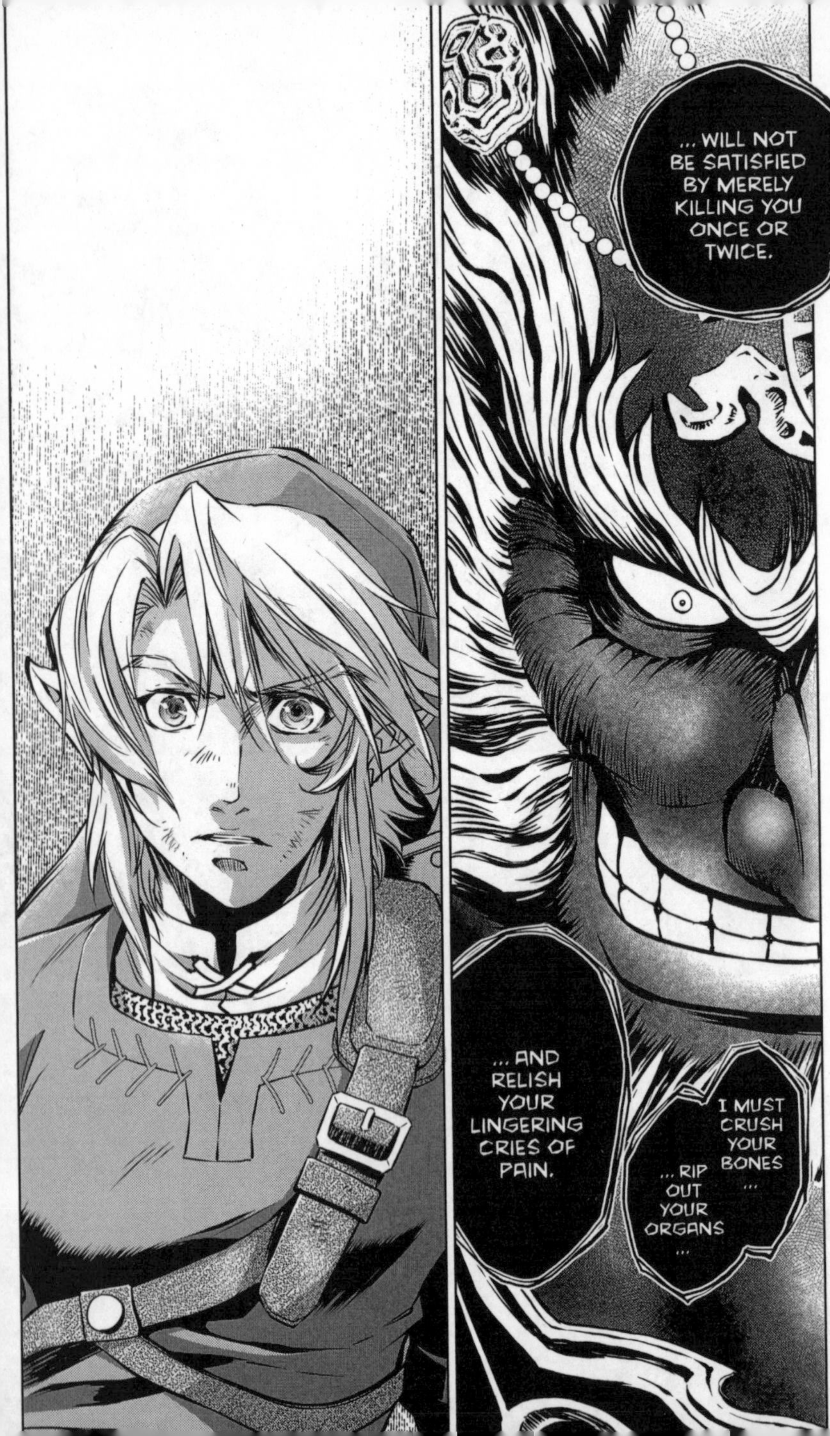
...WILL NOT BE SATISFIED BY MERELY KILLING YOU ONCE OR TWICE.
I MUST CRUSH YOUR BONES...
...RIP OUT YOUR ORGANS...
...AND RELISH YOUR LINGERING CRIES OF PAIN.

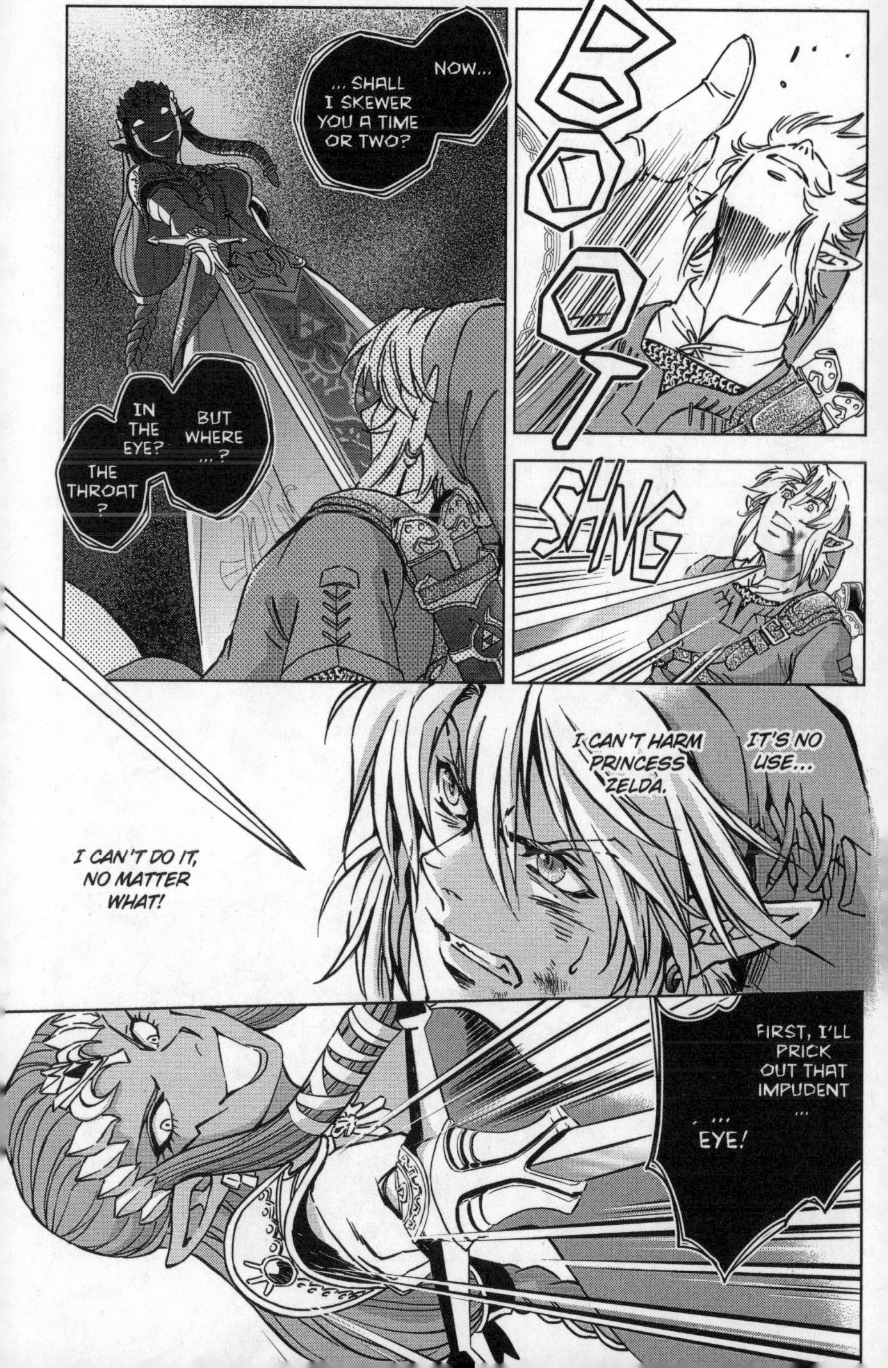
BOOT
SHNG
NOW... ... SHALL I SKEWER YOU A TIME OR TWO?
BUT WHERE ...? IN THE EYE? THE THROAT?
IT'S NO USE...
I CAN'T HARM PRINCESS ZELDA.
I CAN'T DO IT, NO MATTER WHAT!
FIRST, I'LL PRICK OUT THAT IMPUDENT ... ... EYE!

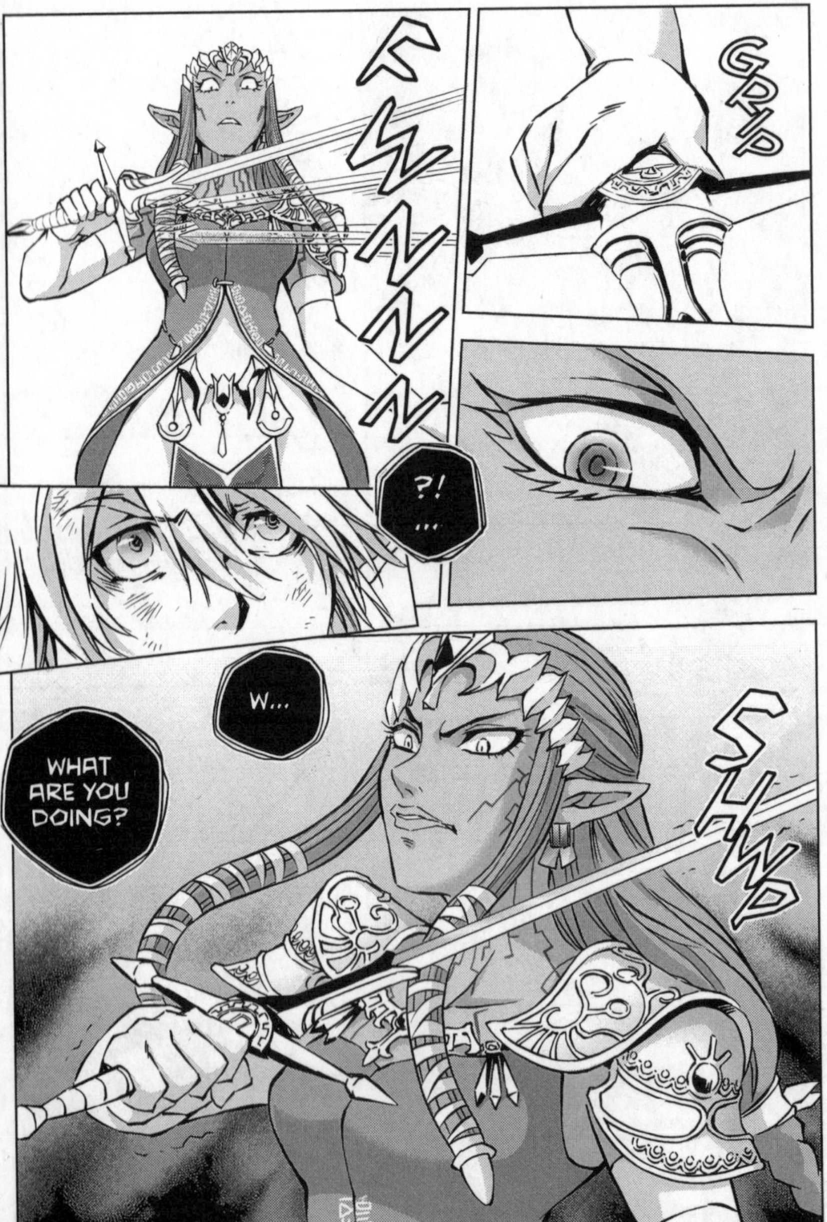
GRIP
?!
...
SHWP
W...
WHAT ARE YOU DOING?

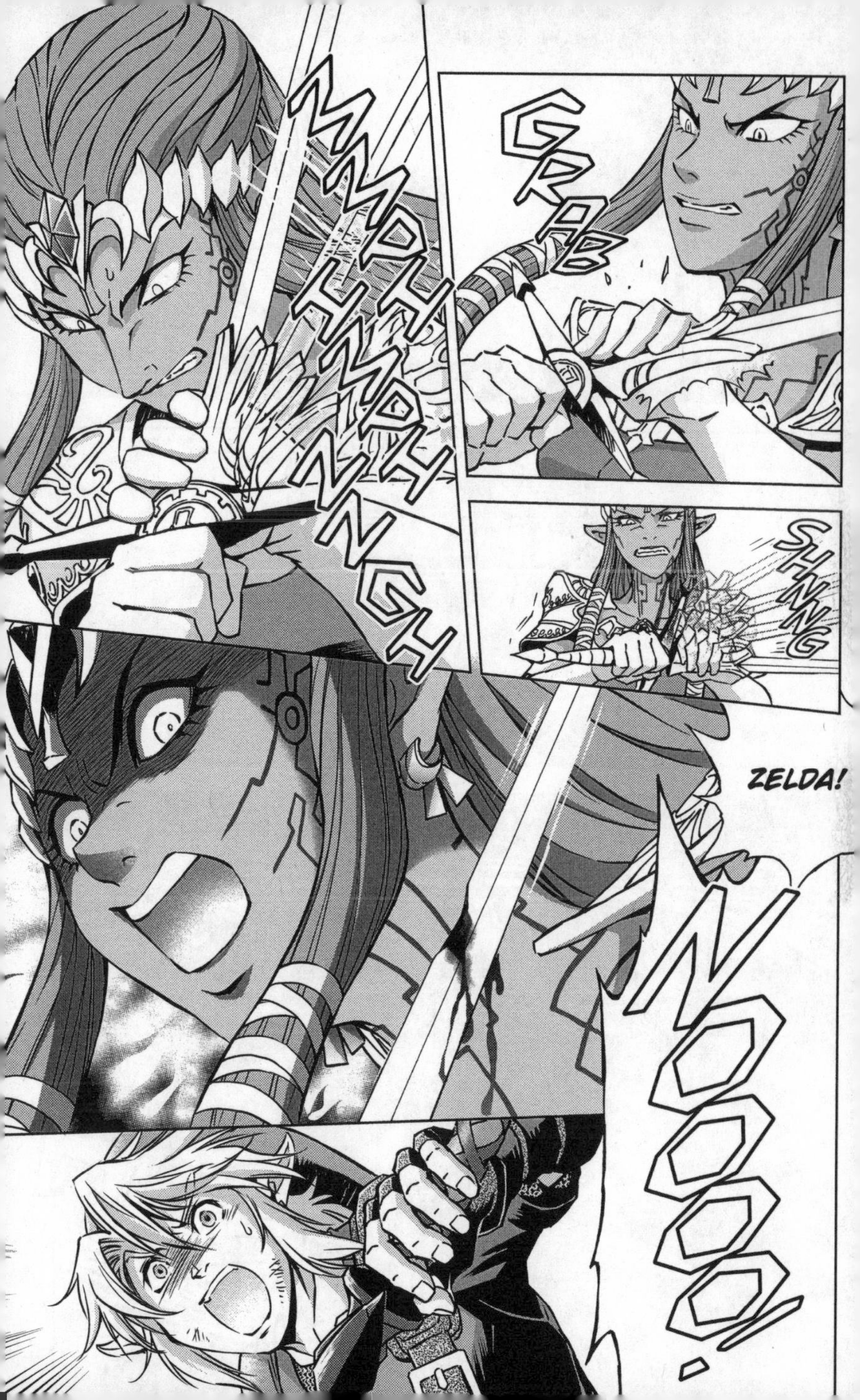
GRAB
SHNNNG
MMMPH HMMPH NNNGH
ZELDA!
NOOOOO!

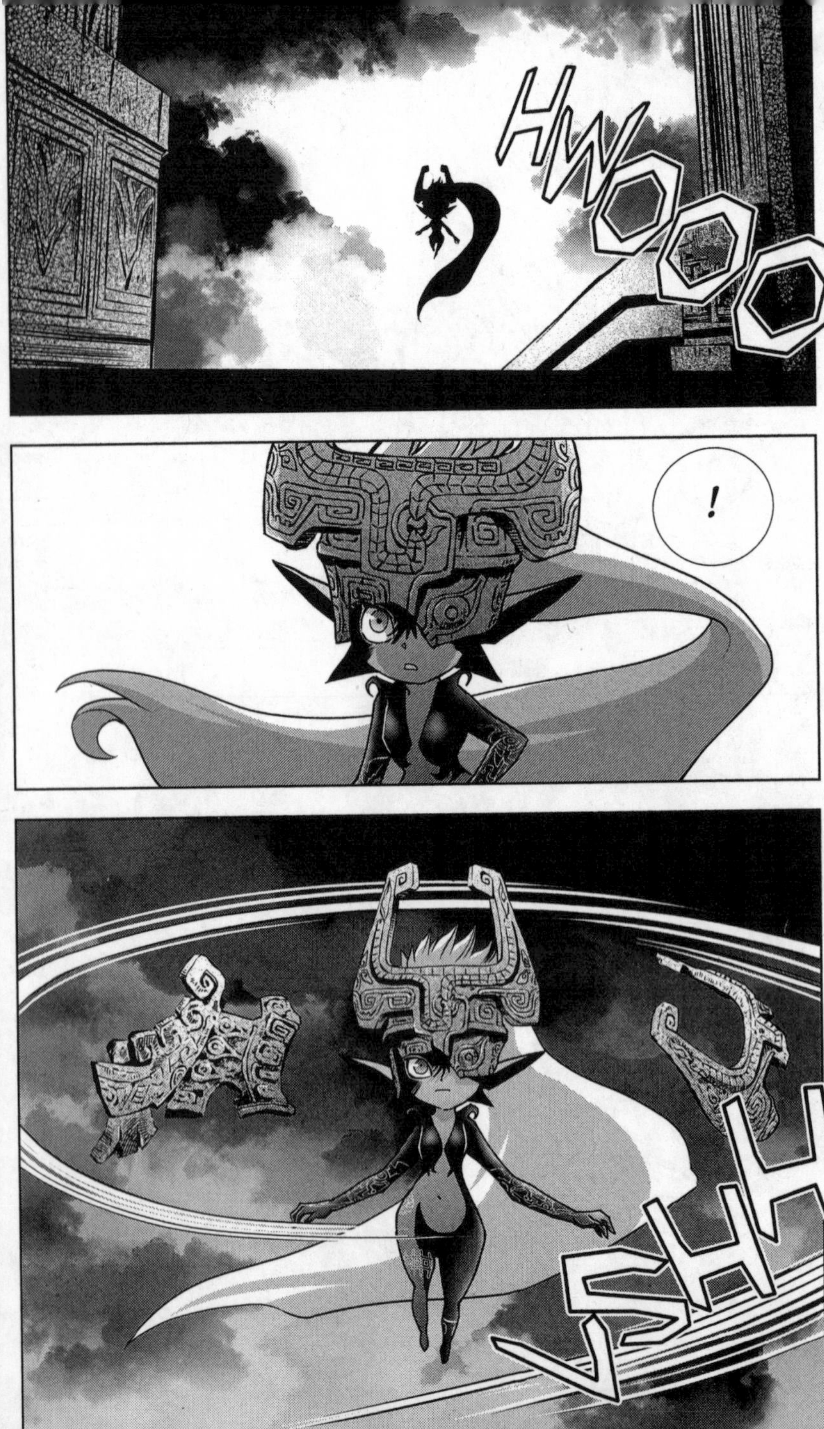
HWOOOO
!
VSHH

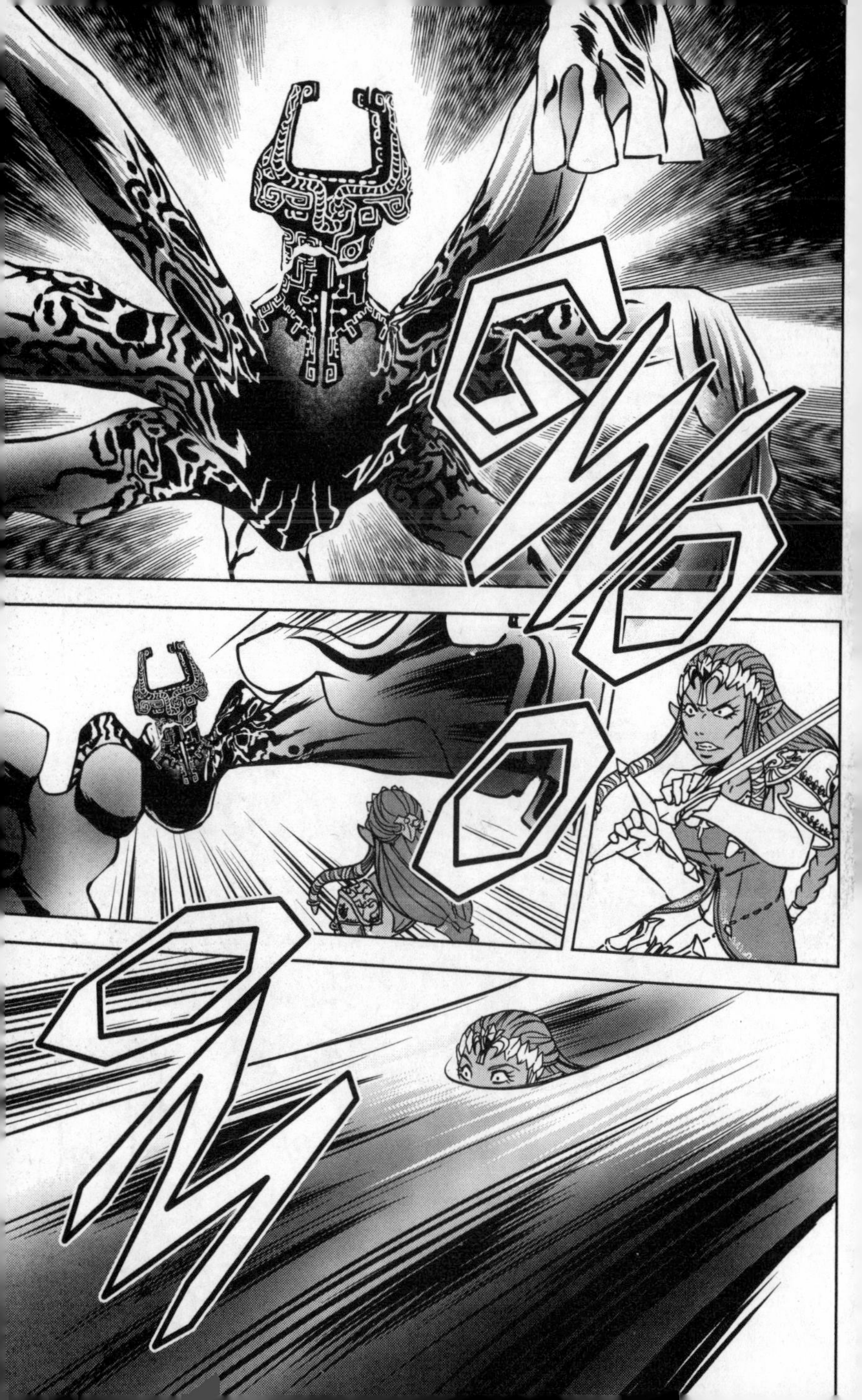

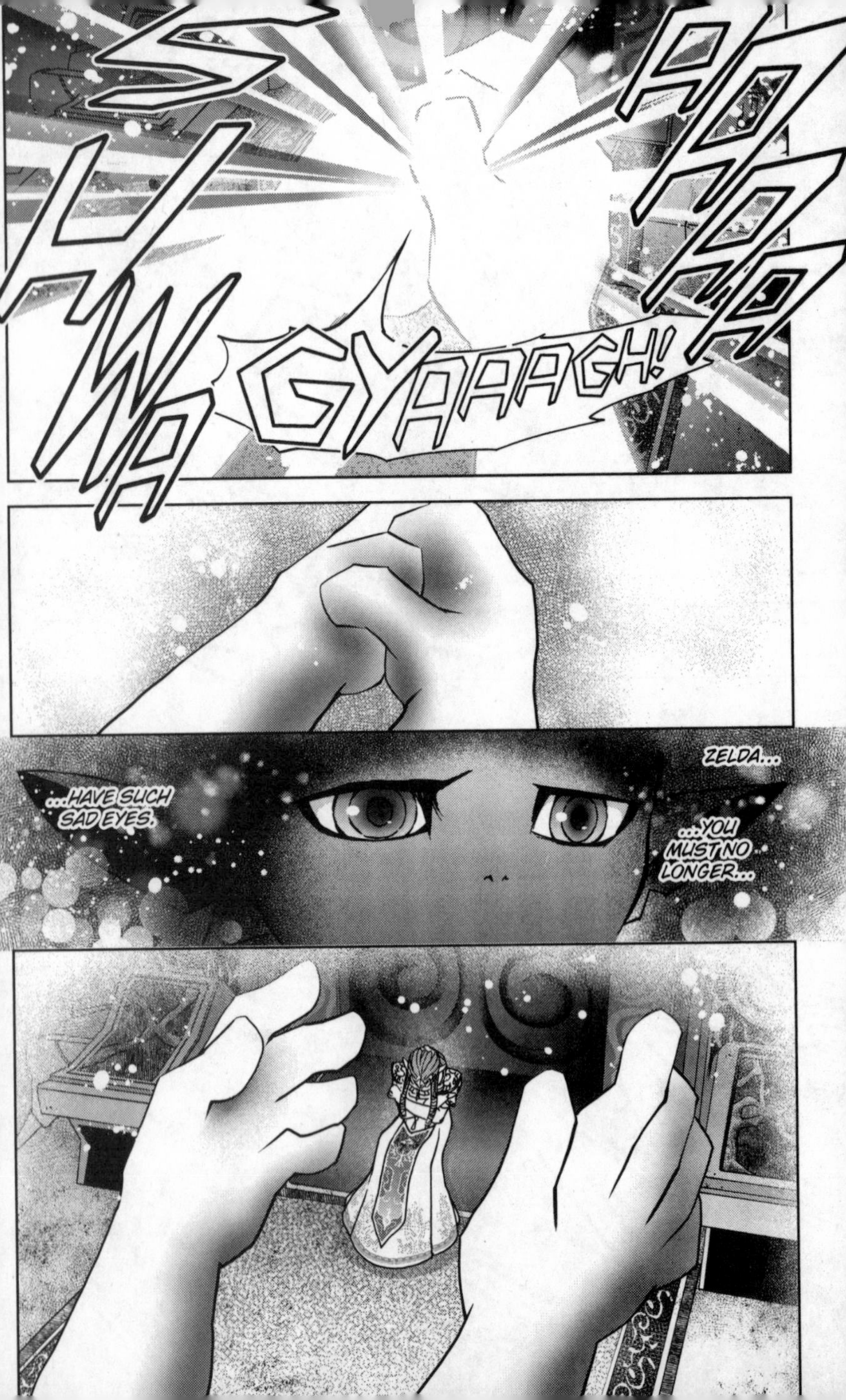
AAAAA
SHWAA
GYAAAAGH!
ZELDA...
...YOU MUST NO LONGER...
...HAVE SUCH SAD EYES.

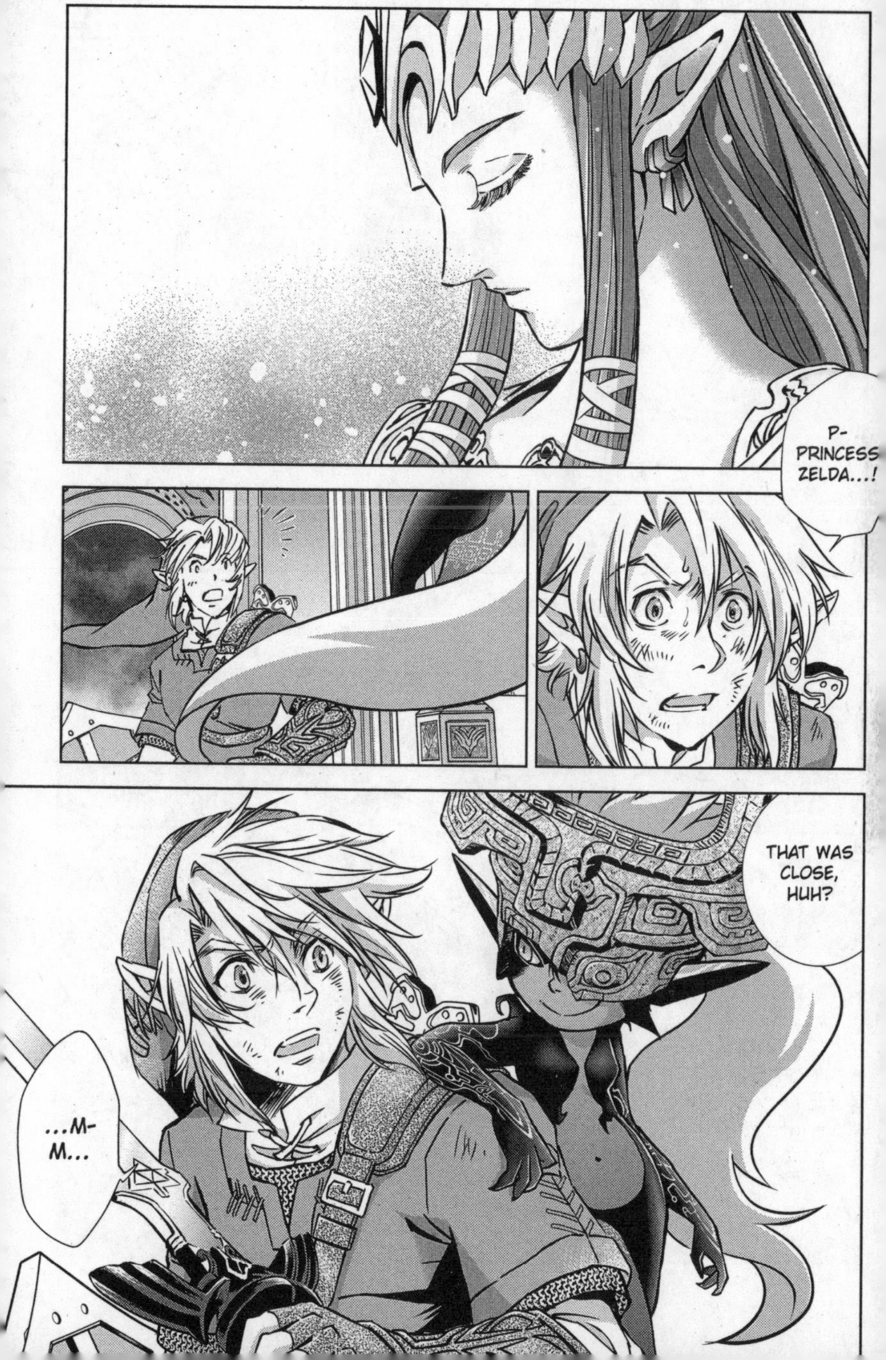
P-
PRINCESS
ZELDA...!
THAT WAS
CLOSE,
HUH?
...M-
M...

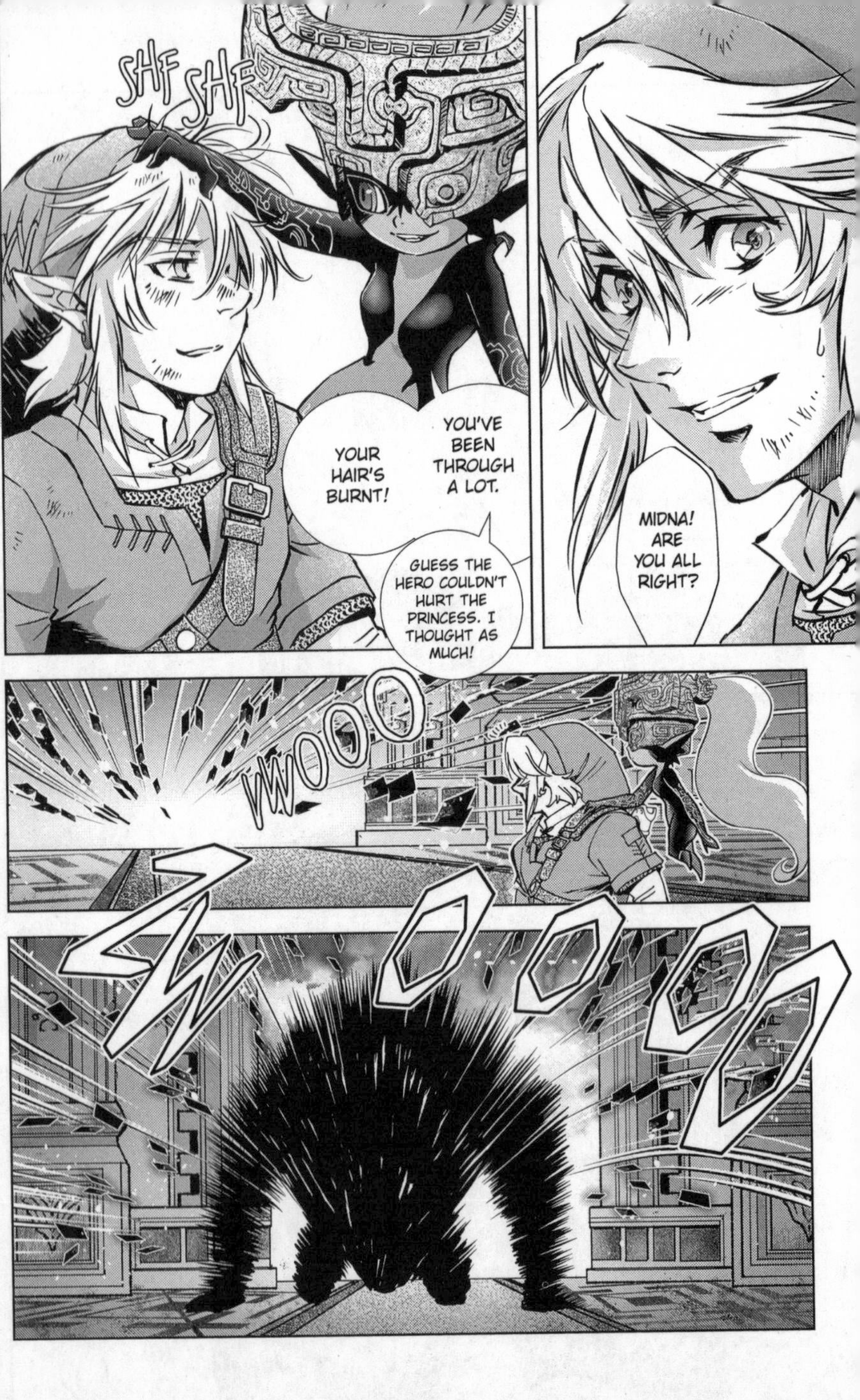
MIDNA! ARE YOU ALL RIGHT?
SHF SHF
YOU'VE BEEN THROUGH A LOT.
YOUR HAIR'S BURNT!
GUESS THE HERO COULDN'T HURT THE PRINCESS. I THOUGHT AS MUCH!
VWOOO
VWOOOO

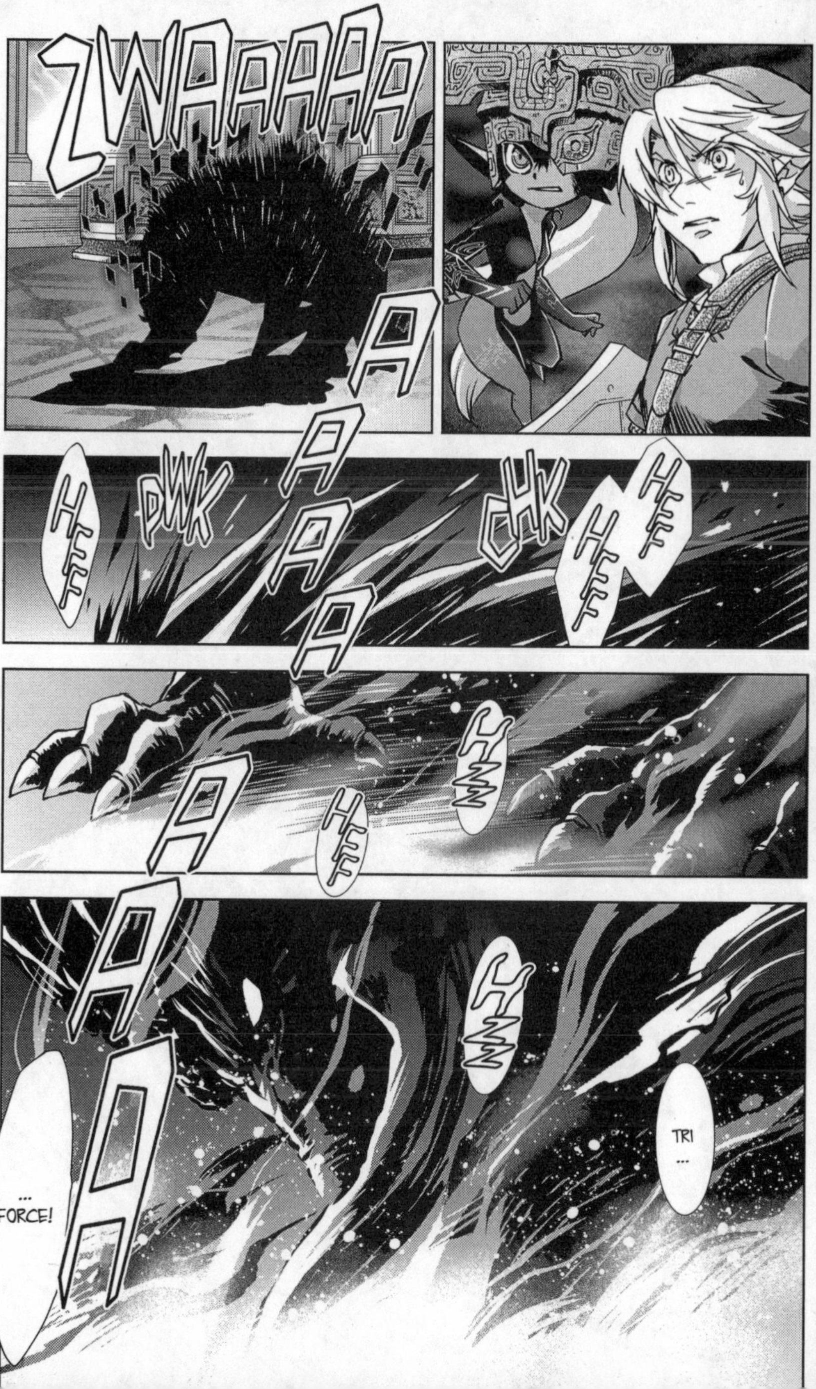
ZWAAAAAA
AAAAAAA
HEF HEF
HEF
CHK
DWK
HEF
HMM
HEF
HMM
TRI...
...FORCE!

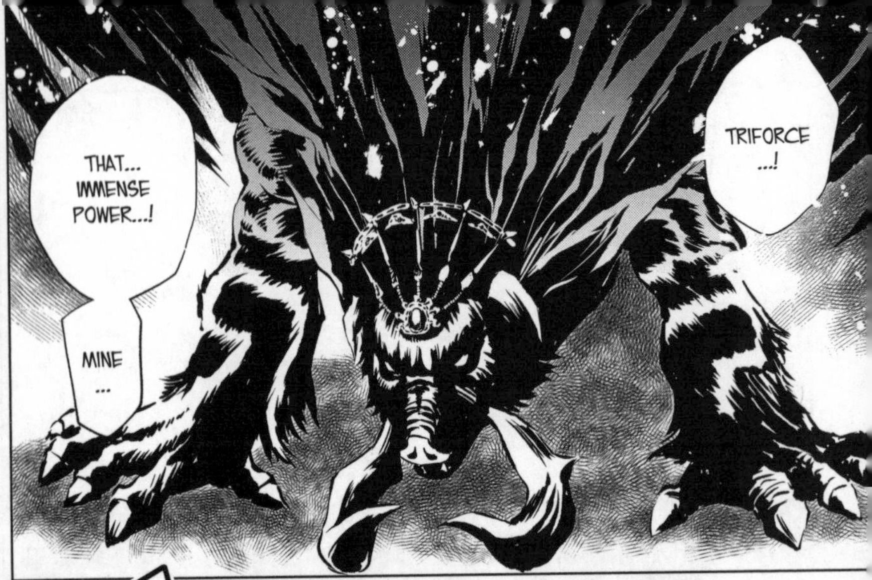
TRIFORCE ...!
THAT... IMMENSE POWER...!
MINE ...

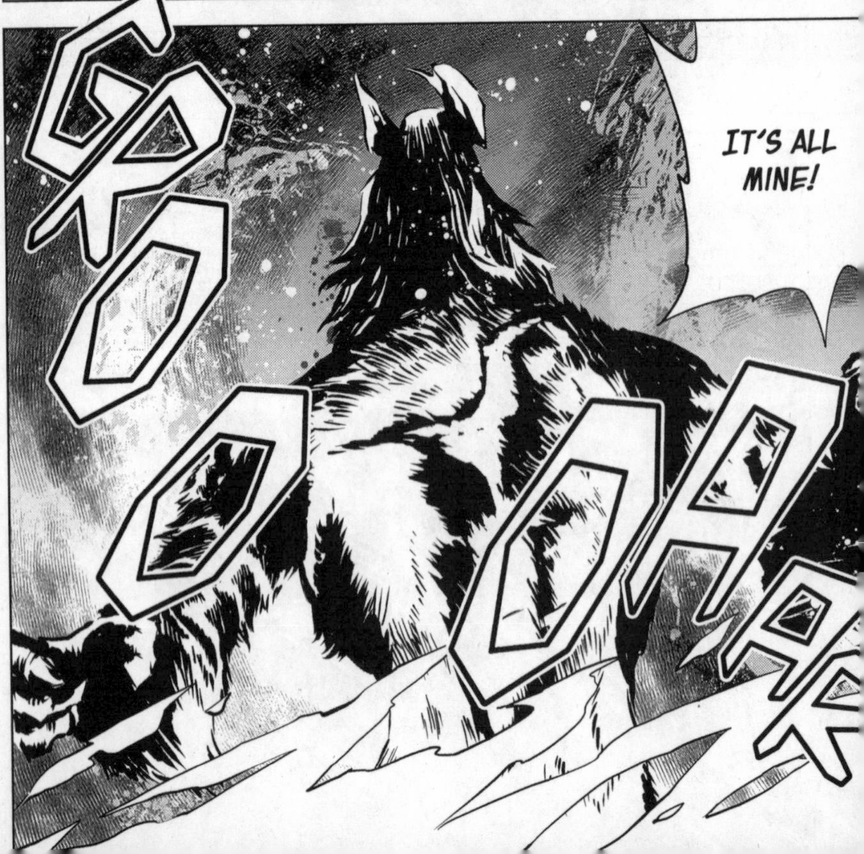
IT'S ALL MINE!
GROOAH

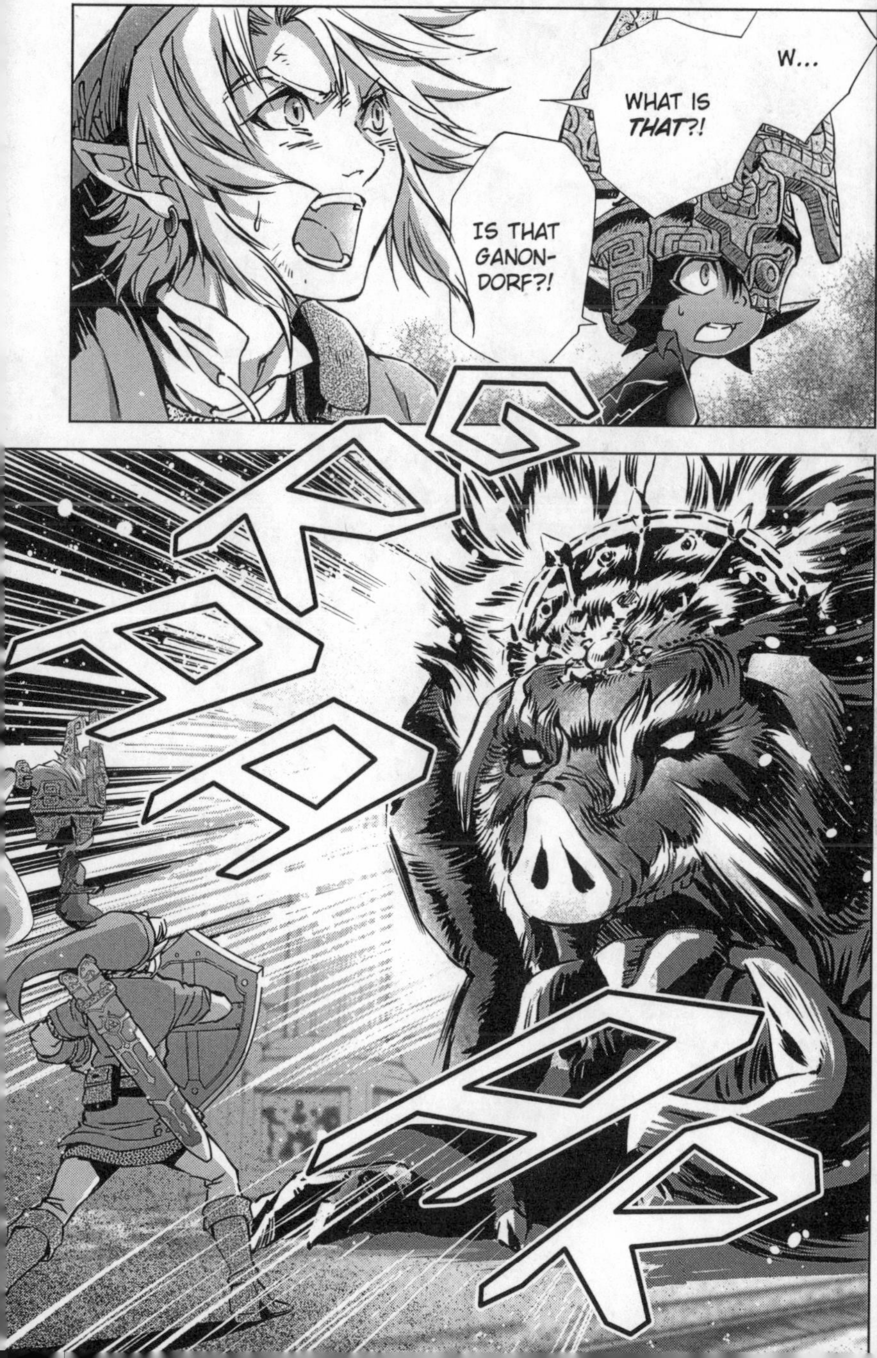
W...
WHAT IS THAT?!
IS THAT GANON-DORF?!

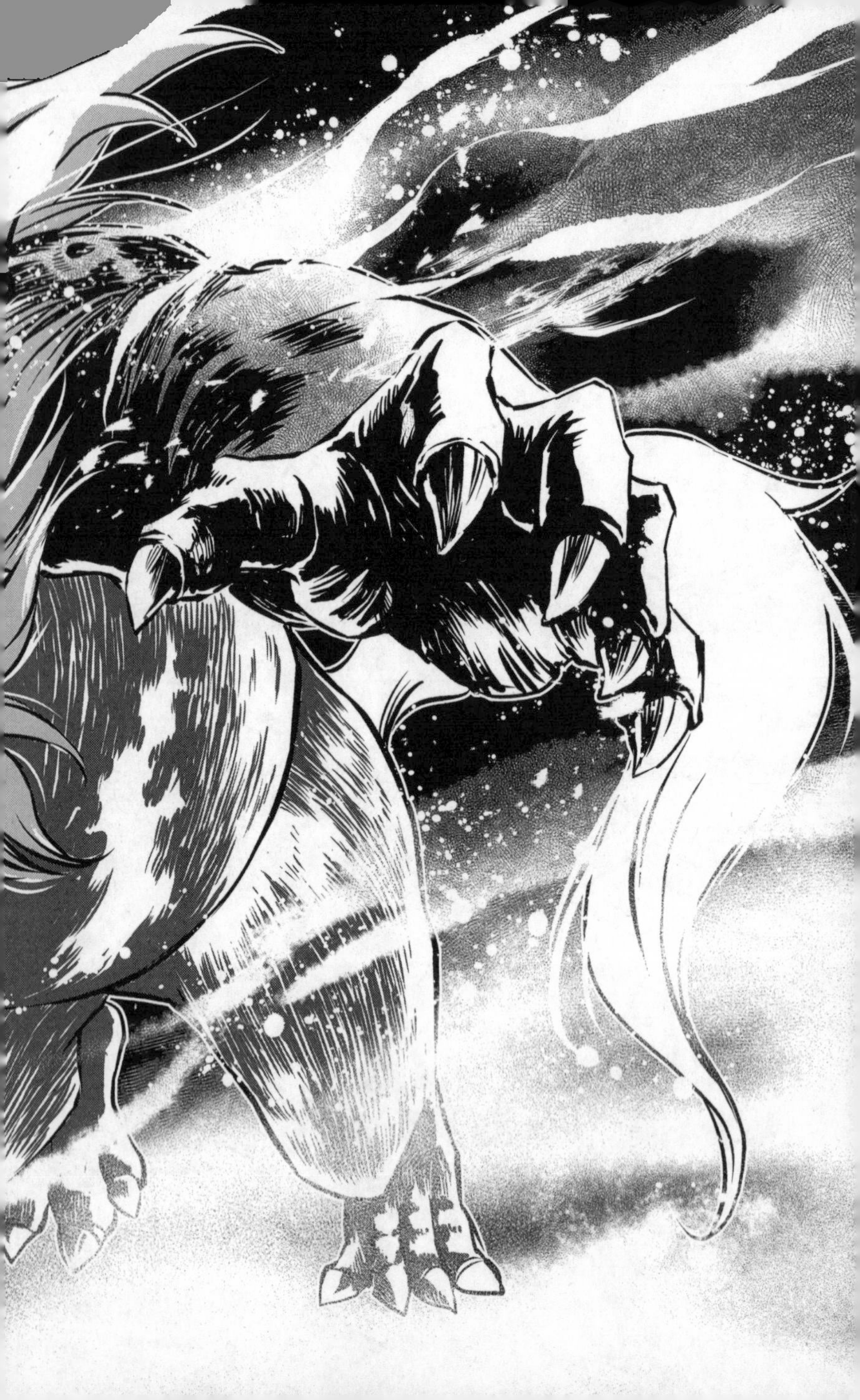

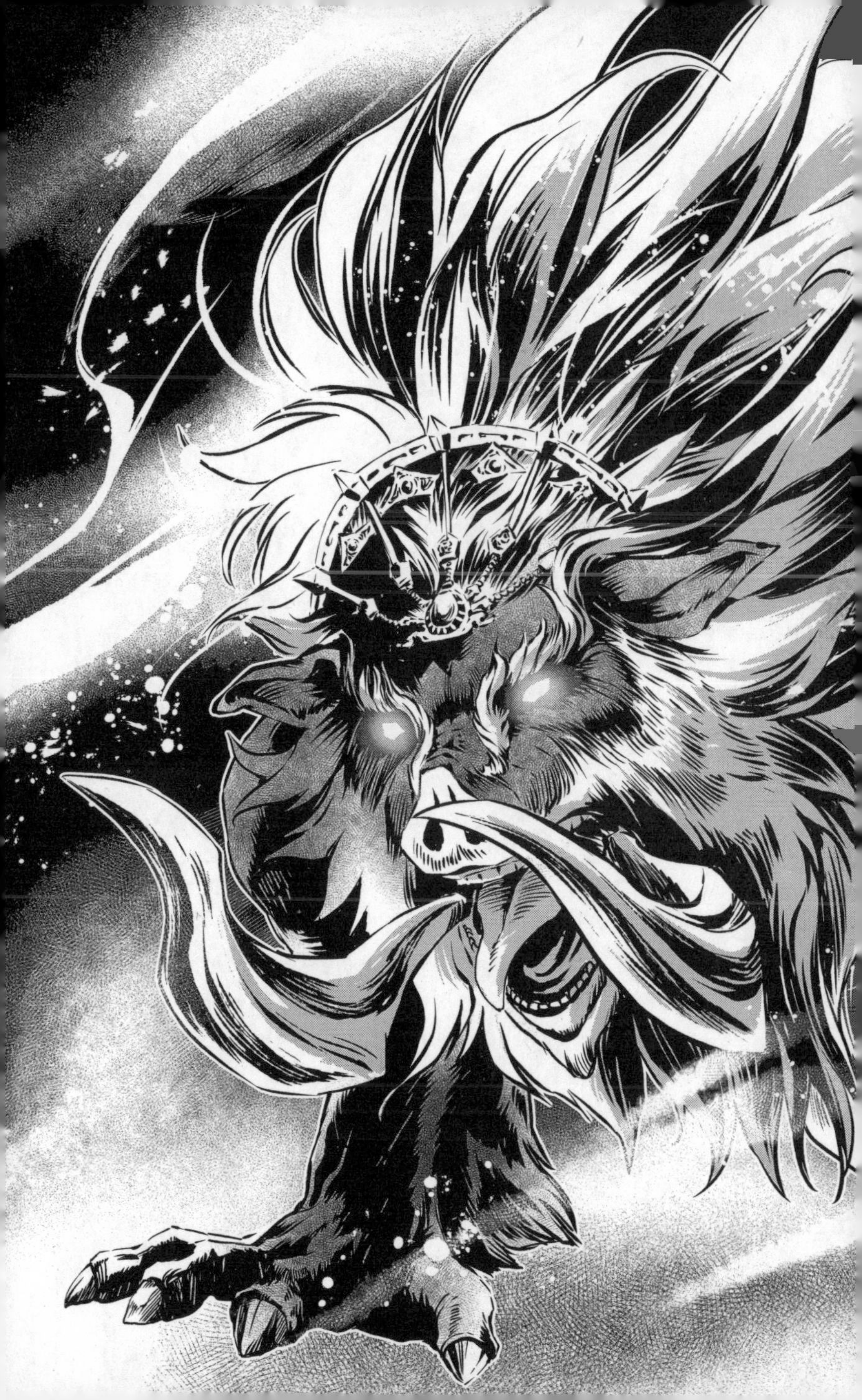

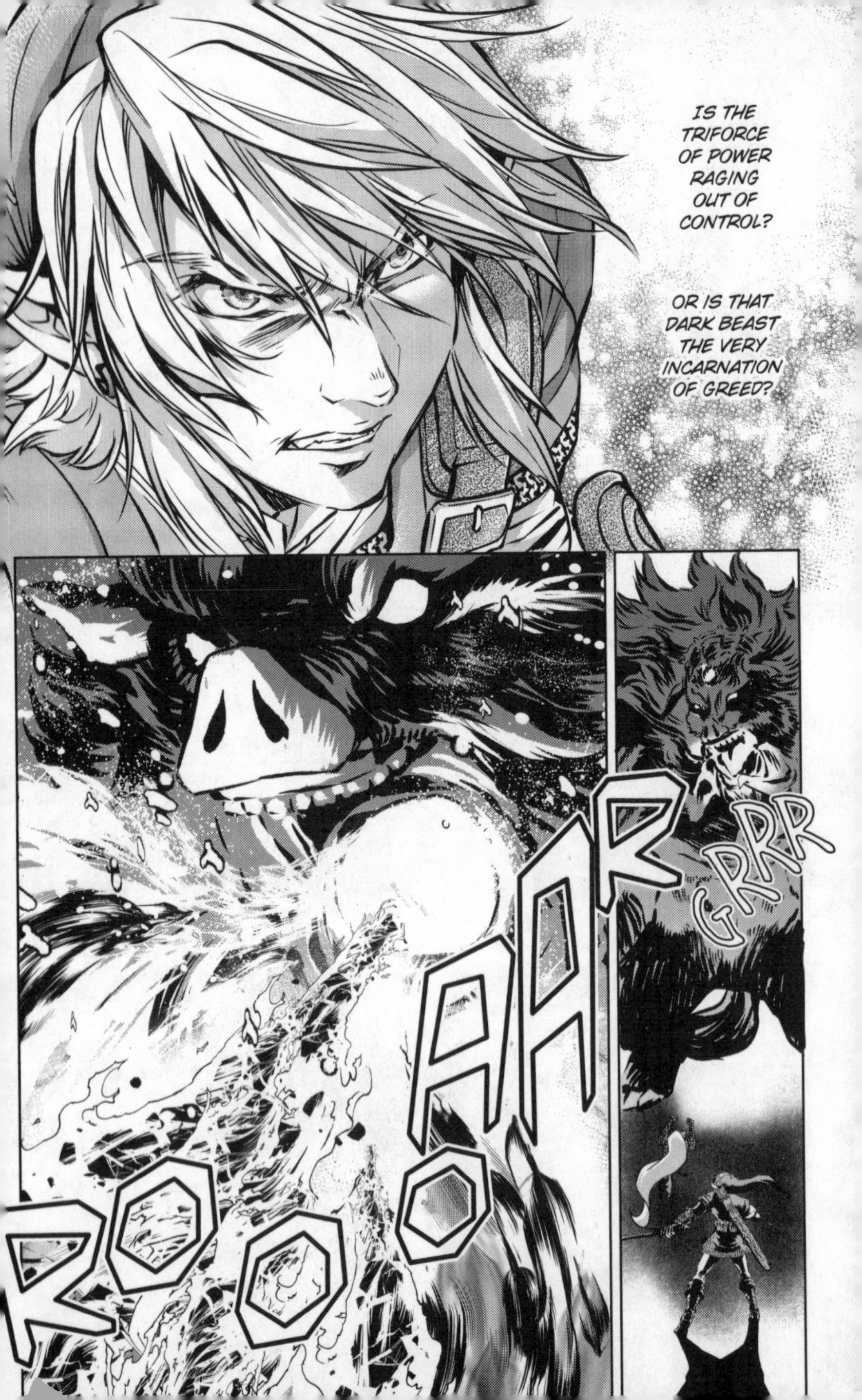
IS THE TRIFORCE OF POWER RAGING OUT OF CONTROL?
OR IS THAT DARK BEAST THE VERY INCARNATION OF GREED?
GRRR
ROOOAAR

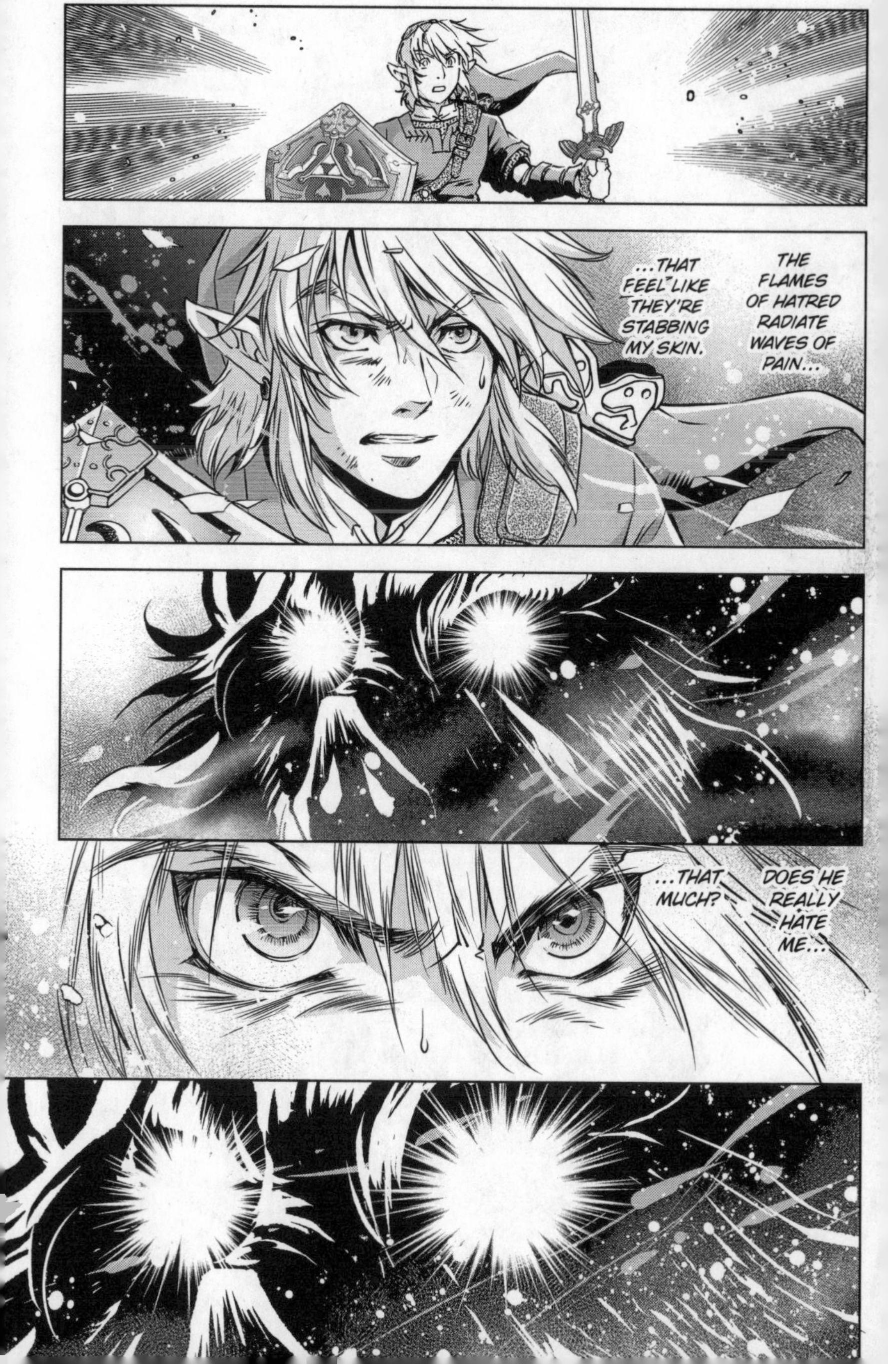
THE FLAMES OF HATRED RADIATE WAVES OF PAIN...
...THAT FEEL LIKE THEY'RE STABBING MY SKIN.
DOES HE REALLY HATE ME...
...THAT MUCH?

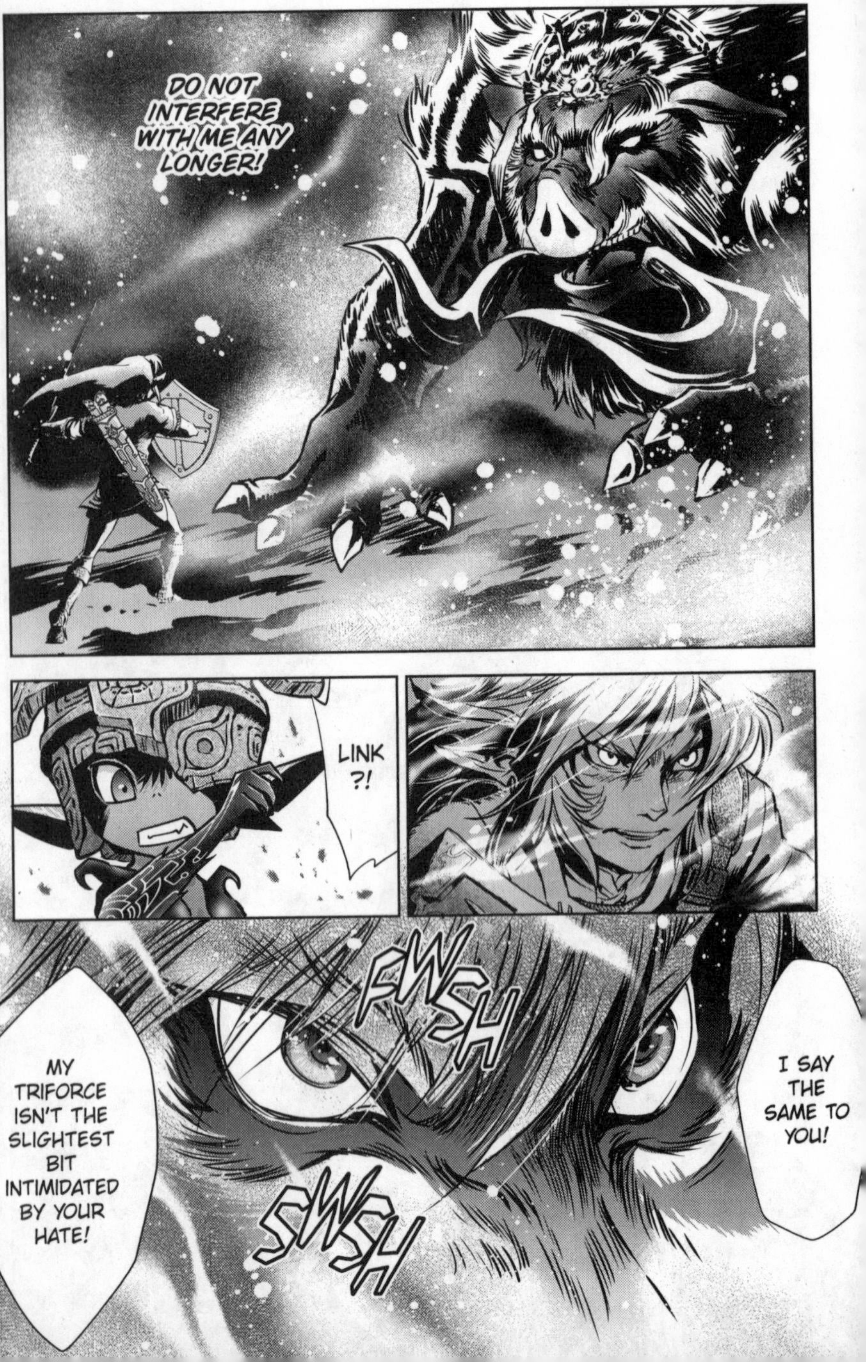
DO NOT INTERFERE WITH ME ANY LONGER!
LINK ?!
I SAY THE SAME TO YOU!
FWSH
MY TRIFORCE ISN'T THE SLIGHTEST BIT INTIMIDATED BY YOUR HATE!
SWSH

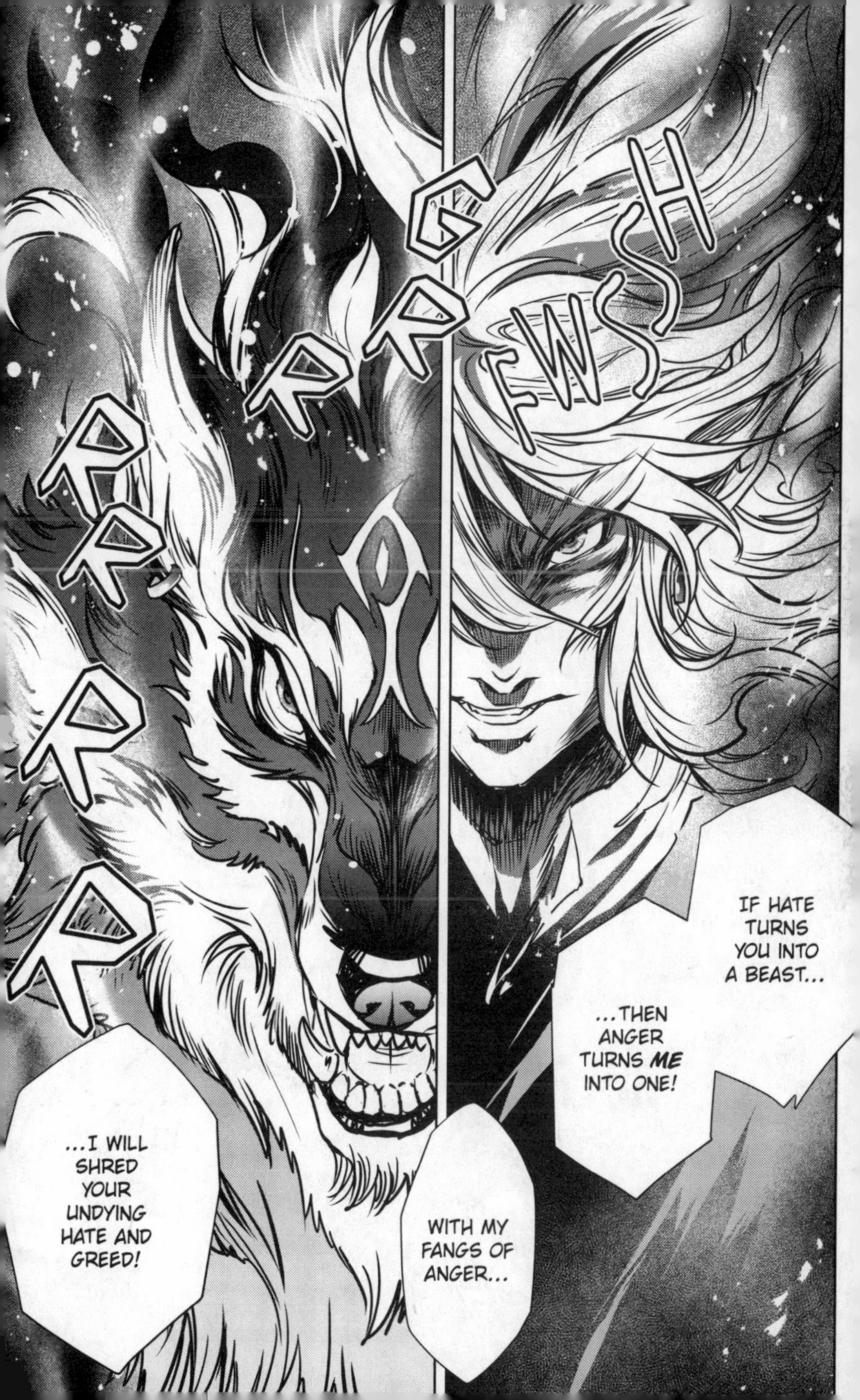
FWSH
IF HATE TURNS YOU INTO A BEAST...
...THEN ANGER TURNS *ME* INTO ONE!
WITH MY FANGS OF ANGER...
RRRRRG
...I WILL SHRED YOUR UNDYING HATE AND GREED!

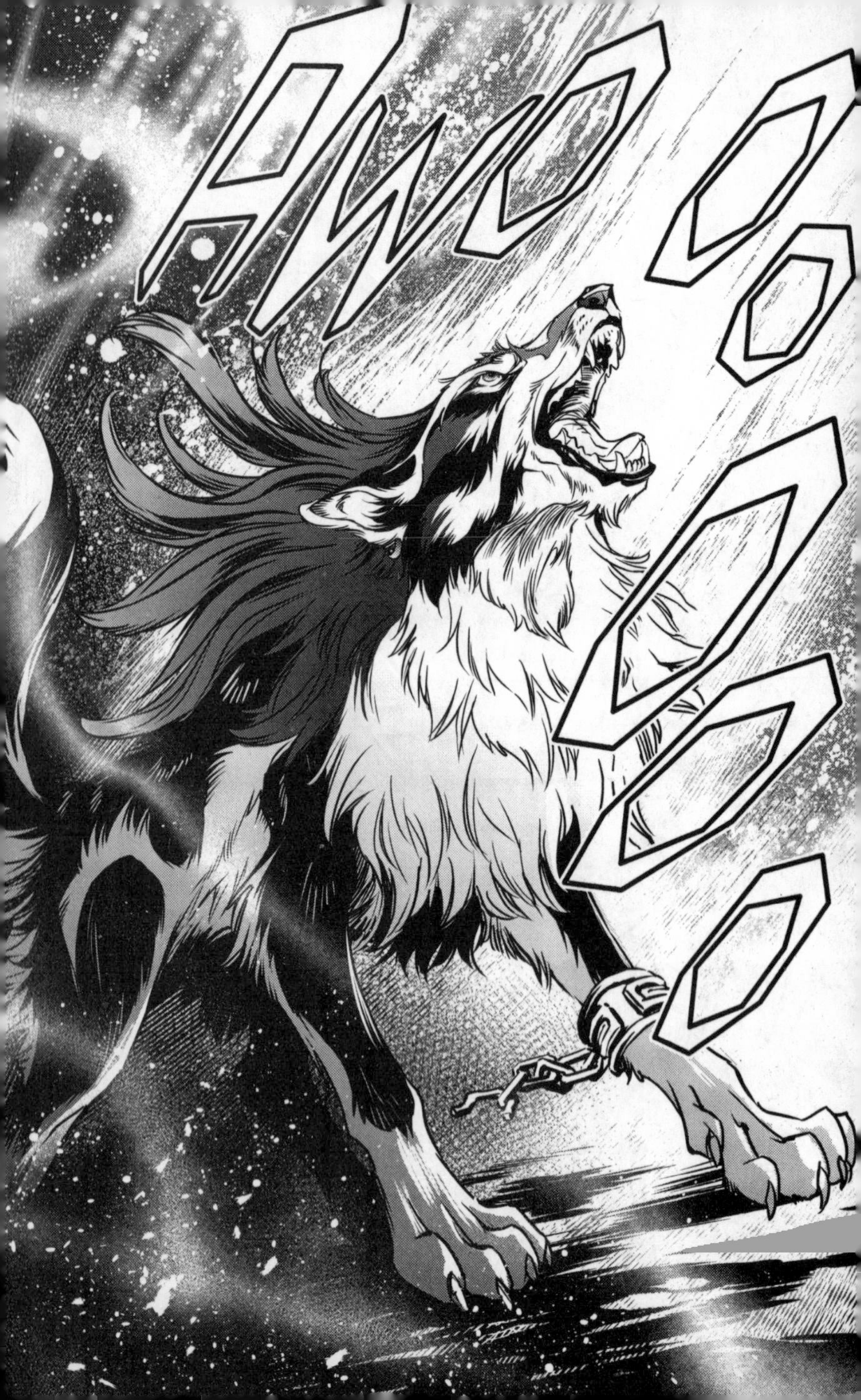
AWOOOOOO

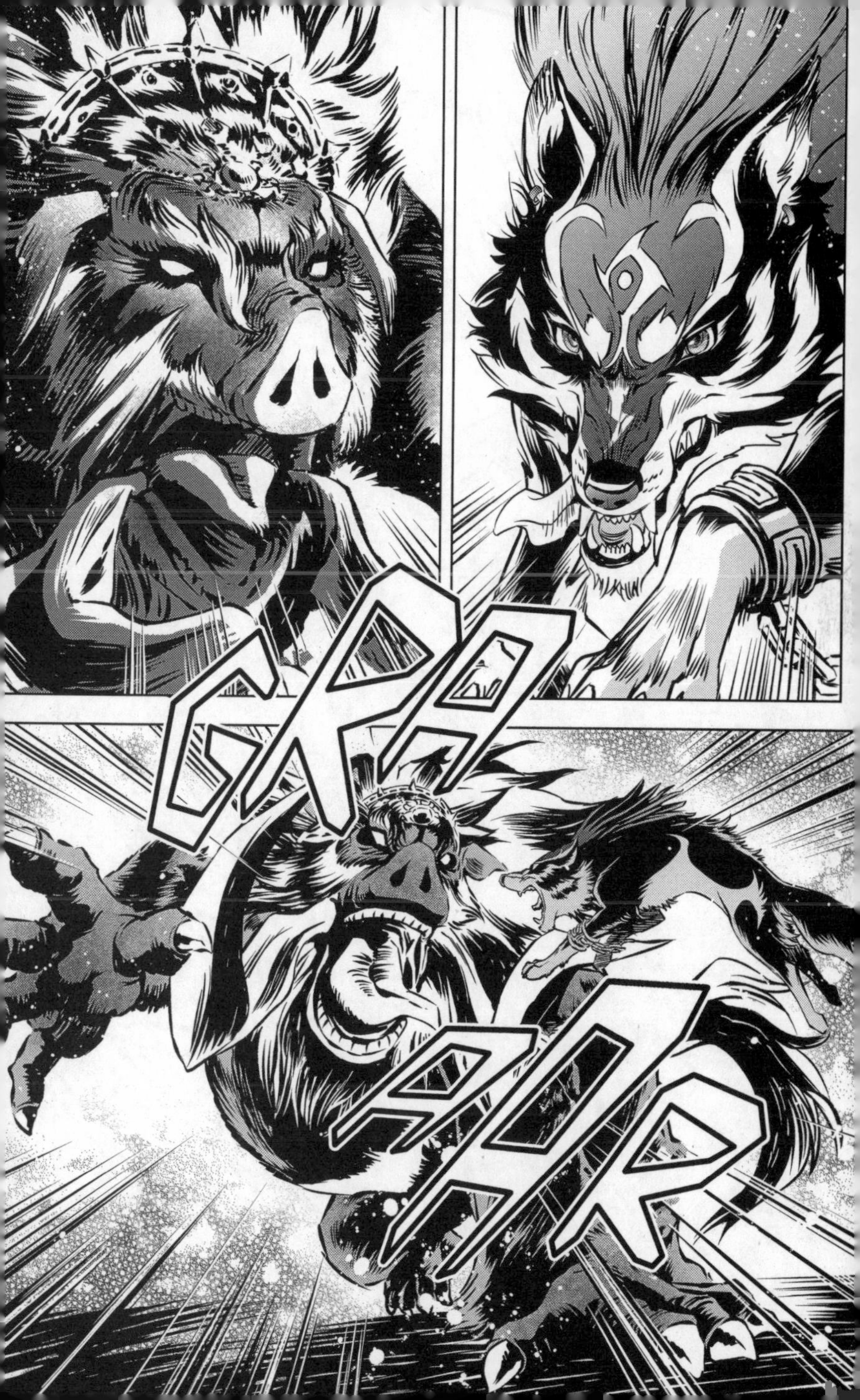
GRAAAR

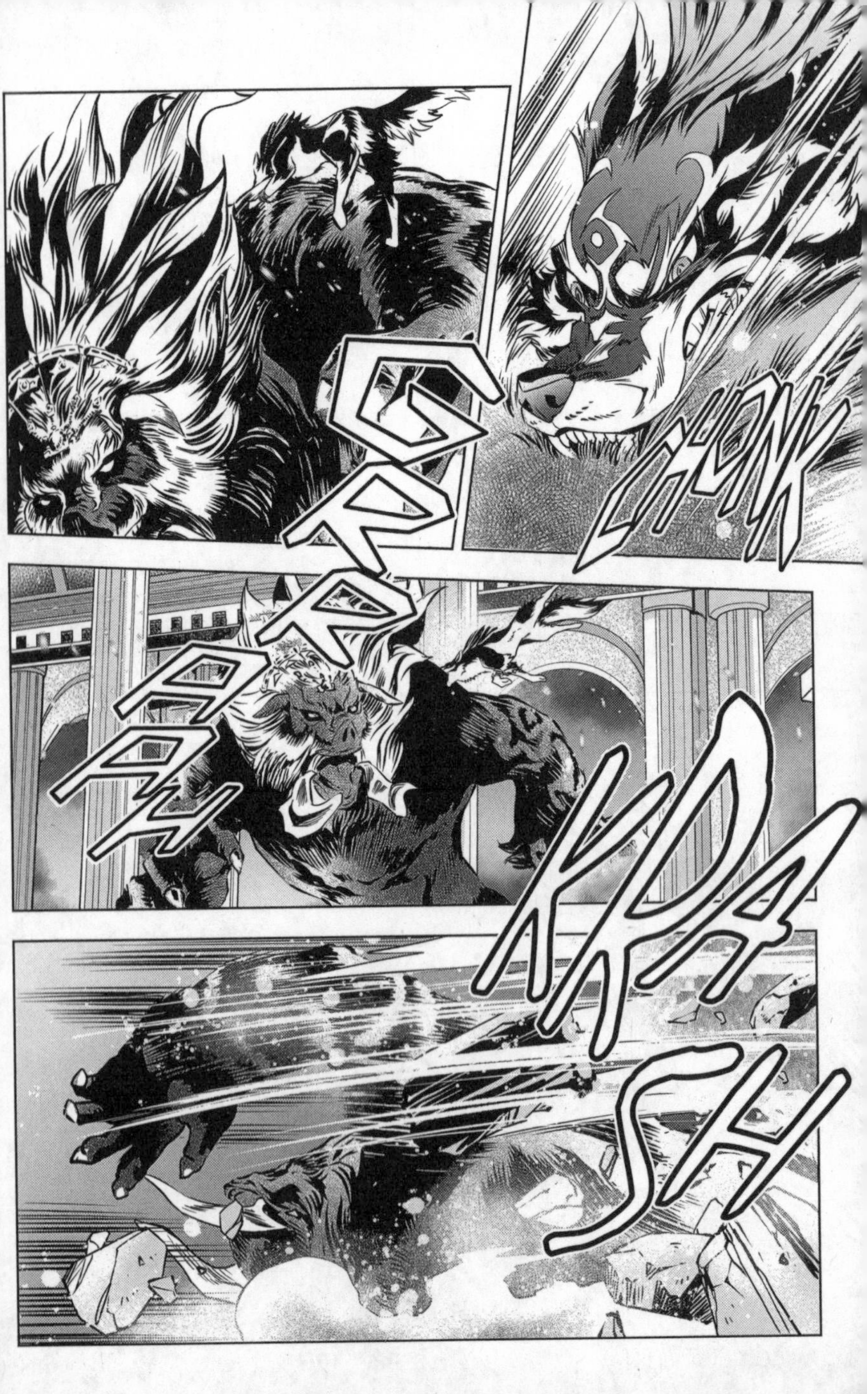
CHOMK
GRRAAAH
KRASH

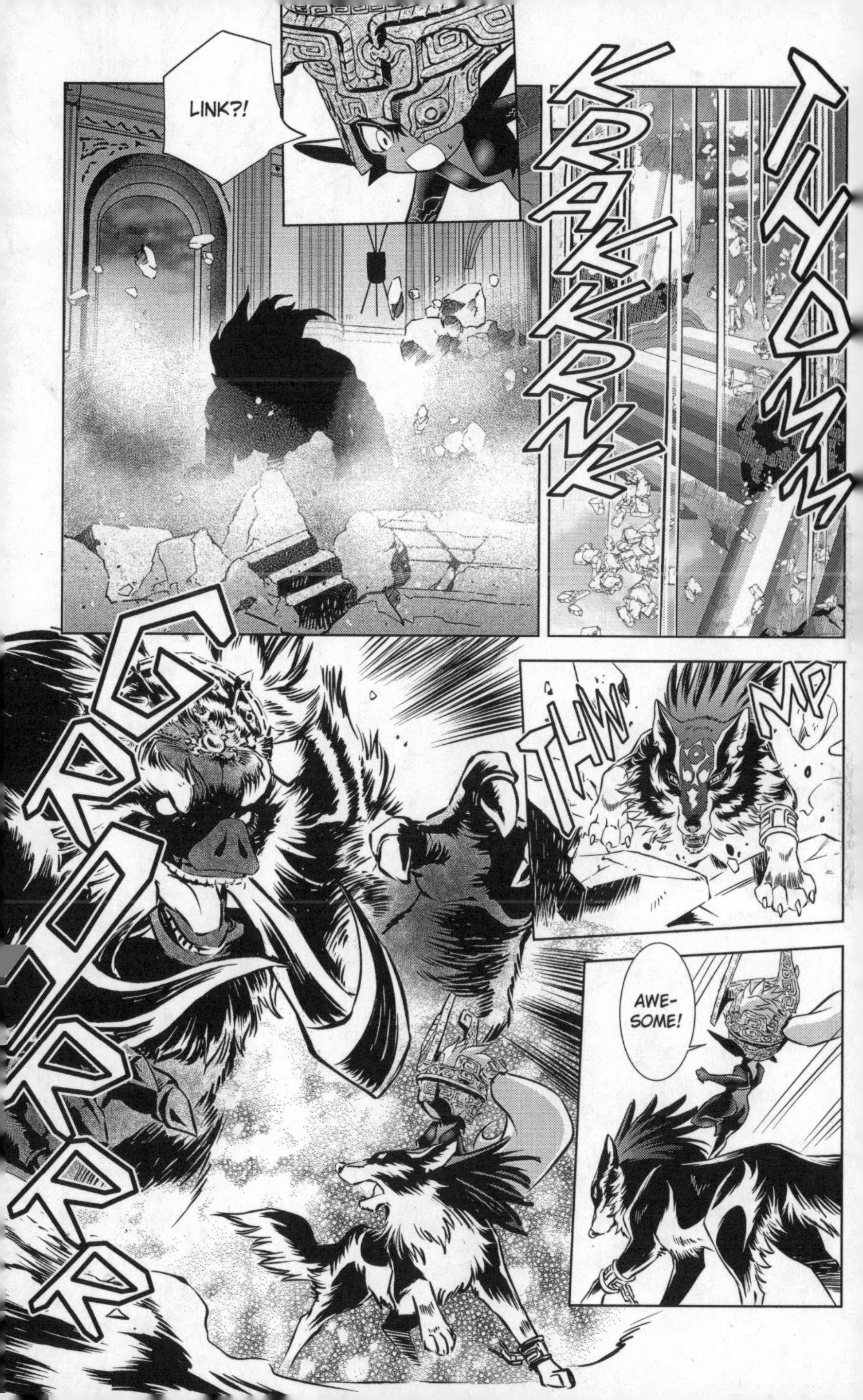
THOMMM
KRAKKRNK
LINK?!
THWMP
AWE-
SOME!
GRRRRRRR

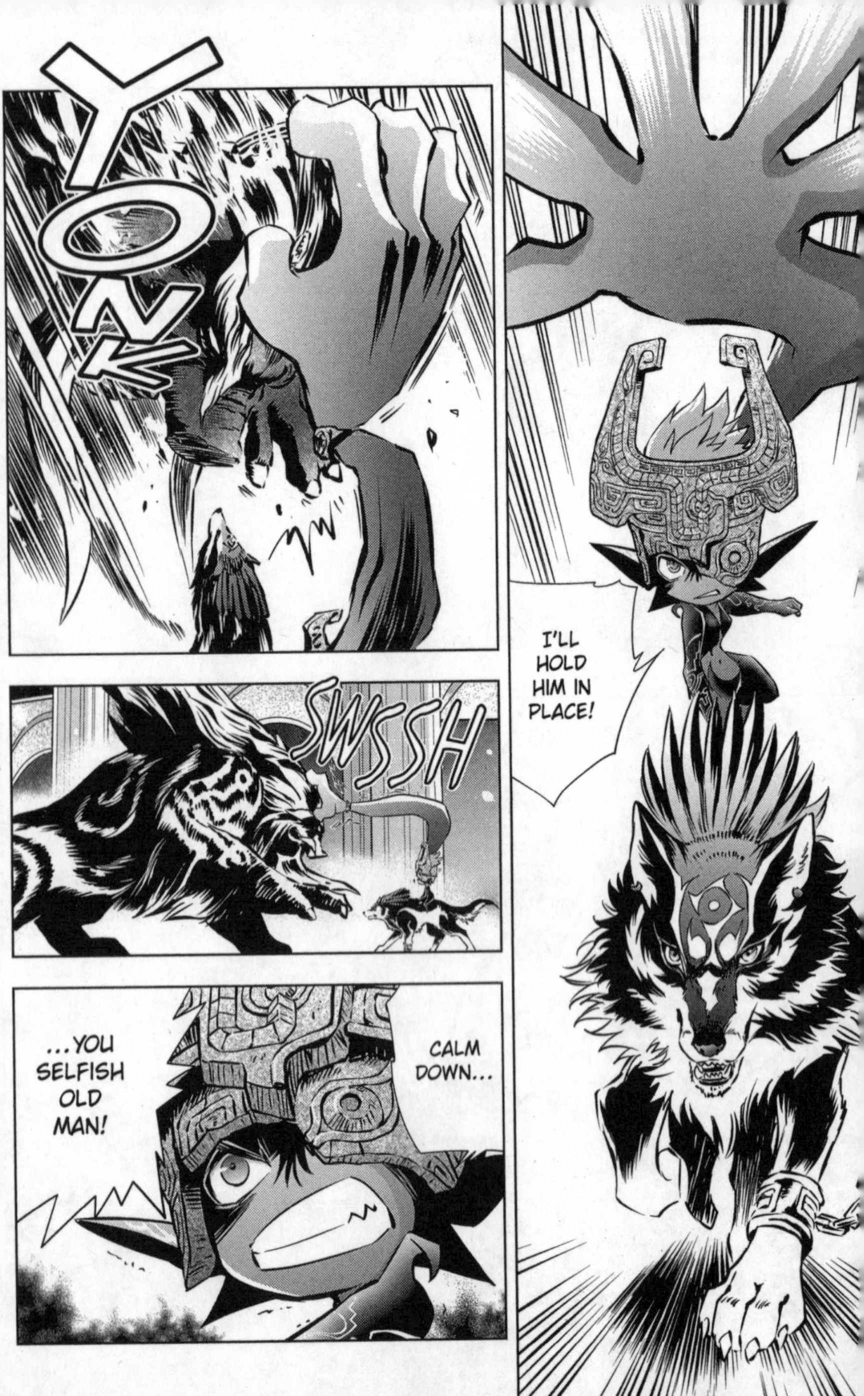
I'LL HOLD HIM IN PLACE!
YONK
SWSSH
CALM DOWN...
...YOU SELFISH OLD MAN!

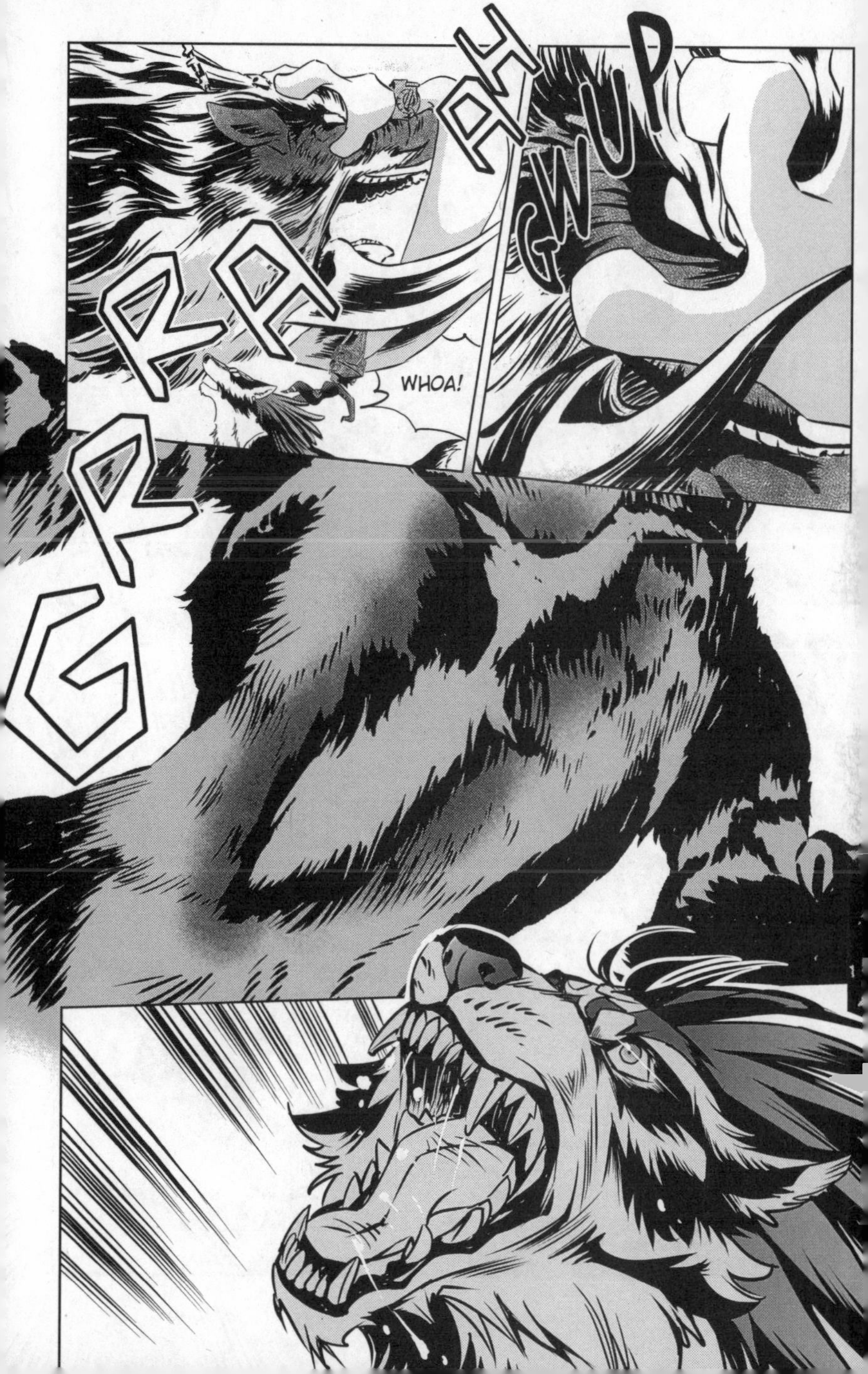
GWUP
WHOA!
GRRAAH

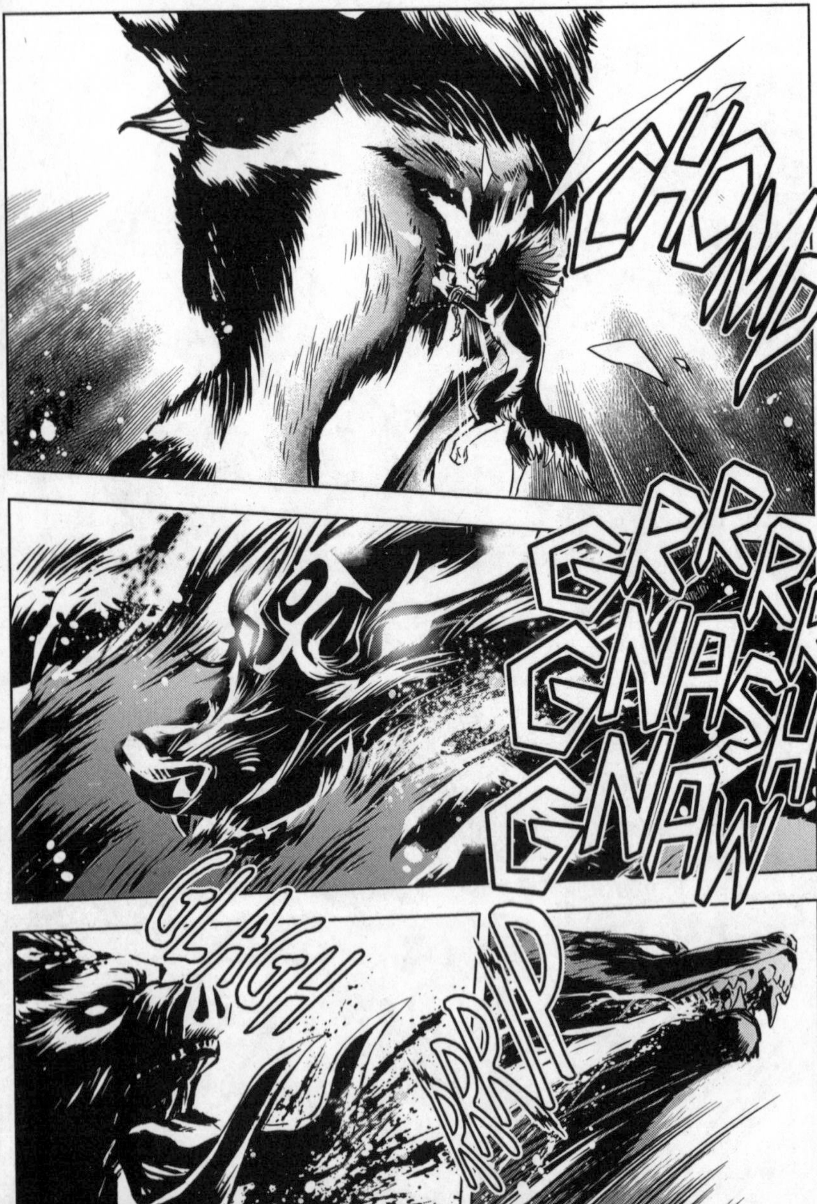
CHOMP
GRRRR
GNASH
GNAW
RRRIP
GLAGH

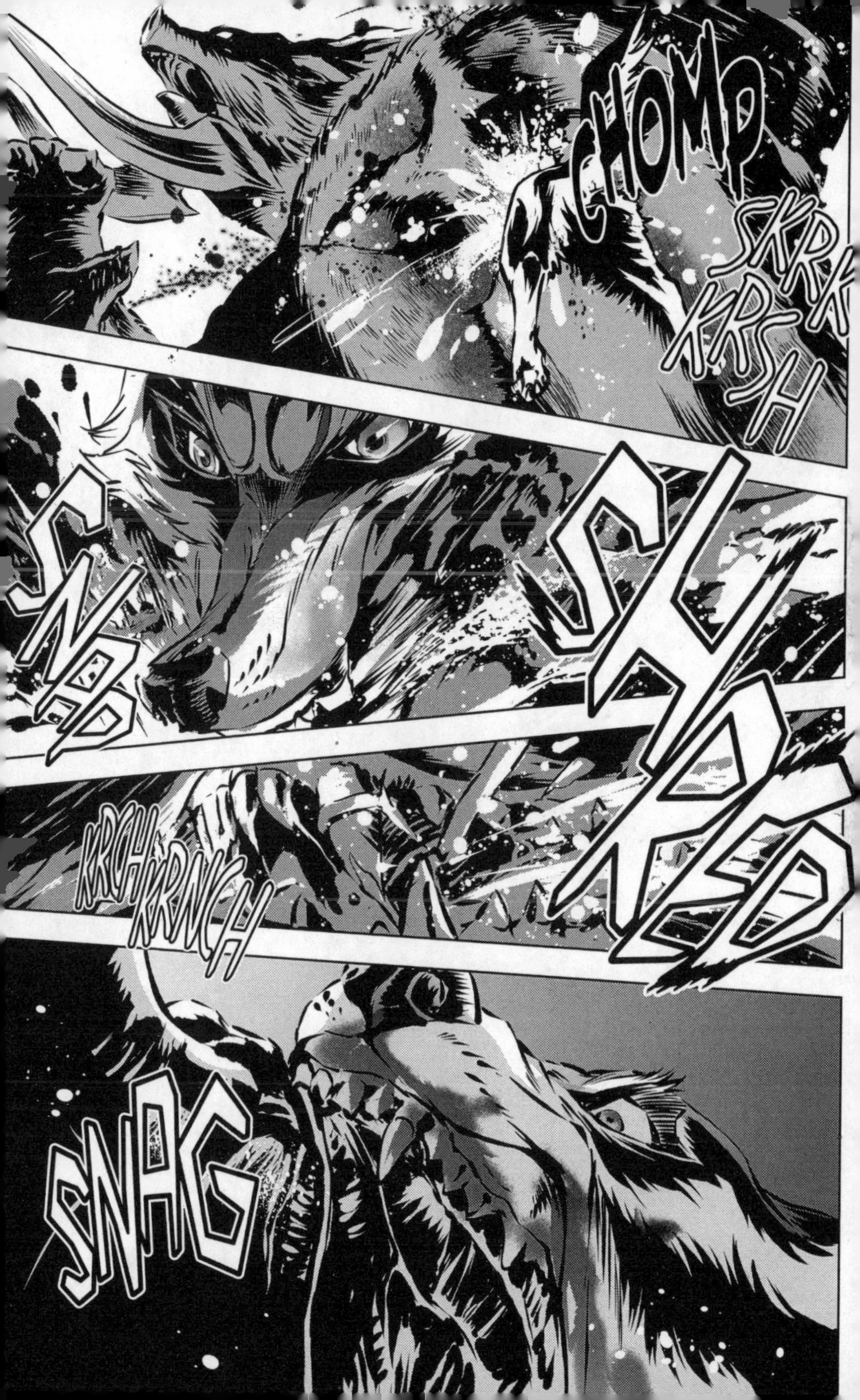
CHOMP
SKRK KRSH
SNAP
KRCH KRNCH
SNAG

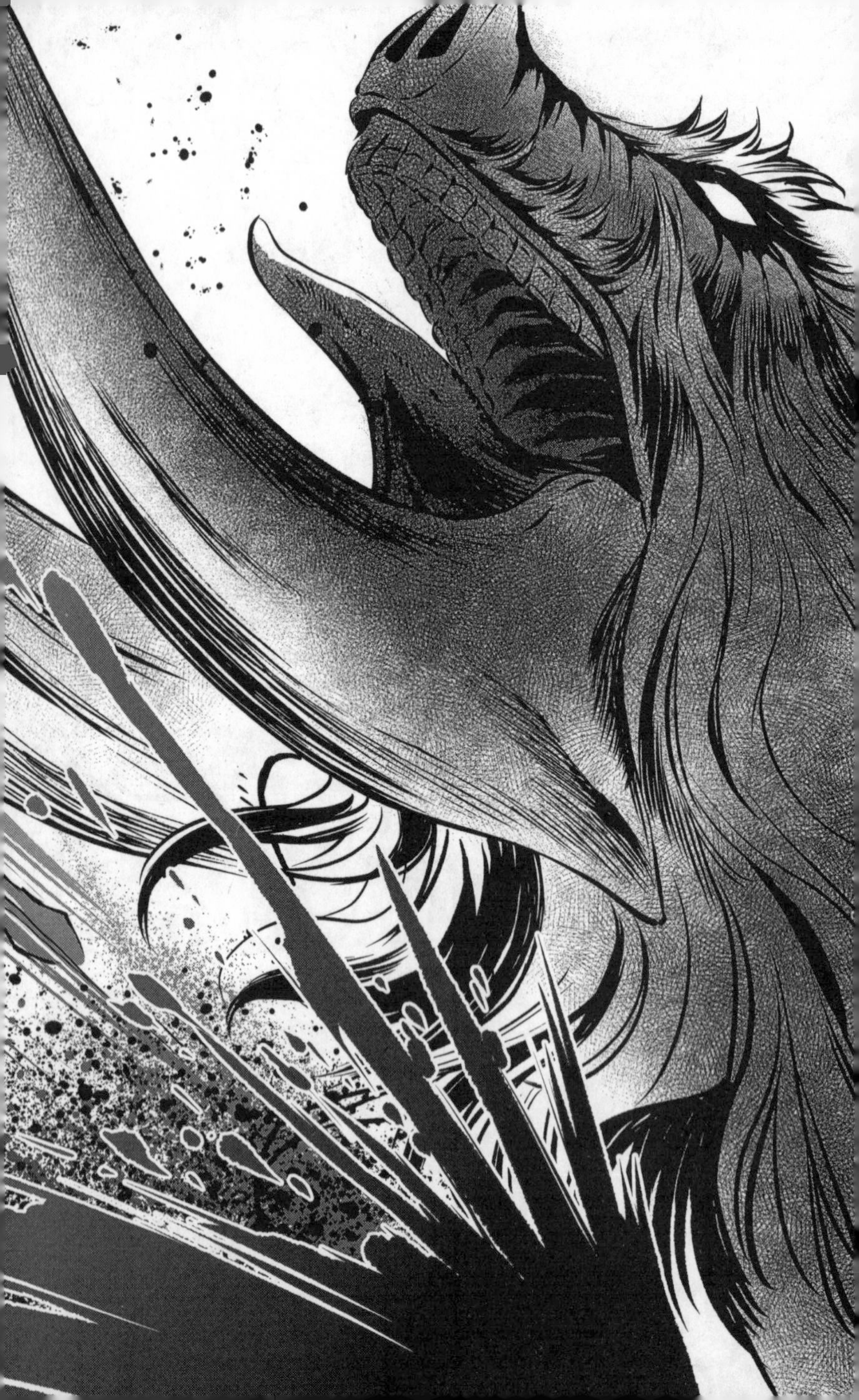

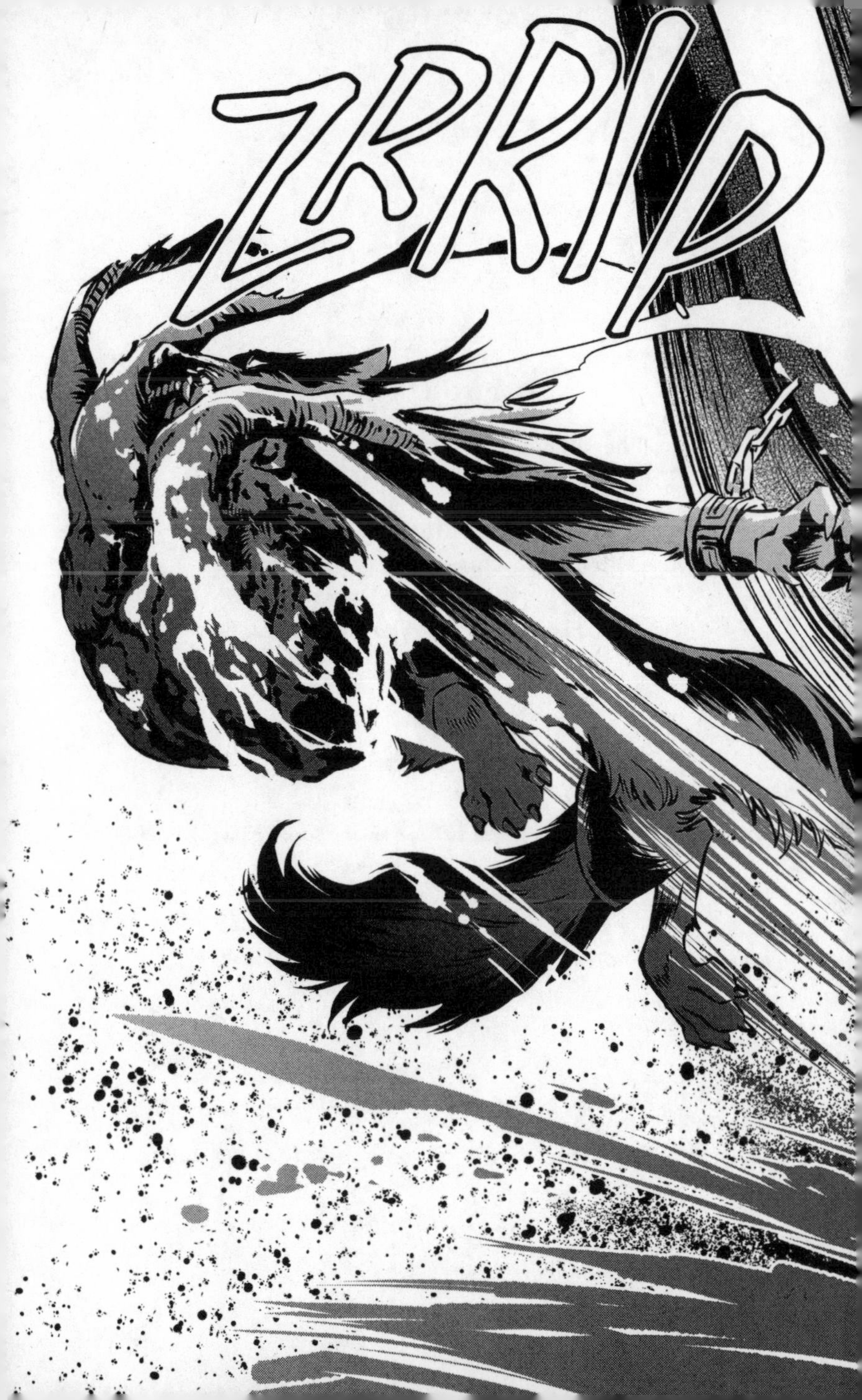
ZRRIP

AUTHOR'S NOTE

The final boss in *The Legend of Zelda* is always Ganondorf (Ganon), but Link in *Twilight Princess* is confronting him for the first time. Why must they fight? What does he believe in?

He has finally arrived at this place.

Akira Himekawa is the collaboration of two women, A. Honda and S. Nagano. Together they have created ten manga adventures featuring Link and the popular video game world of *The Legend of Zelda*™. Their most recent work, *The Legend of Zelda*™: *Twilight Princess*, is serialized digitally on Shogakukan's MangaONE app in Japan.

THE LEGEND OF ZELDA™

•TWILIGHT PRINCESS•

Volume 10—VIZ Media Edition

STORY AND ART BY
Akira Himekawa

DRAWING STAFF **Akiko Mori** / **Sakiho Tsutsui** / **Kanan**

TRANSLATION **John Werry**

ENGLISH ADAPTATION **Stan!**

TOUCH-UP ART & LETTERING **Evan Waldinger**

DESIGNER **Shawn Carrico**

EDITOR **Mike Montesa**

THE LEGEND OF ZELDA: TWILIGHT PRINCESS
TM & © 2022 Nintendo. All Rights Reserved.

ZELDA NO DENSETSU TWILIGHT PRINCESS Vol. 10
by Akira HIMEKAWA
© 2016 Akira HIMEKAWA
All rights reserved.
Original Japanese edition published by SHOGAKUKAN.
English translation rights in the United States of America,
Canada, the United Kingdom, Ireland, Australia and
New Zealand arranged with SHOGAKUKAN.

Original design by Kazutada YOKOYAMA

The stories, characters, and incidents mentioned in this publication are entirely fictional.

Printed in the U.S.A.

Published by VIZ Media, LLC
P.O. Box 77010
San Francisco, CA 94107

10 9 8 7 6 5 4 3 2 1
First printing, September 2022

VIZ MEDIA
viz.com

PARENTAL ADVISORY
THE LEGEND OF ZELDA is rated
T for Teen and is recommended
for ages 13 and up. This volume
contains fantasy violence.

RATED
TEEN

Hey! You're Reading in the Wrong Direction!

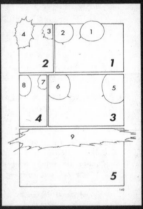

This is the **end** of this graphic novel!

To properly enjoy this VIZ graphic novel, please turn it around and begin reading from **right to left.** Unlike English, Japanese is read right to left, so Japanese comics are read in reverse order from the way English comics are typically read.

Follow the action this way

This book has been printed in the original Japanese format in order to preserve the orientation of the original artwork. Have fun with it!